EU, Europe Unfinished

Radical Cultural Studies

Series Editors: Fay Brauer, Maggie Humm, Tim Lawrence,
Stephen Maddison, Ashwani Sharma and Debra Benita Shaw
(Centre for Cultural Studies Research, University of East London, UK)

The *Radical Cultural Studies* series publishes monographs and edited collections to provide new and radical analyses of the culturopolitics, sociopolitics, aesthetics and ethics of contemporary cultures. The series is designed to stimulate debates across and within disciplines, foster new approaches to Cultural Studies and assess the radical potential of key ideas and theories.

Titles in the Series

Sewing, Fighting and Writing: Radical Practices in Work, Politics and Culture,
  Maria Tamboukou
Radical Space: Exploring Politics and Practice, edited by Debra Benita Shaw
  and Maggie Humm
EU, Europe Unfinished: Mediating Europe and the Balkans in a Time of Crisis, edited
  by Zlatan Krajina and Nebojša Blanuša
Science Fiction, Fantasy and Politics: Transmedia World-Building Beyond Capitalism,
  Dan Hassler-Forest (forthcoming)
Austerity as Public Mood: Social Anxieties and Social Struggles, Kirsten Forkert
  (forthcoming)
Metamodernism: Historicity, Affect, Depth edited by Robin van den Akker, Alison
  Gibbons and Timotheus Timotheus Vermeulen (forthcoming)
Pornography, Materiality and Cultural Politics, Stephen Maddison (forthcoming)

EU, Europe Unfinished

Mediating Europe and
the Balkans in a Time of Crisis

Edited by
Zlatan Krajina and Nebojša Blanuša

ROWMAN &
LITTLEFIELD
——INTERNATIONAL——

London • New York

Published by Rowman & Littlefield International, Ltd.
Unit A, Whitacre Mews, 26-34 Stannary Street, London SE11 4AB
www.rowmaninternational.com

Rowman & Littlefield International, Ltd. is an affiliate of Rowman & Littlefield
4501 Forbes Boulevard, Suite 200, Lanham, Maryland 20706, USA
With additional offices in Boulder, New York, Toronto (Canada), and Plymouth (UK)
www.rowman.com

British Library Cataloguing in Publication Data
A catalogue record for this book is available from the British Library

ISBN: HB 978-1-7834-8978-7
     PB 978-1-7834-8979-4

Library of Congress Cataloging-in-Publication Data Available
ISBN 9781783489787 (cloth : alk. paper)
ISBN 9781783489794 (pbk. : alk. paper)
ISBN 9781783489800 (electronic)

♾™ The paper used in this publication meets the minimum requirements of American
National Standard for Information Sciences—Permanence of Paper for Printed Library
Materials, ANSI/NISO Z39.48-1992.

Printed in the United States of America

*To all who define themselves beyond their homelands
and forever postpone defining others.*

Contents

Acknowledgements

This book began with a question, concerning the place of the Balkans in a changing Europe, which circulated certain academic networks for a period of time. The editors are grateful to all who accepted our challenge to reflect on this issue. We thank those whose valuable work in the end did not feature in this volume, for sharing their curiosity, and we thank the contributing authors for investing this book's journey with their creativity and perseverance.

Europe kept changing during the production of the book. While the refugee and economic crises in the summer of 2015 informed our analyses, the momentous EU membership referendum held in the UK in June 2016, when 51.9% of voters chose "leave", coincided with the finalization of our project. However, we believe that our key argument, which sees the shifting terrains of cohesion and fragmentation as a core problem of an "unfinished" Europe, will have much to say about "Brexit" and events to follow.

The chapter featuring the conversation between Slavenka Drakulić and David Morley would not have been possible without the willingness of our invited participants to commit to the many stages of its production. We are particularly grateful to Slavenka Drakulić for her very kind hospitality in Istria. Viktor Koska and the research assistants at the Centre for the Study of Ethnicity, Citizenship and Migration (CEDIM) at the Faculty of Political Science, University of Zagreb, provided invaluable help in transcribing the conversation.

Zlatan Krajina thanks Martina O'Sullivan for her editorial assistance, Debra Shaw for her enthusiasm and encouragement, Paul Stubbs for his convivial and selfless help, Dave Morley for the generosity of his intellectual support and friendship, Jasenka Pregrad for her comradery and wisdom in thinking about the book and beyond and Mario Malčak for being there.

Nebojša Blanuša thanks Zrinka, Buga and Zlatan for their patience and support during difficult times.

Part I

INTRODUCTION

Why the Balkans, Why Now, Who Cares?

Zlatan Krajina

This book explores what it means for the Balkans to belong in Europe, and for Europe to find a home in the Balkans, 25 years after the fall of the Iron Curtain. At a moment of a particular political and economic crisis in Europe, the Balkans return to global screens to haunt Western Europe, and to remind it of its own incompleteness as the self-perceived source and centre of the modern world. Some time ago, in the 19th century, the Balkans were known only to a few Western European travellers who side-tracked from their trips to the Orient, discovering a scenic, "open-air Volksmueum of Europe" that conserves Europe's pre-Enlightenment ways of life[1]. In the early 20th century, following regional wars, the Balkans were made into an image of violent nationalist self-determination, where nationalism, imported from Western Europe, was found in a displaced, and extreme, form. This image was rehabilitated in the early 1990s, when postmodern Europe found itself pulled back, travelling back in time, to once again witness medieval barbarism as socialist Yugoslavia disintegrated. At the same time, the concept of the Balkans retained its plural definition (even linguistically), encompassing the Greek classicist heritage (resourced, inter alia, by Germany during the Nazi regime for an image of pure Europe), the former Yugoslav non-aligned orientation ("socialism with a human face") and the former communist countries where the mountain carrying the region's name is located. Even though the European Union (EU) has sought to rename the Balkans as the "Western Balkans" and "South-eastern Europe", certain common ways of perceiving the Balkans negatively have continued to inform dominant definitions of critical European developments, currently staged in the continent's South-eastern peninsula.

Firstly, the "Western Balkan Route" (straddling parts of Turkey, Greece, Macedonia, Serbia, Hungary or Croatia, Slovenia and Austria) has appeared as the most frequent path taken by nearly a million refugees on their journey from countries like Syria, Iraq, Afghanistan and Eritrea, to Germany and Nordic countries during 2015. In what has been unfolding as the largest exodus since the Second World War, media reports on refugees' troglodyte existence and disputes over who should accept refugees have reactivated the notion of the "Balkan powder keg". Secondly, the Greek Balkans have generated suspicion about the future of the EU's monetary union, the Eurozone, after Greece's de facto bankruptcy in July 2015. The failure of its economic system, linked to Balkan laziness and trickery, also showed leading European institutions to be torn between profitable lending and political solidarity. Thirdly, the Balkans have been constructed as a space of conditional EU enlargement for those in former Yugoslavia who forever seek to become recognised as part of what Ivaylo Ditchev calls "the heavens of modernity, currently called 'Europe'"[2]. And while we acknowledge the first two developments (the refugee and economic crises), which have dominated headlines in the global media during the completion of the book, in this collection we focus on the third one, which we argue provides a crucial background against which the former two processes are to be usefully observed in further studies. It is precisely the occasionally visible Balkans which provide a lens onto the transformations of Europe as a multiple, self-reflexive and contradictory space, defined relationally and stratified geographically.

Having adopted the continent's name, the EU has also brought those central characteristics of Europe into sharp relief. As the 2014 Nobel Peace Prize laureate, the EU consolidated post-war cooperation in Western Europe, but simultaneously built, dissolved and re-built a series of boundaries, both formal and informal, to its nearest East. The EU is a transnational, voluntary, political and economic association, a polity of 500 million people, the world's seventh largest territory, a leader in the world economy, a legislative system, a confederation and, not least, a laboratory: in a word, a project "unprecedented" in human history[3]. The EU's trajectory has been one of expansion, both in territory and in form: starting in 1952 as a peace-building economic alliance between former Second World War enemies (namely West Germany and France), as well as Belgium, the Netherlands, Luxembourg and Italy, it evolved into the European Community (from 1957) and then into a Union (from 1993), encompassing also the UK, Denmark, Ireland, Spain, Portugal, Greece, Austria, Finland and Sweden. In the aftermath of the Cold War, the EU admitted twelve former Soviet and "Central and Eastern European" (CEE) countries between 2004 and 2007: Poland, the Czech Republic, Slovakia, Slovenia, Estonia, Latvia, Lithuania, Cyprus, Malta, Hungary, Bulgaria and Romania. Croatia became an EU member in 2013 after the longest accession process, while negotiations with other former Yugoslav countries (Montenegro and Serbia) began in 2012 and 2014, respectively. Macedonia, Albania and Bosnia and Herzegovina have also applied for membership, while Kosovo awaits the start of the Stabilisation and Association Agreement[4]. Yet key motifs behind EU enlargement (sustaining peace and expanding the market) have come to be clouded by an unprecedented sense of uncertainty, which seems to be here to stay.

The professed EU identity – a commitment to democracy and a market economy – has been refracted through a specific crisis which has affected both of Europe's key forms of social organisation: multiculturalism and the welfare state. The former, specifically modelled as a coexistence of difference rather than assimilation, including free transnational movement, has been openly proclaimed "dead" by German, British and Hungarian political leaders. The latter, which began to decline sharply in the 1970s with the "neoliberal revolution"[5], is currently being demolished during an epidemic of austerity following the global "credit crunch". In that context, Europe considers Greece as inept for global business, former Yugoslavia as insufficiently competitive and "economic" Islamic refugees as covert social welfare scroungers – even though the killing of Europe's key offspring, the welfare state, contradicts the predominant argument for keeping the migrants out[6]. In this contradictory but paired promotion of capital mobility and ethnic conservatism[7], old issues, concerning the imaginary locations of "east" and "west", re-emerge in new guises. This ongoing debate has brought back a topography of ancient and modernist pedigrees, such as locating "barbarians" and assessing the East's "development" through the West's criteria of "complexity" and "civility". Barriers were unenthusiastically and only gradually removed for workers from countries like Poland, Romania, Bulgaria and Croatia, while the gates for nearly a million people floating or hiking into EU's inner borderless cosmos (the "Schengen" zone) from Europe's war-torn periphery are closing down entirely. Lights glimmering from remote Greek islands, as spotted from North African shores during clear nights, signal only leftovers of a Europe that once was. Reaching their first stop, refugees themselves encounter a humanitarian trauma caused by Greece's financial collapse, while, progressing further into the continent, in some places more than others, they confront state-authorised tear gas and water cannons, as well as civic first aid and improvised friendly greetings.

To make sense of this disturbing moment, one may reach for historical reasoning. The 1683 Battle of Vienna, the 1848 revolutions, the 1914 Great War, the antifascist movement, the 1989 Velvet Revolution and the wars of the 1990s form a narrative in which the Balkans "again" provide the location and the occasion for Europe to question its cohesive basis. But rather than historicity, defined by Chakrabarty as a Eurocentric narration of a straightforward accumulation of events leading to "development"[8], we need an understanding of Europe and the Balkans as co-constitutive of each other. Lest we rehearse methodological essentialism – creating that which is the focus of a non-essentialist investigation – we need to be wary of re-creating the Balkans as an isolated (coherent) reality resulting from the adoption of a single focus. We might better dislocate (de-centre) the Balkans from the geography of our enquiry, and instead explore its becoming through its interaction with universes other than itself.

One obvious danger of this approach is that the reader may already feel shoved through a labyrinth-like souk of frontiers (from former Yugoslavia to the Maghreb). Nevertheless, we find this to be a necessary price to be paid for the advantage of portraying a haunting absence of totality in the current European-Balkan conjuncture of "crisis". As so many times before, Europe turns out having very different meanings from different vantage points: in the West, "European" is an identity marker inherited by birth; in the Balkans, it is a badge that can be earned through adaptation; and for unfortunate stow-aways, Europe's outer borders are the nearest shelter. As we learn from the leading figure of multi-dimensional cultural analysis, Stuart Hall, to under-stand how dominant interpretations of the world (such as the "inevitability" of events) smuggle in a politics of inequality, our task is to penetrate "the mechanisms which connect dissimilar features"[9]. His own parallel attention to the British/French occupation of the Suez Canal and the Soviet quashing of the Hungarian uprising in 1956 demonstrated the relevance of looking at seemingly very different events for a better understanding of how domi-nant conceptions (such as imperialist and communist promises of welfare) function as ideologies, enforcing limits on their subjects[10]. Too messy for a disciplinary research agenda, conjunctures are always "historically specific articulations of concrete social forces" which play out at the intersection between overarching policy and daily practice[11].

The present European-Balkan moment of "crisis" shows that there is always more to cultural spaces than cartographic positions; history is not only made of geopolitical manoeuvres but also glances and gestures. Before 1989, the border officers at the Iron Curtain "looked down on us" Easterners[12]. In the meanwhile, the border moved east, but so has the practice of keeping Others out, as it is now former Soviet bloc countries like Poland, Slovakia and Hungary that are determined to form a military defence against refugees arriving in flip-flops from an even further East. For Hall, joint analysis of politics and culture allows us to recognise novel developments emerging from existing elements, which in our case involves showing that estab-lished phenomena like "Euroscepticism" and "Western Balkans" are being given important refinements such as "Euroapathy" and "Restern Balkans". If "difference" from the start defines European identity, and Europe thus cannot do without it[13], and if identity is both to do with discourse and mate-rial practice[14], then neither Europe nor the Balkans *are*; they *emerge*, from what Hall called "a conversation between spaces"[15]: a conversation between unequal partners, but one that is unceasing.

Crucially, this conversation is about the negotiations of belonging in Europe. Having never been "discovered", "dominated" or "conquered by another continent", Europe is a space where the search for "essence" generates territory[16]. And since all European regions want to be "essentially" European, they are set on an endless search for a source of their European belonging, thus seeking an opportune beginning and end of Europe. In other words, Europe's unfinished character is constitutive of its definition. Observing Europe through the Balkans uncovers Europe to be far from "united", implicated though it may seem through the centrality of its "union". The failure of post-war reconciliation and the delayed EU accession of the countries of the former Yugoslavia, the reactivation of national border controls as a response to the arrival of Islamic refugees via the "Western Balkans" and the popular support won by extremist nationalist and Eurosceptic parties in the 2014 European elections have cast considerable doubt on the EU's founding motto of "unity in difference". European "unity" has rather come to denote a predominantly white, Christian and technocratic fortification. In contemporary Europe, "difference" is a specific breed of variety, which is generated by a politics of borders and the inequality of geographical access. Crucially, European difference is about a spatial hierarchy, which involves the positioning of Others in the East and the imagined centrality of the West.

In this book, we investigate how Europe's specific visions of the Balkans, as the essence of unrest and a potential object of "Europeanisation", interact with the Balkans' dreams of Europe, as a hopeful refuge from prejudice and from the burdens of its own post-socialist transition. We seek to hijack those transactions from "common sense" and uncover their deeper orientations. More specifically, we explore whether the gradual EU accession of the former Yugoslav countries, and the parallel renaming of the Balkans, involves a completion of its "transition" into Europe and a diminution of "Balkanism". Is European identity consequently being re-defined, through a de-centring or a "provincialising" of the West? While many in the EU increasingly doubt its future, what does still make the EU a preferred home for the future to those residing in, to use Dejan Jović's term, "Restern" (non-yet-but-hopeful-EU) Balkans[17]: Serbia, Bosnia and Herzegovina, Montenegro, Kosovo, Albania, the former Yugoslav Republic of Macedonia (henceforth, Macedonia), but also Turkey? If the appearance of various Others on the European centre stage, whether following decolonisation, EU enlargement or the refugee crisis, shows that "European identity can no longer be, simply . . . a matter of Western intellectual and cultural traditions"[18], where is Europe headed next, with the Balkans in its skein? To unpack those difficult questions (never mind answering them!), the following discussion will first trace the evolving conjuncture of Balkanism, Europe and EU enlargement, uncoupling them one by one, and will then move on to provide a brief overview of contributions to this collection.

SPACE AS METHOD

Though physically within Europe and never colonised formally, the Balkans continue to be a space whose preconceived "character" is a concern in postcolonial critique of Eurocentric stereotypes. The central interpretive framework for social and cultural phenomena residing in South-eastern Europe, Balkanism, stems mainly from Western (European and American) reports, historiography, documents and actions mainly from the 19th century onwards. As has been notably demonstrated by Maria Todorova, a nearly two-millennia-long rivalry between empires and a tradition of representation concerning the space positioned along their fault lines have made the Balkans "the 'other' of Europe"[19]. Once positioned along the borders of the Byzantine empire (4th–14th centuries), whose Orthodox culture was considered by Rome a "heretic deviation" of Christianity, it was the subsequent, Ottoman rule (14th–early 20th centuries), once encompassing much of today's Balkans (ending roughly where Croatia meets Bosnia and Herzegovina), that confronted Europe with Islamic culture, the "boundary" to which was deemed "unbridgeable"[20]. After the Ottoman demise, for Europe, the Balkans remained suspiciously ambiguous.

Ideas of "evolutionism" met forms of reasoning such as Saussurean linguistics, which defines signs as negative to others, and made the Balkans what Todorova calls an "incomplete self": neither entirely Islamic ("European Turkey"), nor "coloured", but "mixed"[21]. Unlike the Orient, which was imagined as an opposition to the West[22], the Balkans were coded as a hybrid state of humanity. Geopolitically too, they were nowhere precisely: "between West and East, Europe and Asia, Christianity and Islam"[23]. In the early decades of the 20th century a "testing" and "training" field for Western European elite personages[24], the Balkans continued being a "laboratory" for such professed actions as the protection of human rights with the 1999 NATO bombing of Serbia[25]. The 20th century made "violence" its defining characteristic[26]. Though neither Spanish nor Greek civil wars were described in regional terms, the violent dissolution of Yugoslavia was defined as Balkan violence, to stand for the kind of violence which was drawn from reports on the Balkan Wars (1912–1913), when Balkan violence was found to be specifically "archaic": "born of clan societies"[27]. Even though nation states were consolidated in Europe through "social engineering", European "fundamental hostility to heterogeneity" made the undefined status of the region "frustrating"[28].

Imaginary descriptions have, by far, outweighed the historiography of the Balkans. Travel writing, referring to "filth, passivity, unreliability, misogyny, propensity for intrigue, insincerity, opportunism, laziness, superstitiousness, lethargy, sluggishness, inefficiency, incompetent bureaucracy"[29], inspired authors like Christie, Welles and Stocker in creating an imaginary space (like

Ruritania) with "spies, murderers, various suspicious characters or supernatural creatures" as central figures[30]. An invented environment in turn informed the accounts by politicians and journalists, many of whom confessed to have "never visited" the Balkans in person[31].

Even though Balkanism is a Eurocentric discourse, which makes the Balkans appear as a "backyard" of Europe[32], one defining feature of the discourse of Balkanism is its adoption *within* the Balkans. In fact, "the surest sign of Balkan identity", writes Ditchev, is "the resistance to Balkan identity"[33]. Many Balkan cities brand themselves as "Central" European (creating places like Vienna Café or Amelie Sweetshop). But, as Bjelić explains, "While Gandhi and the Hindi internalized Orientalized stereotypes to resist their colonial identifications . . . something else happened in the Balkans, where people subverted their own identities by orientalising one another"[34]. Balkan is always that which lies on the east, even if within sight: Slovenes orientalise Croats, Croats pride themselves in being better than Serbs and so on[35]. In the current context, the EU decided to negotiate with each country individually, thus fostering a spirit of competition which couldn't but acquire nationalist-Orientalist overtones. Slovenia blocked Croatia's EU journey for two years over disputes regarding a stretch of sea border; after Croatia entered, any unresolved issues with Serbia soon activated the "blocking" game (the right of veto on the admittance of new members). Just as Sofia proclaimed being "ahead of Bucharest" in the Bulgarian advancement towards the West[36], Croatia was happy to announce the uncoupling of its negotiations with the EU from the Turkish one, which had begun at the same time. Greeks, voting on the referendum in the summer of 2015 on "bailout" measures, were divided between being against new cuts in public spending and "for" the Troika's offer as a wish "to stay in Europe". For the latter, austerity was an acceptable price for securing an amiable geographical location. They won the referendum. If anything, "nesting orientalisms"[37] within the East says something about how regressive the East's adoption of Eurocentric geography can be, when the West is believed to be the centre and the East the periphery (for an array of illustrations, see chapters 4 and 9 in this volume). In fact, refuting the Balkan heritage in the Balkans evolved into a wide-ranging politics of renaming – as if resolving the region's problems was only obstructed by a lack of precise names.

BALKANISM AFTER THE BALKANS

While semi-visibility, transition and violence are established Balkanist assumptions about the Balkans, more recent discursive practice includes an unparalleled amount of renaming. Initially mapped in the 15th century as the Balkan Mountain located mainly in Bulgaria, the Balkans gradually came to refer to the entire South-eastern European peninsula, stretching from the Black Sea to the Alps, only to shrink to a "Western" or "Restern"[38] version more recently, to specify where the rest of the trouble is: the non-EU parts of former Yugoslavia.

A country (Yugoslavia) had "withered away"[39], a war had ended and a new hope was evoked by adding the "West" to the "Balkan" pairing, even though there is no geographic "North or South in the Balkans", as there is in Europe[40]. A parallel refinement came with the EU's "Stability Pact", which began referring to "South-eastern Europe", this time in the aftermath of the war in Kosovo[41]. The latter term seeks a "politically correct" abandonment of the Balkans altogether, given that "it has become impossible to define a country as 'Balkan' without having to explain oneself"[42]. Policy analysis has adopted "SE Europe" as a territorial reality, while the term "Balkans" has become reserved for studies of history and culture. A tsunami of renaming marched through former Yugoslavia as well (see particularly chapter 3 in this volume). Following public outrages, especially in Croatia and Slovenia, against any "regional" identification, their Yugoslav and Balkan roots have been nearly wiped out from names of countless public spaces like institutions and streets. The Balkans only remained useful as a name for "authenticity" in the international tourism industry. Recent media developments like the launch of "Al Jazeera Balkans" and CNN's competitor "N1" both sought to appeal to their ex-Yugoslav audiences by referring to a more neutral, however empty a concept, "region" (invented by local politicians), all the while reproducing versions of Yugoslavia's old map in weather forecasts[43].

The absence of a shared definition is not exclusive to the Balkans: the EU also fails to create supranational identification and a sense of strong, joint leadership[44]. As Pearson argues, the EU lacks a formal and histori-cal capital city and other signage that could evoke connections as strong as national ones[45]. According to Förnas, key EU symbols – the flag, with a dislocated space of yellow stars circle on a blue background, and the "euro" money showing generic doors and bridges – abound in ambivalence, articu-lating the Union's forever unresolved tension between fragmentation and homogenisation[46].

LIVING IN A MOBILE CONTINENT

"Europe is not something you discover", Bauman writes, paraphrasing the classic Greek myth of Cadmon's search for his sister Princess Europa, captured forever by Zeus. Rather, Europe is "something to be made, created, built", involving "a labour that never ends"[47]. Historically part of "the great landmass of Eurasia"[48], Europe became a distinct worldwide legacy through colonialism, while postcolonial processes have worked on de-centring Europe from available visions of the world. Europe's sophistication in the creation of borders, be it CCTV surveillance of "suspicious" behaviour in urban neigh-bourhoods, construction of anti-refugee fences in Hungary and their leaders' fear of becoming a racial "minority", proposals for "Grexit", prospects for "Brexit" or "enlargement fatigue", signals a newer stage in the search for Europe's end. Even though during the Second World War, Europe was an origin rather than merely destination for refugees, the EU has invested in the maintenance of its border controls far more than in the creation of asylum centres[49], resulting in scenes of chaos as the member states proved to be unprepared for the massive wave of refugees arriving in the summer of 2015.

Nevertheless, refugees who made it into Fortress Europe advise those left behind via social media, "every time you fall down the map, get climb-ing up again"[50], evoking the centuries old heritage of border-crossing in the Mediterranean basin, of which the Balkans are a part. An organic space of meeting that belonged to everyone, the Mediterranean Sea fostered exchanges and co-authorship of arts and crafts, thus delaying nationalistic appropria-tions of history[51]. As "a repressed alterity within modernity" with its "sunlit sloth, civic chaos and corruption" now to be exorcised, the Mediterranean contains another set of unwanted European lineages, the "Jewish, Christian and Muslim origins of the Occident", legacies which imported into Europe, skills like agriculture and mathematics[52]. The migrant is now a "criminal" but for centuries "central" to the formation of modernity, through modern colonialism, which commenced (in 18th) and ended (in 20th centuries) in the Mediterranean[53] – currently, for many on rubber boats, the "sea of death".

Those who succeed in moving into Fortress Europe are likely to find the economic component of European integration corroding the political com-ponent, as the neoliberal pressure for transnational profit accumulation over-powers solidarity and the state. The weakening of the welfare state loosened the essential pairing between employment and citizenship[54]. Migrants can find low-paid jobs but not citizenship, while half of educated youth in countries like Spain, Greece and Croatia have EU citizenship but not employment. This mistaking of political union (solidarity) for an economic one (market profits) has been most visible in the demands made by "the international financial industry" from Greece in 2015 to achieve both "fiscal consolidation" and "prospect of future economic growth"[55]. Though allowed to borrow at lower, collective, Eurozone rates, Greece's failure to return debts was treated as a single nation's problem, without prospects of a rapid recovery. The travel-ling scenario of the financial "vicious circle", whereby cuts in public spending block the circulation of money in the national market, landed even harder in the non-EU parts of former Yugoslavia, where protection from the European financial institutions is unavailable[56]. Though assessed by the EU as insufficiently "Europeanised", these countries are heavily "Euro-ised" (debts and earnings denominated in foreign euros), which made deficit rates comparable to Greece's[57], long before Europe developed a concern for "Grecovery". Nonetheless, *Euroscepticism* inside the EU has come to be firmly paired with what appears to be *Eurofixation* at its fringes, creating an idealised Europe, which, like any other dream, thrives best in imagination.

CULTURAL ECONOMY OF ACCESSION

An Occidentalised perception of Europe is a familiar image in the Balkans. Drakulić recalls that for former Soviet countries, the Iron Curtain was "made of silky, shiny images of pretty women dressed in wonderful clothes, of pictures from women's magazines", where "the other world" seemed like nothing less than "a paradise", particularly because neither the magazines nor their ideas of femininity were accessible in communist Europe[58]. And just as countries like France or the Netherlands were debating the dangers of the American "cultural industry" for their national cultures, in Yugoslavia, large-scale import of pop magazines, Hollywood films and chewing gum was gauged "as a conscious de-sovietisation", even if that which remained firmly abroad was "liberty" itself[59].

To be in the Balkans means to idealise Europe as a container of things lacking so dearly at home, things to be attained in Europe rather than achieved at home. While only about a tenth of EU citizens equate the EU with "economic prosperity" or "rule of law", in Serbia, Macedonia and Albania these figures are in the range of 30–60%[60]. And whereas the West is desirable to the Balkans as a complete opposite of itself, the Balkans are acceptable to the West only as versions of themselves. In the pre-accession period, the EU portrayed former Yugoslav countries, in a series of video promos, by showing only their Austro-Hungarian, rather than also communist, architecture. Candidate countries themselves, like Croatia, sought to discourage any public debate about EU accession[61], even at the cost of ridiculing also the pro side, by disseminating de-contextualised glossy propaganda materials[62]. The grand public celebration of the latest, Croatian EU entry, staged in Zagreb's central square, was a spectacular multi-screen showcase of Croatia's historic contributions to Europe like pre-modern crafts, omitting reference to Yugoslavia or the "homeland" war in the 1990s.

Even though it is precisely the Balkans which counterpose to their difficult past (which drags on into the present), a rare expression of optimism about the EU's future[63], membership is a receding horizon for those waiting in the wings. The more time passes, the more new EU regulations (*acquis communitaire*) accumulate to be adopted, and as the EU draws "lessons" from each enlargement, new candidates are given more tasks to fulfil. Transition has become a permanent state of being, and its aim has been lost from view. Democratization turned into Europeanisation: a series of quasi-post-colonial "civilising missions", which involve the East in the work of "adaptation to the exigencies of the advanced models of the West"[64]. Negotiations, such as those in 2004 with Central and East European countries, assigned former Soviet bloc countries "the position of 'a client' or 'pupil' of the EU", whereby the status of "a truly equal partner" was to be gained only upon the "transmission" of EU regulations[65]. Similar to postcolonial relations where "peripheries are . . . primarily defined as takers, rather than givers of meaning"[66], in the Balkans, "European civilization was held responsible for even the tiny improvements in the Balkan civilization"[67].

It is thus unsurprising that the aspiring EU members from the Balkans sense their relationship with the EU as one of inequality. The prevailing image of the EU in Serbian, Bosnian, Montenegrin and Macedonian media is that of a "rider" carrying a "carrot and a stick", whereas individual countries are "'donkeys' that unsuccessfully keep trying to get the carrot"[68]. EU representatives are portrayed as addressing the Balkans via a "bureaucratic language" and in a "pedagogical" tone, keeping the Other at a distance[69]. News about EU announcements, treaties, initiatives and projects portray it being "concerned", "caring" or "disappointed", and the candidates being "euroapathic" (in Serbia, where the elites suggest "our [task] is only to listen"), "rejected" (in Bosnia and Herzegovina, a "black hole of the Western Balkans"), "responsible" (Macedonia) or a "front runner" in Europeanisation (Montenegro)[70]. Reports about neighbours are predominantly about "disassociation", that is, "strengthening the boundaries between 'us who are not in the EU' and 'them [Slovenia and Croatia] in the EU'"[71]. Consequently, accession (essentially, a bulk of legal work) is couched in spatial terms:

> There are not only course, map, track, roads, staircases and approaching in general, but also passengers (countries who are joining the EU, their state officials and/or citizens), various ways of movement on the road – forward, backward, pacing, jogtrotting, running … various means of transport (train, ship), obstacles (blockage, barrier, red light) and finally aim, destination (membership in the European Union)[72].

In lieu of conscious reform, there is a race for geographical position. This is most obvious in the former Yugoslav countries of Slovenia and Croatia, where the EU's "post ante conditionality" (the carrot and stick model) resulted in "unwilling, recalcitrant Europeanization"[73]. Instead of a non-violent "open exchange" between any two traditions (such as positioning

Viennese Sachertorte right next to Turkish baklava in any Balkan sweet-shop), EU membership negotiations for the former Yugoslav countries were "violent" in as far as they were "guided" by "one tradition"[74].

This problem also takes us back to 1989. Whereas CEE countries like the Czech Republic and Poland felt that the Soviet regime "violated their identi-ties" and thus they actively sought liberal democracy, non-aligned Yugoslavia took a different course[75]. People's dissatisfaction with Yugoslavia, "the most open and westernized country in the really existing socialist world", never sought a fundamentally different system strongly enough[76]. The post-1989 "liberalisation" was taken up by "anti-liberals", and even though new insti-tutions were created, political culture switched from socialism to violent nationalism, instead of liberal democracy[77]. In turn, as Jović recalls, "Post-Yugoslav states [like Bosnia and Herzegovina] collapsed just as Yugoslavia did: along ethnic fault lines"[78]. The breakdown actually went all the way to "the very bottom of the social structure", including cities like Mostar, fami-lies and "in the sense of personal identity, many individuals fell apart too"[79]. Twenty-five years since the break-up of Yugoslavia, its societies in fact "still bear with the consequences of 1989, a year which never happened to us"[80].

While an important form of Balkanism is the fact that "European leaders only discuss Balkan problems when they become absolutely impossible to ignore"[81], the former Yugoslav states themselves invest heavily in fashioning a separate existence. Preparing this book in Croatia, where the proportion of ethnic minorities dropped from 22% in 1991 to only 10.5% in 2001[82], we have the advantage to witness the national media routinely passing over in silence any ordinary reference to daily life in neighbouring countries. Reports from Slovenia and Serbia will seek to update viewers about "territorial disputes" or "belated apologies for the war", but the discussion of quotidian issues like "surviving the summer heat" just kilometres away, remains inconceivable. In this mediated geography, Croatia borders untrustworthy neighbours on one side, whose sole existence is a reminder of an undigested past, and, on the other, the West (the EU), which has grown into a metonym for the coun-try's imagined future. Reporters exclaim that "Western" visitors praise "our" coastline (the governors of which have changed numerously) and consider "us" as "European", even if only during a passing summer vacation. Serbs, Bosnians or the Italian minority are not even "Others" (a European invention) but are entirely invisible (though linguistically perfectly understandable). As Todorova reminds us, it has become far more acceptable to be mapped as the periphery of Europe rather than the "centre" of the Balkans[83]. A range of EU initiatives for regional cooperation, such as the "Balkan Free Trade Zone", have been jettisoned by successor states' fears of a "return" to Yugoslavia and a suspicion of their neighbours' intentions[84]. The region "lacks cohesion" in terms of transport infrastructure too[85]. If "a road always has two ends" and the stronger partner can have a positive effect on the weaker[86], it is difficult to imagine a united Europe without a more united Balkans.

Those wishing to subvert the regressive post-Yugoslav piecemeal geography resort to mourning over the Yugoslav past. This is present not only in serious academic work on so-called "Coca-Cola Socialism," but can also be seen in museum exhibitions, TV series, documentaries or flea market gatherings that commemorate the progressive impulse of Yugoslav multiculturalism and its notable "new wave" culture in the 1980s. Though nostalgic – going as far as portraying electricity shortages and consumer scarcity as charming – these projects say something about an irredeemable loss that was created by nationalist self-determination in the early 1990s[87]. Étienne Balibar goes a step further, to argue, quite rightly, that the "Balkan patchwork" remains a reminder to Europe itself of what it has lost. The pre-nationalist Balkan rainbow is "an epitome and an allegory of Europe as such": identities which have never been "pure" but "constructed" out of "encounters between 'civilizations'"[88]. A consciousness of there being "a mosaic of nations"[89], as formulated in Yugoslav multiculturalism, was massacred during the establishment of nation states in the 1990s. Though originating from the (still recent) past, this notion of coexistence has not as yet been made useful in tackling the failures of post-Yugoslav reconciliation or Europe's treatment of refugees. Of course, as Morley reminds us, some distinction has a vital function in the provision of "any minimal coherence which would allow the subject or community to formulate any sense of itself, at all"[90]. What needs recovery, however, is the post-war heritage of Europe – as being not about escape from, but about living with neighbours, both those nearer and farther away.

"EUROPE UNFINISHED": AN INVENTORY OF PERSPECTIVES

If self-reflexivity is one crucial tenet of the European "adventure"[91], it is also one distinguished feature of this book. Readers won't only travel across different aspects of cultural relationships between Europe, the EU and the Balkans, but also across spaces from which contributors have arrived into the shared space of the book to discuss this specific geographical space. If the majority of existing books raises the important issue of whether the Balkans "belong" in Europe, one strategic emphasis of this book is on the necessity to also raise the same question from the opposite point of view – of whether Europe can ever "find a home" in the Balkans. Drawing from the well-known commitment of British cultural studies to appreciating a diversity of voice and style as a necessary precondition for any democratic (if, in Chantal Mouffe's terms, necessarily "agonistic"[92]) encounter, and evoking the essential political intent of the postcolonial critique to provide the space for the various "subalterns" to express themselves in their own terms[93], we gathered a wide variety of authors. For most of them, the Balkans is their present home or else their point of origin; for some, the Balkans is a space to which they have other modes of "adopted" relationships. In listening to this variety of "Balkan" voices, readers may find that, in places, they perhaps encounter some unfamiliar forms of presentation, involving stylistic characteristics such as polemic, elliptical forms of association, and references to sources of existing knowledge outside the Anglo-American academy, about which they are perhaps less knowledgeable. Indeed, as part of their respective surveys, some of the contributors themselves highlight the ways in which uneven access to forms of social capital based around English language skills and cultural reference points works to set regrettably narrow limits to contemporary forms of trans-European communication[94]. Our editorial decision not to standardise the contributions here, from voices beyond those linguistic and stylistic frontiers, stems from our determination to practise formally what the book endorses in terms of its theoretical framework, which is an appreciation of dialogue and counterpoint across a wide range of different – and, in many cases, previously marginalised, if not silenced – positions[95].

Our will to provide a wide understanding of different, mutually related, dimensions of the Europe-Balkan conjuncture involved us assembling contributors from different intellectual backgrounds. Our joint horizon weaves together a variety of their macro- and micro-perspectives (media analysis, art history, autobiography), whereby individual chapters read as complementary pieces of a mosaic, a notion we seek to recover in the understanding of the Balkans. From "civilising" Europeanisation via EU policy transfer and politics of renaming, to the more local phenomena like turbo-folk television, architectural kitsch and utopian motivations for westbound migration, the studies presented in this collection uncover the less known face of contemporary Balkan and European identities. However, as incomplete as any collection will always be, on what is a developing conjuncture, editors and contributors hope to have inspired, with our shared interdisciplinary curiosity and consciously unconventional approach, further "discoveries" of Europe, an "unfinished" continent.

The chapters in this book are organised thematically. We begin with policy discussions about the *Europeanisation* of the Balkans (Stubbs and Lendvai; Metykova). Our focus then moves to diffuse practices of *renaming*, both in the realm of state politics and the arts (Milevska; Ditchev). Following the debates about identity, we look at various struggles around the symbolic *representation* of the region (Castro Seixas; Marinkova; Rexhepi). In the final part of the book, we explore different accounts of *accessing* Europe (Čvoro; Obad; Ciobanu), concluding with a conversation on the issues raised, as well as identifying roads for further research (Drakulić, Morley,

Krajina and Blanuša). Given the multiple geographical and methodological focus of each chapter, the presented sequence is more about emphasis, rather than direction of movement (such as from state to state) or clear-cut level of analysis (micro/macro). Each chapter, whether on policy or media, will gain further significance when read in conjunction with pieces focusing on autobiography and cultural production.

We set out on our journey with a discussion laid out by policy analysts Paul Stubbs and Noémi Lendvai, which seeks to build into this project an awareness of Europe's imperial past as a necessary preamble to any understanding of Europe's preferred mode of addressing the Balkans today, via EU projects, deadlines and benchmarks. Stubbs and Lendvai demonstrate Europeanisation to be a one-directional translation of policies not only in geographical (West-to-East) but also in sociological terms (widening the space of neoliberalism). Nevertheless, the authors find in the Balkans much needed seeds of optimism for Europe on the whole. Various parts of the Balkans perform difference in the form of recalcitrance (public occupations, civic plenums and protests), evoking a "social Europe otherwise" with "a commitment to [developing] politics as interruption" rather than as coherent "narrative". This is precisely what, in a distinctly forceful manner, media scholar Monika Metykova articulates in her exploration of the media landscape of post-war Bosnia and Herzegovina in the subsequent chapter. "Pink TV", a turbo-folk commercial television network, constructs a productive (anti-nationalist) representation of local ethnic diversity far more than state-owned media outputs ever do. "Pink's" staging of shows like music or reality television with participants from across the post-Yugoslav space manages to create what one of Metykova's sources called a "metanational" space that speaks to everyone residing there, as opposed to national public media, which, like the state, remain crippled by international supervision and territorial/ethnic divisions, thus failing to address and engage anyone in particular.

The following two chapters, by Suzana Milevska and Ivaylo Ditchev, uncover the other, rarely documented, side of Europeanisation, namely the immense force of post-socialist self-fashioning into an imagined Europe, with a focus on the relevance of linguistic practice in that process. Milevska's exploration of "violence by signification" in a number of cases (from the post-socialist renaming of streets in Balkan cities to international disputes over names of countries and regions) shows that a "renaming machine" is operative across the Balkans as a form of maintenance of old ethnic, gender and other dominance within the "Europeanising" countries. For Ditchev, given that Balkan nation states have been engaged in a frivolous "catch-up" modernisation, the practices of "renaming" can go as far as emptying cultural forms like architectural construction or historical narration of content altogether and producing replicable "kitsch" as a handy resource in nationalist "comparison and competition". Unlike the older figure of "Kulturträger" who translated major civilisations to peripheries, the "kitsch-manager" operates on an international tourism market, branding their country as a truer root of European virtues than any other (e.g. the erection of a Triumphal Arc in Macedonia as an "anti-modern"[96] manoeuvre to commemorate antique events in the 21st century). Renaming itself, however, has not involved a wholesale abandonment of Balkanism.

When the people of Bosnia and Herzegovina took to the streets in 2014, after decades of sustained corruption as well as failed local politicians' and EU promises of democratic consolidation, international media represented the situation as having to do with a curiously unvaried Balkanist fate: life forever locked amidst violence and human suffering, past and present. Even though personal testimonies of activists like young professionals and elderly factory workers were qualified as "brave" (ironically, such depiction was inconceivable to those media during events like the 2012 London riots), the actual organisation of protests or their relationship with the country's EU aspirations remained unobserved. Where Castro Seixas shows, in chapter 5, how a particular Balkan country figured in the international media (an "unresolved, unfinished question for the EU"), the undecided fate of "post-socialist" Balkans becomes particularly accessible in the following, Milena Marinkova's analysis, based on her reading of Mikhail Veshim's 2008 novel "The English Neighbour". The plot revolves around a variety of mishaps surrounding the arrival of an Englishman in a Bulgarian village, such as the disappearance of a "stop" sign facing west. Subsequent interactions between Mr Jones and the locals over his possible investment projects uncover the mutual Balkan and European hesitations in the rocky enlargement of Europe. The former functions as "a disruptive presence", by "obstructing", through its "inefficiencies" (such as nationalism), "the free flow of goods and money", and the latter acts from a position of "weakened public governance". In that constellation, "Balkanness" and "Europeanness" become vessels for performing "strategic", rather than essentialised, identities. Such is the status of parallel codifications of Islam and homosexuality in Piro Rexhepi's analysis of select "historical Albanian novels" and "Bosnian films". Here, dominant cultural production provides a specifically vivid insight into how those countries seek to relieve their Islamic otherness, so as to be perceived as European, through expulsion of gays (in the former case, a lover is killed in an Ottoman battle and in the latter, a partner must emigrate to Europe during the Yugoslav wars, in order to live). Rather than "writing back to Europe", here the Balkans adopt what they recognise as a "right" European orientation by "correcting" its queer folk.

As Uroš Čvoro's analysis of select post-Yugoslav art projects suggests, underprivileged cultural formations, like the lack of language proficiencies, can unsettle dominant binaries, particularly when addressing unequal access to dominant modes of cross-European interaction. Art projects, he explores, thematise the long procedures behind "marrying for papers" and linguistic (in)competences for participating in European fan cultures, demonstrating that Europeanness is reserved for those who display a double capacity: "to speak English and ... to move freely across borders". In fact, the desire for European recognition can be such that it can produce what, in her chapter, Orlanda Obad terms "deliberately naïve and utopian narratives of progress and Europeanness", narratives which can run in parallel to professed Euroscepticism. As Obad's anthropological research on select groups of people related with the Croatian EU accession (agricultural entrepreneurs successful in applying to the pre-accession funds and Croatian negotiators with the EU and Croatian EU officials) demonstrates, usual assumptions that a whole aspiring nation's society enjoys the privileges of EU entry are wide off the mark. Different segments of the population have different dispositions for participation, which in Obad's study appeared to be class based: it is mainly the young, highly educated and polyglot members of society who gain easier access to EU's resources such as mobility and employment. Nonetheless, as we read from Romanian journalist Claudia Ciobanu's autobiographic text on her own experience of returning (in her case to Poland) upon completing higher education in "Western" Europe, "back and forth" migration of "the lucky ones" always requires the handling of important affectual issues like the feeling of "guilt" and uselessness in relation to family members "left behind". Far from dissipating the relevance of home, cross-European mobility can stimulate the search for home, particularly for "dark souls of the Erasmus generation", who seek to orient themselves at once in the geography of Europe and in "the geography of heart".

To move further with this notion, in the final chapter, the editors of this volume seek ways of understanding Europe as being at home in the Balkans by engaging two acclaimed writers on European issues in a conversation: Slavenka Drakulić speaking from Istria, a region in Croatia which would be "offended" to be linked with the Balkans; and David Morley, speaking from the UK, a country which has long been "at the edge of Europe". The speakers go back to their earlier, formative arguments, about the Yugoslav states in the Balkans as a space of partial, often regressive, post-1989 transition (Drakulić), and about Europe being about "spaces of identity", spaces which are not necessarily consistent with national state borders (Morley). In their exchange, the speakers reflect on issues ranging from reconciliation, history as ideology, global geopolitics, regionalism, migration and politics of representation. Drakulić espouses a view of the Balkans as a space specifically damaged by a historical absence of a democratic revolution. Morley, on the other hand, wary of essentialism, argues for a recognition of analogies between some phenomena in the Balkans and those in spaces far away.

This book hopes to have made evident that Europe and the Balkans have no meaningful existence outside their relationship. Europe can only be admirable and pleasing from the perspective of the "troubled" Balkans idealising Europe and setting on a journey – defined as impossible from the start – towards Europe's recognition and acceptance. Instead of a search for Europe (as a specific set of social, political and economic relations) we submit that analysis should focus on what makes up the space where Europeans live, especially if to feel European they have to mentally leave the Balkans. If "we do live on the same planet . . . but not in the same world"[97], the fact that Europe without the Balkans remains unfinished makes its narration an ongoing conversation.

NOTES

1. Maria Todorova, *Imagining the Balkans* (New York and Oxford: Oxford University Press, 1997), 111.

2. Ivaylo Ditchev, "The Eros of Identity," in *Balkan as Metaphor: Between Globalization and Fragmentation*, eds., Dušan Bjelić and Obrad Savić (Cambridge, MA and London: The MIT Press, 2002), 235–50. See also chapter 9 in this volume.

3. Damir Grubiša, "Politički sustav Europske unije i europeizacija hrvatske politike," in *Politički sustav Europske unije i europeizacija hrvatske politike*, Damir Grubiša, Nataša Beširević and Hrvoje Špehar, eds. (Zagreb: Politička misao, 2012), 8.

4. EU enlargement is formally "Unstoppable," Grubiša, "Politički sustav," 16. Eastern Partnership strategy also mentions Ukraine and the Caucasus countries as possible future members.

5. Stuart Hall, "The Neo-liberal Revolution," *Cultural Studies* 25, no. 6 (2011).

6. Zygmunt Bauman, *Europe: An Unfinished Adventure* (Cambridge and Malden MA: Polity, 2004), 80.

7. Hall, "Neoliberal".

8. Dipesh Chakrabarty, *Provincializing Europe: Postcolonial Thought and Historical Difference* (Princeton and Oxford: Princeton University Press, 2007).

9. Stuart Hall, "Race, Articulation and Societies Structured in Dominance," in *Sociological Theories: Race and Colonialism* (Paris: UNESCO 1980), 325. Quoted in Jennifer Daryl Slack "The Theory and Method of Articulation in Cultural Studies," in *Stuart Hall: Critical Dialogues in Cultural Studies*, David Morley and Kuan-Hsing Chen, eds. (London: Routledge, 1996), 113–29.

10. Stuart Hall, "Life and Times of the First New Left," *New Left Review* 61, January–February (2010).

11. Slack, "Articulation," 119.

12. Slavenka Drakulić, *Café Europa: Life after Communism* (New York: Penguin Books, 1999/1996), 15.

13. David Morley and Kevin Robins, *Spaces of Identity: Global Media, Electronic Landscapes and Cultural Boundaries* (London and New York: Routledge, 1995), 45.

14. Stuart Hall, "Who Needs Identity?" in *Questions of Cultural Identity*, Stuart Hall and Paul du Gay, eds. (London: Sage, 1996), 1–17.

15. Kuan-Hsin Chen, "Cultural Studies and the Politics of Internationalization: An Interview with Stuart Hall by Kuan-Hsing Chen," in *Stuart Hall: Critical Dialogues in Cultural Studies*, David Morley and Kuan-Hsin Chen, eds. (London: Routledge, 1996), 408.

16. Bauman, *Europe*, 9, 45, 5.

17. Dejan Jović, "Instead of Enlargement, 'Restern Balkans' in Consolidation," *European Western Balkans*, July 29, 2015, http://europeanwesternbalkans. com/2015/07/29/instead-of-enlargement-restern-balkans-in-consolidation/ Accessed August 15, 2015.

18. Morley and Robins, *Spaces*, 41.

19. Todorova, *Balkans*, 3.

20. Ibid., 18.

21. Ibid., 18–19, 27.

22. Edward Said, Orientalism (London: Penguin Books, 2003).

23. Katarina Luketić, *Balkan: od geografije do fantazije* (Zagreb: Algoritam, 2013), 20.

24. Luketić, *Balkan*, 130.

25. Ibid., 191.

26. Todorova, *Balkans*, 122.

27. Ibid., 137.

28. Ibid., 162, 187, 128.

29. Ibid., 119.

30. Luketić, *Balkan*, 55–69. See also chapter 6 in this volume.

31. Ibid., 67.

32. Luketić, *Balkan*.

33. Ditchev, "Identity," 244.

34. Dušan Bjelić, "Introduction: Blowing up the 'Bridge'," in *Balkan as Metaphor: Between Globalization and Fragmentation*, Dušan Bjelić and Obrad Savić, eds. (Cambridge, MA and London: The MIT Press, 2002), 4.

35. This argument is drawn from a well-known notion of the intra-Balkanist "gradation of 'Orients'," which, according to Bakić-Hayden's definition, involves "all ethnic groups defin[ing] the 'other' as 'East' of them" (Bakić-Hayden, "Nesting," 918–919), as was persuasively illustrated in Žižek's earlier discussion of the issue (Žižek, *Negative*, 223). The "gradation of Orients" can crop up in a variety of suggestive contexts, including everyday television (see Krajina, "Mapping the Other"). For a reverse perspective of EU being seen as a version of Yugoslavia just before disintegration see Blanuša, "Yugoslav Syndrome".

36. Ditchev, "Identity," 244.

37. Bakić-Hayden, "Nesting".

38. Jović, "Restern".

39. Dejan Jović, *Yugoslavia: A State that Withered Away* (West Lafayette, IN: Purdue University Press, 2009).

40. Luketić, *Balkan*, 187.

41. Bjelić, "Introduction," 16.

42. Vesna Goldsworthy, "Invention and In(ter)vention: The Rhetoric of Balkanization," in *Balkan as Metaphor: Between Globalization and Fragmentation* Dušan

Bjelić and Obrad Savić, eds. (Cambridge, MA and London: The MIT Press, 2002), 34.

43. See also Pero Maldini and Davor Pauković, eds., *Croatia and European Union: Changes and Development* (Farnham: Ashgate, 2015).

44. Charles Grant, *Europe's Blurred Boundaries: Rethinking Enlargement and Neighbourhood Policy* (London: Centre for European Reform, 2006), 1–2.

45. Caspar Pearson, "EUtopia? The European Union and the Parlamentarium in Brussels," *City* 17, no. 5 (2013): 637.

46. Johan Förnas, *Signifying Europe* (Bristol: Intellect, 2011), 264.

47. Bauman, *Europe*, 1–2.

48. Jan Nederveen Pieterse, "Unpacking the West: How European Is Europe," *Racism, Modernity and Identity: On the Western Front*, Ali Rattansi and Sally Westwood, eds. (Cambridge: Polity Press, 1994), 131.

49. Amnesty International, *Europe's Borderlands: Violations against Refugees and Migrants in Macedonia, Serbia and Hungary.* (London: Amnesty International, 2015), 62.

50. "Migrants' Newest Route to Europe Means an Epic Balkans Trek," *New York Times*, March 26, 2015, http://www.nytimes.com/aponline/2015/03/26/world/europe/ap-eu-migrants-journey-to-europe-abridged.html?_r=1. Accessed July 10, 2015.

51. Fernand Braudel, "Definicija mediteranske kulture," *Zbornik Trećeg Programa Radio Zagreba* 11, Zagreb: RTZ (1985): 78, 81.

52. Iain Chambers, "A Fluid Archive," in *Transculturality and Interdisciplinarity: Challenges for Research on Media, Migration and Intercultural Dialogue* (Barcelona: Centre for International Affairs, 2014), 13, 17.

53. Chambers, "Archive," 17–18.

54. See Bauman, *Europe*, 76, 101.

55. Wolfgang Streeck, "The Crises of Democratic Capitalism," *New Left Review* 71, September–October (2011): 29, 25.

56. Will Bartlett and Ivana Prica, "The Deepening Crisis in the European Super-periphery," *Journal of Balkan and Near Eastern Studies* 15, no. 4 (2013): 368.

57. Ibid.

58. Slaveka Drakulić, *How We Survived Communism and Even Laughed*, (Zagreb: VBZ, 2013/1992), 40. See also chapter 8 in this volume.

59. Radina Vučetić, *Koka-kola socijalizam* (Beograd: Službeni glasnik, 2012), 16, 411.

60. Eurobarometer, "Standard Eurobarometer 83 Fieldwork May 2015," http://ec.europa.eu/public_opinion/archives/eb/eb83/eb83_en.htm. Accessed August 10, 2015.

61. See, on "Euroindifference," Dejan Jović, "Hrvatski referendum o članstvu u Europskoj uniji i njegove posljedice za smanjeni Zapadni Balkan," *Anali Hrvatskog politološkog društva* IX (2012): 163–182.

62. See Zlatan Krajina, "EU nije YU – EU je fora: Analiza predreferendumskih televizijskih spotova Vlade RH za ulazak Hrvatske u Europsku uniju," *Politička misao* 50, no. 2 (2013): 98–123.

63. Whereas the "positive image" of the EU is held amongst an average of only 41% of the surveyed EU citizens (32–45% in "older" member states), the Balkans

see the EU much more positively, ranging 47–75% in Croatia, Bulgaria, Romania, Macedonia and Albania (Eurobarometer, 2015). Amongst the few countries which are optimistic about the future of the EU are Romania (75%) and Croatia (74%); least optimism countries are France, Austria and the UK (ibid.).

64. Othon Anastasakis, "The Europeanization of the Balkans," *Brown Journal of World Affairs,* Summer/Fall, XII, no. 1 (2005): 78. See in particular chapter 1 in this volume.

65. Kristi Raik, "EU Accession of Central and Eastern European Countries: Democracy and Integration as Conflicting Logics," *East European Politics and Society* 81, no. 4 (2004): 582–83.

66. David Morley, *Media, Modernity and Technology: The Geography of the New* (London and New York: Routledge, 2006), 165.

67. Todorova, *Balkans*, 133.

68. Brankica Drašković and Jelena Kleut, "Discursive Representation of Euro-peanization Process Actors in Print Media," in *Europe, Here and There: Analysis of Europeanization Discourse in the Western Balkans Media,* Dubravka Valić Nedeljković and Jelena Kleut, eds. (Filozofski fakultet: Novi Sad, 2013), 135.

69. Drašković and Kleut, "Representation," 136, 145.

70. Ibid., 136–140.

71. Ibid., "Representation," 144.

72. Ibid., 141.

73. Zoran Kurelić, "No Carrot and No Stick: Croatia's Simulated Democracy and the EU," in *Kroatien in der EU: Stand und Perspektiven*, ed., Beate Neuss (Hamburg: Verlag Dr. Kovač, 2015b), 61, 48.

74. Zoran Kurelić, "Anti-Liberal Permanent Transition," Keynote lecture at the *Policy Networks in the European Union Conference*, March 27–28, 2015 (Zagreb: House of Europe, 2015a).

75. Kurelić, "Simulated Democracy," 49.

76. Ibid., 53.

77. Ibid.

78. Dejan Jović, "1989: godina koja nam se nije dogodila," *Politička misao portal* 2014, http://politickamisao.com/1989-godina-koja-nam-se-nije-dogodila/. Accessed September 1, 2015.

79. Ibid.

80. Ibid.

81. Francisco de Borja Lasheras, "Europe Must Not Neglect the Western Balkans," *European Council on Foreign Relations,* September 5, 2014, http://www.ecfr.eu/article/commentary_europe_must_not_neglect_the_western_balkans307. Accessed July 15, 2015.

82. Jović, "1989".

83. Todorova, *Balkans*, 54.

84. Jim Seroka, "Issues with Regional Reintegration of the Western Balkans," *Journal of Southern Europe and the Balkans* 10, no. 1 (2008): 21. For a fuller overview of such proposals see Blanuša, "Yugoslav Syndrome".

85. Pantoleon D. Skayannis and Haralambos Skyrgiannis, "The Role of Transport in the Development of the Balkans," *Eastern European Economics* 40, no. 5, (2002): 42.

86. Skayannis and Skyrgiannis, "Transport," 45.

87. Velikonja's archaeology of *"Titostalgia"* demonstrates that the proliferation of popular memorabilia commemorating Tito's persona and regime testifies to the sense of dissatisfaction with the unclear direction of transition in the post-Yugoslav space. See Mitja Velikonja, *Titostalgia – A Study of Nostalgia for Josip Broz* (Ljubljana: Mirovni inštitut, 2008).

88. Étienne Balibar, "Europe as Borderland," *The Alexander von Humbolt Lecture in Human Geography*, University of Nijmegen, November 10, 2004. http://gpm. ruhosting.nl/avh/Europe%20as%20Borderland.pdf. Accessed May 1, 2015.

89. Todorova, *Balkans*, 187, 13.

90. David Morley, *Home Territories: Media, Mobility and Identity* (London and New York: Routledge, 2000), 253, 252.

91. Bauman, *Europe*.

92. Chantal Mouffe, *On the Political* (London: Routledge, 2005).

93. Cf. Gayatri Chakravorti Spivak, "Can the Subaltern Speak?" in *Marxism and the Interpretation of Culture* Cary Nelson and Lawrence Grossberg, eds. (Urbana: University of Illinois Press, 1988).

94. See chapters 3, 8 and 10 in this volume.

95. We thank David Morley for his assistance in developing this point.

96. I borrow this characterisation of the project from Zlatko Uzelac's remark made in the public panel "Urbana plastika i politika forsiranih korijena" (Urban sculptures and the politics of forced roots), held as part of the EUROKAZ Festival in Zagreb, on 2 July 2012.

97. Slavenka Drakulić, *Café Europa: Life after Communism* (New York: Penguin Books, 1999/1996), 142.

BIBLIOGRAPHY

Amnesty International. *Europe's Borderlands: Violations against Refugees and Migrants in Macedonia, Serbia and Hungary*. London: Amnesty International, 2015.

Anastasakis, Othon. "The Europeanization of the Balkans." *Brown Journal of World Affairs*, Summer/Fall, XII, no. 1 (2005): 77–88.

Bakić-Hayden, Milica. "Nesting Orientalisms: The Case of Former Yugoslavia." *Slavic Review* 54, no. 4 (1995): 917–931.

Balibar, Étienne. "Europe as Borderland." *The Alexander von Humbolt Lecture in Human Geography*. University of Nijmegen, November 10, 2004. http://gpm. ruhosting.nl/avh/Europe%20as%20Borderland.pdf. Accessed May 1, 2015.

Bartlett, Will and Prica, Ivana. "The Deepening Crisis in the European Super-periphery." *Journal of Balkan and Near Eastern Studies* 15, no. 4 (2013): 367–382.

Bauman, Zygmunt. *Europe: An Unfinished Adventure*. Cambridge and Malden MA: Polity, 2004.

Bjelić, Dušan. "Introduction: Blowing Up the 'Bridge'." In *Balkan as Metaphor: Between Globalization and Fragmentation*, edited by Dušan Bjelić and Obrad Savić. Cambridge, MA and London: The MIT Press, 2002, 1–22.

Blanuša, Nebojša. "The Political Unconscious of Croatia and the EU: Tracing the Yugoslav Syndrome through Fredric Jamesons's Lenses." *Journal of Balkan and Near Eastern Studies* 16, no. 2, (2014): 196–222.

Braudel, Fernand. "Definicija mediteranske kulture." *Zbornik Trećeg Programa Radio Zagreba* 11, Zagreb: RTZ (1985): 47–90.

Chakrabarty, Dipesh. *Provincializing Europe: Postcolonial Thought and Historical Difference*. Princeton and Oxford: Princeton University Press, 2007.

Chambers, Iain. "A Fluid Archive." In *Transculturality and Interdisciplinarity: Challenges for Research on Media, Migration and Intercultural* Dialogue, 11–22. Barcelona: Centre for International Affairs, 2014.

Chen, Kuan-Hsin. "Cultural Studies and the Politics of Internationalization: An Interview with Stuart Hall by Kuan-Hsing Chen." In *Stuart Hall: Critical Dialogues in Cultural Studies*, edited by David Morley and Kuan-Hsin Chen, 393–409. London: Routledge, 1996.

Ditchev, Ivaylo. "The Eros of Identity." In *Balkan as Metaphor: Between Globalization and Fragmentation*, edited by Dušan Bjelić and Obrad Savić, 235–250. Cambridge, MA and London: The MIT Press, 2002.

Drakulić, Slavenka. *Café Europa: Life after Communism.* New York: Penguin Books, 1999/1996.

Drakulić, Slavenka. *How We Survived Communism and Even Laughed.* Zagreb: VBZ, 2013/1992.

Drašković, Brankica and Kleut, Jelena. "Discursive Representation of Europeanization Process Actors in Print Media." In *Europe, Here and There: Analysis of Europeanization Discourse in the Western Balkans Media*, edited by Dubravka Valić Nedeljković and Jelena Kleut, 133–145. Filozofski fakultet: Novi Sad, 2013.

Eurobarometer. "Standard Eurobarometer 83 Fieldwork May 2015." http://ec.europa. eu/public_opinion/archives/eb/eb83/eb83_en.htm. Accessed August 10, 2015.

Förnas, Johan. *Signifying Europe.* Bristol: Intellect, 2011.

Goldsworthy, Vesna. "Invention and In(ter)vention: The Rhetoric of Balkanization." In *Balkan as Metaphor: Between Globalization and Fragmentation*, edited by, Dušan Bjelić and Obrad Savić, 25–38. Cambridge, MA and London: The MIT Press, 2002.

Grant, Charles. *Europe's Blurred Boundaries: Rethinking Enlargement and Neighbourhood Policy.* London: Centre for European Reform, 2006.

Grubiša, Damir. "Politički sustav Europske unije i europeizacija hrvatske politike." In *Politički sustav Europske unije i europeizacija hrvatske politike*, edited by Damir Grubiša, Nataša Beširević, and Hrvoje Špehar, 7–42. Zagreb: Politička misao, 2012.

Hall, Stuart. "Race, Articulation and Societies Structured in Dominance." In *Sociological Theories: Race and Colonialism*, 305–345. Paris: UNESCO, 1980.

Hall, Stuart. "Who Needs Identity?" In *Questions of Cultural Identity*, edited by Stuart Hall and Paul du Gay, 1–17. London: Sage, 1996.

Hall, Stuart. "Life and Times of the First New Left." *New Left Review* 61, January-February (2010), http://newleftreview.org/II/61/stuart-hall-life-and-times-of-the-first-new-left. Accessed April 15, 2014.

Hall, Stuart. "The Neo-liberal Revolution." *Cultural Studies* 25, no. 6 (2011): 705–728.

Jović, Dejan. *Yugoslavia: A State that Withered Away*. West Lafayette, IN: Purdue University Press, 2009.

Jović, Dejan. "Hrvatski referendum o članstvu u Europskoj uniji i njegove posljedice za smanjeni Zapadni Balkan." *Anali Hrvatskog politološkog društva* IX (2012): 163–182.

Jović, Dejan. "1989: godina koja nam se nije dogodila." *Politička misao portal* 2014, http://politickamisao.com/1989-godina-koja-nam-se-nije-dogodila/. Accessed September 1, 2015.

Jović, Dejan. "Instead of Enlargement, 'Restern Balkans' in Consolidation." *European Western Balkans*, July 29, 2015. http://europeanwesternbalkans.com/2015/07/29/instead-of-enlargement-restern-balkans-in-consolidation/. Accessed August 15, 2015.

Krajina, Zlatan. "'Mapping' the 'Other' in Television News on International Affairs: BBC's 'Pre-Accession' Coverage of EU Membership Candidate Croatia." *Croatian Political Science Review* 46, no. 5 (2009): 140–170.

Krajina, Zlatan. "EU nije YU – EU je fora: Analiza predreferendumskih televizijskih spotova Vlade RH za ulazak Hrvatske u Europsku uniju." *Politička misao* 50, no. 2 (2013): 98–123.

Kurelić, Zoran. "Anti-Liberal Permanent Transition." Keynote lecture at the *Policy Networks in the European Union Conference*, March 27–28, 2015 (Zagreb: House of Europe, 2015a).

Kurelić, Zoran. "No Carrot and No Stick: Croatia's Simulated Democracy and the EU." In *Kroatien in der EU: Stand und Perspektiven*, edited by Beate Neuss, 47–64. Hamburg: Verlag Dr. Kovač, 2015b.

Lasheras, Francisco de Borja. "Europe Must not Neglect the Western Balkans." *European Council on Foreign Relations,* September 5, 2014, http://www.ecfr.eu/article/commentary_europe_must_not_neglect_the_western_balkans307. Accessed July 15, 2015.

Luketić, Katarina. *Balkan: od geografije do fantazije*. Zagreb: Algoritam, 2013.

Maldini, Pero and Pauković, Davor, eds., *Croatia and European Union: Changes and Development*. Farnham: Ashgate, 2015.

Morley, David. *Home Territories: Media, Mobility and Identity*. London: Routledge, 2000.

Morley, David. *Media, Modernity and Technology: The Geography of The New*. London and New York: Routledge, 2006.

Morley, David and Robins, Kevin. *Spaces of Identity: Global Media, Electronic Landscapes and Cultural Boundaries*. London and New York: Routledge, 1995.

New York Times, "Migrants' Newest Route to Europe Means an Epic Balkans Trek," March 26, 2015, http://www.nytimes.com/aponline/2015/03/26/world/europe/ap-eu-migrants-journey-to-europe-abridged.html?_r=1. Accessed July 10, 2015.

Mouffe, Chantal. *On the Political*. London: Routledge, 2005.

Pearson, Caspar. "EUtopia? The European Union and the Parlamentarium in Brussels." *City* 17, no. 5 (2013): 636–653.

Pieterse, Jan Nederveen. "Unpacking the West: How European is Europe." In *Racism, Modernity and Identity: On the Western Front*, edited by Ali Rattansi and Sally Westwood, 129–149. Cambridge: Polity Press, 1994.

Raik, Kristi. "EU Accession of Central and Eastern European Countries: Democracy and Integration as Conflicting Logics." *East European Politics and Society* 81, no. 4 (2004): 567–594.

Said, Edward. *Orientalism.* London: Penguin Books, 2003.

Seroka, Jim. "Issues with Regional Reintegration of the Western Balkans." *Journal of Southern Europe and the Balkans* 10, no. 1 (2008): 15–29.

Skayannis, Pantoleon D. and Skyrgiannis, Haralambos. "The Role of Transport in the Development of the Balkans." *Eastern European Economics* 40, no. 5 (2002): 33–48.

Slack, Jennifer Daryl. "The Theory and Method of Articulation in Cultural Studies." In *Stuart Hall: Critical Dialogues in Cultural Studies*, edited by David Morley and Kuan-Hsing Chen, 113–129. London: Routledge, 1996.

Spivak, Gayatri Chakravotri. "Can the Subaltern Speak?" In *Marxism and the Interpretation of Culture*, edited by Cary Nelson and Lawrence Grossberg, 271–313. Urbana: University of Illinois Press, 1988.

Streeck, Wolfgang. "The Crises of Democratic Capitalism." *New Left Review* 71, September–October (2011): 5–29.

Todorova, Maria. *Imagining the Balkans.* New York and Oxford: Oxford University Press, 1997.

Todorova, Maria. *Imagining the Balkans.* Updated Edition. New York and Oxford: Oxford University Press, 2009.

Velikonja, Mitja. *Titostalgia – A Study of Nostalgia for Josip Broz.* Ljubljana: Mirovni inštitut, 2008.

Vučetić, Radina. *Koka-kola Socijalizam.* Beograd: Službeni glasnik, 2012.

Žižek, Slavoj. *Tarrying with the Negative: Kant, Hegel, and the Critique of Ideology.* Durham: Duke University Press, 1993.

Part II

EUROPEANISING

Chapter 1

Re-assembling and Disciplining Social Europe

Turbulent Moments and Fragile F(r)ictions

Paul Stubbs and Noémi Lendvai

WHEN ALICE MET HUMPTY DUMPTY

The Commission is not keen on the word "austerity." They prefer "fiscal consolidation."[1]

The use of words within the European Union (EU) is about much more than mere linguistic choices. In the statement above, the preference for "fiscal consolidation" rather than "austerity" reveals, perhaps more dramatically than usual, the intimate connection between linguistic representations, policy schemas and disciplinary practices. "Austerity" is no longer a neutral term. It has become saturated, even before the election of Syriza in Greece in January 2015, with negative connotations, not merely in terms of a raft of unpopular policy prescriptions but, perhaps even more so, with massive and unnecessary human suffering. A report by the International Federation of the Red Cross[2] paints a stark picture of millions queuing up for food in hastily arranged soup kitchens, of endemic youth unemployment in many parts of Europe and, above all, of a crisis whose long-term consequences are yet to hit us. "Fiscal consolidation" attempts to return the political genie into the technical bottle, in a vain hope that the vague neutrality of the term, its purportedly abstract, bureaucratic character, will mask, at least partially, and at least for a while, the real and symbolic violence being performed in its name.

We write as increasingly disenchanted observers of the EU, Europeanisation, the social dimension of the EU and, above all, of mainstream academic attempts to grasp them. As, respectively, Hungarian-born and UK-based (NL), and UK-born and Croatian-based (PS) scholars, we find ourselves continually attempting to understand the variegated social in the EU, currently within the context of austerity neo-liberalisms[3]. We have focused, over a long period of time, on South East Europe as a privileged positionality from which to see the shifting "social" as embedded in the complex articulation of post-socialism, conflict and post-conflict, new nation-state building and variegated capitalisms, often simplistically termed "transition"[4] Over time, we have seen many concepts rise and fall in the pecking order of "Eurospeak."[5] Phrases are introduced, mobilised, put to work and discarded with an alarming frequency. Policy domains are constantly being constructed and deconstructed and, in the process, reconfigured, reframed and recoupled. Who outside of a narrow policy community has any idea what is meant by "The Open Method of Co-ordination," much less the "Social OMC"? Who understands what is meant by "social inclusion" and "social cohesion," or what might be the difference between them? Is it really important that policy processes be "benchmarked," "mainstreamed," and "streamlined" to ensure that there is "feeding in and feeding out" across policy areas? Do the concepts of "investment," "entrepreneurship" and "innovation" really change their meaning if the word "social" is added in front of them? Can we find in these phrases the new "commonsense" of the neo-liberal settlement, working to inscribe "the supposed naturalness of 'the market', the primacy of the competitive individual, the superiority of the private over the public?"[6]

Some of these words and phrases sound "unbearably foreign"[7] even to English language speakers, within a complex *mélange* of "international Englishes."[8] It may be, in fact, that because they do not mean anything they can, indeed, mean anything[9]. We are reminded of the encounter between Humpty Dumpty and Alice in *Through the Looking Glass*. Humpty Dumpty scornfully tells Alice: "When I use a word . . . it means just what I choose it to mean – no more or no less." Alice, in thrall to a peculiar brand of relativistic postmodernism, replies: "The question is . . . whether you can make words mean so many different things." Humpty Dumpty retorts in a way a critical Gramscian scholar would be proud of: "The question is . . . which is to be master – that's all."[10]

In this chapter we trace European integration not as a linear, modernist process of catch-up, convergence and mutual learning but as a set of mediated, postcolonial encounters and translations, marked by the enactment and embodiment of performative fictions and frictions, as a series of "contact zones," involving "the spatial and temporal co-presence of subjects previously separated by geographic and historical disjunctures, and whose trajectories now intersect."[11] A focus on performativity allows us to focus on sites of practice, on "acting, speaking, feeling and doing" implying "the presence of simultaneous dynamics of creativity and constraint, activism and incorporation, and retreat and proliferation."[12] "Fictions," as "discursive strategies," whilst "intangible and weightless," are always embedded in material relations and often inform how policies and politics are "understood, performed,

enacted, enforced, resisted, or colonised."[13] At the same time, these relations are marked by what Tsing terms "frictions" or "the awkward, unequal,
unstable, and creative qualities of interconnection across difference."[14]

Conceiving of Europeanisation as a misplaced, catch-all term for multiple
and discontinuous practices of disciplinarity, knowledge and power allows us
to re-examine the realm of "the social" as it has been radically re-assembled
and re-constructed across space and time, here specifically in relation to the
South East European post-conflict, post-Yugoslav space-time assemblage.
To do this, we take postcolonialism as a study of *both* culture and politics
where imperialism, colonialism and agency are linked both discursively and
materially. We take postcolonial theory to be applicable even beyond the
study of the direct effects of colonialism. Even if parts of the post-Yugoslav
space have never been subject to direct colonial social relations, although they
were clearly enrolled in circuits of imperialism, it is postcolonial theory's
focus on the production and reproduction of domination, with parts of the
world constructed as the non-civilised "Other" even as "the epistemic territory of modernity"[15] is expanding, which is most pertinent here. By adding
post-structuralism and cultural political economy into the theoretical mix, we
aim to reflect on social policy, economic development and political economy
as well as cultural encounters and subversive resistances[16].

Highly critical of an orthodox literature on social policy, not least for its
"presentist realism,"[17] tending to ignore the relevance of circuits of imperial and colonial social relations, we explore the politics of and differences
between welfare and well-being, the uneven development of neo-liberalisms,
and the multi-scalar restructuring of welfare assemblages in wider Europe,
not limited to the member states of the EU. We argue that this has to be set
in the context of the reframing of the relationships between "the economic,"
"the political" and "the social" and, crucially between a so-called European
core and periphery, in a period of deep crisis and austerity. Post-communist
Europe is not a flattened map consisting of more or less coherent welfare
regimes. Rather, diverse, and often contradictory, processes of restructuring are emerging, in which variegated peripheralisations occur in different
conjunctures or "moments." Four of these "moments" seem particularly
relevant here: (1) the "wave" of post-communist accession in 2004; (2) the
"aftershock" of the reluctant accession of Bulgaria and Romania in 2007;
(3) the tiny splash caused by Croatia's accession in 2013; and (4) the "not yet"
moment of possible future enlargement to the other countries of the so-called
"Western Balkans" coinciding, for a time at least, with a Syriza-led challenge
to a fundamentalist "austerity" politics.

We argue that exploring "social Europe" in this way forces us to address
how different configurations of neo-liberalism, nationalism and authoritarian-
ism, on the one hand, and movements for direct democracy, social justice and

decommodification, on the other, become central to the contested dynamics of Europeanisation and its variegated impacts. Throughout, we are addressing these processes through a lens of translation[18], tracing movements across languages, jurisdictions, policy domains and practices, not as linear transfer, transmission or transplantation, but rather as active, contested and open processes of complex becoming, modification, distortion and transformation[19]. We treat translation as a flexible, "catch all" concept, albeit heavily influenced by strands of postcolonial theory, understanding translation as "a powerful metaphor to evoke the complex economies of cultural exchange that take place under the sign of empire."[20] Our method is a humble, yet fairly explicit, challenge to the "epistemic modernism" of the European project and much of its associated mainstream scholarship. We urge a shift in direction, a different way of thinking and writing about the EU, which examines "what slips out, does not fit or gets lost in translation."[21]

TRANSLATING EUROPEANISATION: POSTCOLONIALITY, DISCIPLINARITY AND POWER

Whilst there can be no simple or unequivocal answer, then, to the question "What is the EU?", any narrative which fails to take into account "the historicity of empire" or which views the EU "through the looking glass of the West European state"[22] is, at best, partial. It is no accident that the core EU member states are precisely those that "exercised imperial rule . . . just two to three generations ago," creating both "inherited sociocultural patterns of thinking"[23] and dependent political economies. It surely matters that "the political process of European identity construction tries to hide the corpse of colonialism while it continues . . . to partake of the material inheritance of the same colonialism."[24] For Böröcz, a postcolonial analysis asserts that the "structural conditions of dependence on a foreign authority for laws and regulations make the situation of east European applicant states somewhat similar to that of 'dependencies', 'protectorates', and a form of externally supervised government reminiscent of the history of colonial empires as 'indirect rules'"[25].

In our view "Eastern enlargement," in terms of both the accession of postcommunist member states and the prospects of membership for the EU's neighbours, is less a "sharing of the loot"[26] and more an extension and reformulation of the neo-colonialist project within the EU itself. A neo-colonial "dependence on a foreign authority,"[27] like the dependencies and protectorates in colonial history, is now translated into trade, investment and debt dependence within and around the EU itself. In the encounter between "the coloniser" and "the colonised,"[28] the best that is being offered is "integration without inclusion."[29] In the current conjuncture, it may be that the symbolic resonance of "rejoining a Europe to which we have always belonged" has lost its shine in an asymmetrical EU in which the supposed economic and developmental "laggards" face the prospects of prolonged second-class status and neo-colonial disciplinarity, even after having joined the club. Zielonka sees the EU as a neo-medieval empire with polycentric governance asserting economic and bureaucratic control, with the periphery gradually, if fitfully, gaining access to decision-making in the centre[30]. Crucially, however, he argues that successive rounds of enlargements represent "imperial governance," where post-communist countries are not fully "conquered," but where enormous power asymmetries are sustained as a central feature throughout the accession process. He argues that for accession states, "compliance is the essence of imperial relations characterised by structural asymmetries,"[31] and where "the idea of an inferior Eastern Europe, counterpoised to the dominant Western Europe, is embedded in the discourse between the EU and the applicant Eastern European states."[32] Key to this imperial governance is the modernist dream, in which the "EU Accession process looked like the most advanced example of institutional engineering or even the apogee of a modernist dream."[33] For Zielonka:

> Behind the façade of the carefully engineered project there was a great deal of chaos and vagueness. The ultra-modernist pretensions were largely utopian. . . . Under careful scrutiny the accession process looks rather like an imperial exercise of asserting political and economic control over an unstable and under-developed [*sic*] neighbourhood[34].

Crucially, we agree with Gravier, who argues that European integration as "imperialisation" most obviously manifests through continuous enlargements, which "contribute to and reveal the slow but deep dissociation between core states and peripheral states,"[35] with the continued possibility that countries that entered some time ago, such as Greece, Spain, Portugal and Italy, become reclassified as part of the periphery. If the core of the EU is, indeed, part of an "interwoven clique of actors with a set of shared geopolitical interests," it is one where the reproduction of "wealth, power, privilege and . . . cultural superiority" is confined to only some member states, and only to some sub-sections of the population even in those member states[36]. Perhaps the current conjuncture, defined by a narrow emphasis on a fundamentalist neo-liberal economic model, and framed overwhelmingly in terms of debt reduction and austerity, sees the EU no longer able to "sub-contract the dirty work" to others, and unable to avoid direct involvement in "the messy business of the social and environmental violence associated with the extraction of surpluses" as the unfolding renegotiations over Greek debt repayment illustrate as we write[37].

We continue to hold, however, to what has been termed "an inessential view of the EU"[38] as "ambiguous, multiple and contradictory," located within "a contingent, ever-changing 'in-betweenness'"[39]. Although carefully crafted, dominant institutional and social scientific narratives, framing Europeanisation as modernisation, involving processes of "catch up" and "convergence" in terms of both living standards and fundamental values, are merely more or less successful attempts at a "governmentalization of Europe."[40] What is needed, instead, is a critical analysis of "the production of a plurality of Europes within discontinuous regimes and practices of knowledge,"[41] emphasising the active, contested and contradictory construction of "subjectivities and identities, . . . socio-economic trajectories and . . . institutional landscapes."[42] The "work" of combining disciplinary forms of the imperial governance of enlargement with what might be termed "utopian chaos" and "engineered vagueness" is, therefore, highly complex, variegated and messy.

Holding together "four shreds of translation: the performative, the relational, the multiple and the political"[43] is central to our alternative mode of enquiry here. The EU has to be continually performed and enacted, within "multiple spaces of power and resistance."[44] Understanding the EU as a "contact zone"[45] or a "translation zone"[46] involving both "highly asymmetrical relations of domination and subordination" and "the interactive, improvisational dimensions of colonial encounters"[47] questions the omniscient force of "travelling rationalities."[48] When policies travel they not only are "produced, assembled and populated differently"[49] but have very different effects in and across different times and spaces. As such Europeanisation is not a homogenous process with a universal grammar, but a variegated and uneven process. Constructing the EU as a "common space" requires a tremendous amount of work to maintain a kind of "techno-managerial order,"[50] a crowded fictional space of common "indicators," "targets" and "guidelines," where experiences of "best practice" become the material of "peer review" and "mutual learning." It is a work matched, only, by mainstream "Europeanisation" scholarship which served to buttress the techno-managerial order by misconceiving policy change as "technical or expertise-led processes" in the name of "ever more efficient and effective policies,"[51] taking for granted the very concepts, schemes and narratives generated within the EU itself.

Each of the four shreds of a more critical approach reveals something of the ideological work involved in constructing this "common space." The "performative" allows us to address the "enactment" and "staging"[52] of policy; the "relational" addresses processes of domination and subordination, the creation and sustained disciplining of various layered "Others" within the EU itself, and between the EU and non-EUs; the "multiple" challenges any "illusion of similarities"[53] across the EU whilst also grasping "the immense velocity, force and depth of global interconnectedness"[54]; and "the political" returns us to the active production of oppression, violence and ontological flattening within the EU project. Taken together, these four shreds of an alternative analysis mark a turn towards understanding "the dynamic, polycentric and multi-scalar aspects of welfare and its restructuring"[55] within and beyond the EU.

The "work" of the EU is, in part at least, that of trying to "constrain ambiguities," producing that which is "standardized and calculable,"[56] a kind of "structured disciplinarity"[57] which is never quite complete, or where the "the very efforts to constrain . . . ambiguities may create others."[58] Working with a multiplicity of practices and policies does not mean, however, abandoning the political. It is the structuring of the EU in terms of unequal power relations that matters. At the same time, the political work of the EU always contains within it the possibilities of reformulation, as that which is only residually present always contains the capacity to challenge, transform and change. Europeanisation is conceived, therefore, as a multiple translation process, highly political, within unstable assemblages in which the content and dynamics of policy "are constantly being negotiated by diverse, multiple, actors."[59] In "crisis" times, keeping the political genie in the technical bottle becomes ever more difficult. Indeed, in such times, "even complex and very technical issues become prone to resistance,"[60] with many of the most important EU rules and procedures hanging from a very thin thread. In the Greek crisis, when Greek Finance Minister Yanis Varoufakis challenged a decision by the Eurogroup of Euro zone finance ministers to issue a communiqué without him, he was apparently told: "The Eurogroup does not exist in law, there is no treaty which has convened this group," leading Varoufakis to conclude: "What we have is a non-existent group that has the greatest power to determine the lives of Europeans. It's not answerable to anyone, given it doesn't exist in law; no minutes are kept; and . . . no member has to answer to anybody."[61]

Treated discursively, through many of its pronouncements, the EU is a "fictional assemblage," an intangible, discordant, yet performative and agentive, set of policies, strategic frameworks and political commitments. The last iteration of an EU strategic vision, following the two iterations of the Lisbon strategy, is the Europe 2020 strategy, launched in March 2010, as a ten-year strategy for a "social market economy" emphasising "smart, sustainable and inclusive growth."[62] Although it is the case that fictions sustain reality as they enact and perform policies, and "texts" are enrolled in fiction, it is instructive to see that the Europe 2020 strategy has become less important within the European semester, the technical programming of the EU, than mechanisms such as the Annual Growth Survey, the Joint Assessment Framework, Staff Working Documents including Country Specific Recommendations and, above all, the conditionalities associated with the Excessive Deficit

Procedure. The economic and financial crisis has "reanimated and variegated the transnational space"[63] as a kind of European rescue or re-animation of the Washington consensus[64]. The overarching focus on debt and its reduction, at the same time as markets become "disembedded,"[65] and insolvent banks are bailed out, in a new international division of labour between the "troika" of the Commission, through its Directorate General on Economics and Finance, the International Monetary Fund (IMF) and the European Central Bank, has created, in the current conjuncture, not merely an economistic EU but a "fiscal" and "austerity" disciplinary EU with devastating social consequences.

The causes and the consequences of the crisis within the EU are as much spatial as they are economic, political and social[66]. A recalibration of regulation has occurred, with some regulatory mechanisms having reduced significance as others are foregrounded. Debt reduction has become the central, some might say the only, strategic pillar of the EU currently. A set of economic governance and regulatory mechanisms which, inherently, have no greater or lesser significance than mechanisms regarding environmental or social governance have come to occupy centre stage, with the debt of certain member states now reframed as the major cause of the crisis and the reduction of public debt virtually the sole goal of the EU. As Blyth argues, in the crisis "essentially private-sector debt problems were re-labeled as 'the Debt' generated by 'out-of-control' public spending."[67] Indeed, he has gone further to suggest:

> We have grown quite comfortable talking about "creditor nations" and "debtor nations" rather than "European nations," as if being a debtor or a creditor is a national characteristic. Indeed, one of the most poisonous aspects of this period and policy of austerity is the discourse it produces that reduces complex formations of class and institutions to essentials of race and identity[68].

The crisis has induced a double movement, allowing the EU to revert to colonial practices of producing and reproducing the "other," the "debt states," the "new periphery" whilst, at the same time, marginalising social policies. De la Porte and Heins[69] argue that ever since the economic crisis EU governance has shifted away from "soft governance" towards significantly more intrusive and coercive forms of regulation. It is clear that member states are under heavy surveillance in terms of their monetary, fiscal and welfare policies, the "modernisation" of which most often entail cutbacks and "responsibilising" conditionalities. Similarly they assert that, since 2010, novel policy instruments have been introduced containing substantial powers of surveillance and sanction[70]. They see this as part of a changing landscape of EU governance in which macro-economic adjustment programmes are rolled out to public policy reforms including pensions, health care, industrial relations and public administration. The rigid, non-negotiable imperial governance during the accession process[71] then, has been swiftly followed by coercive neo-liberal governance, beginning with, but "spilling out" far beyond, the economic, contributing to a shifting, but continuous, process of residualising and marginalising the "social."

Policies which purport to secure exit from the crisis, then, further discipline the supposedly "laggard" member states via multiple channels of influence which are ever more complex and ever more difficult to control. New waves of structural reforms have recalibrated economic, fiscal and welfare policies,[72] reframing social welfare firmly within the "elsewhere" of public finance and indebtedness. Although the "techno-zone" of a "soft" EU social dimension remains, in terms of the reporting processes within The Open Method of Co-ordination, at least as a useful fiction, it has been weakened dramatically with only a very tangential link to protecting livelihoods and reducing poverty and exclusion. The marginalisation of discourses around "social inclusion" in favour of "social investment" ushers in new disciplinary practices, the "austerity" word in short, through restrictive fiscal policies, a capping of social expenditures and a shift, in the name of "modernisation" and "efficiency," away from "passive" protection to "activation," "innovation" and "investment."[73]

In contrast to the primacy of "the economic," within a debt and austerity frame, the candidate and prospective candidate countries of what have been termed "the W/Restern Balkans" appear to be judged through a neo-colonial lens which focuses primarily on "the political," in terms of "human and minority rights," "corruption" and "the rule of law," key elements of the "Copenhagen criteria," as well as readiness to engage in regional co-operation with each other. In part, this suggests that the EU disciplinary apparatus is more concerned with the issue of "diminished democracy" than with the "brutal capitalism"[74] which goes along with it, only to turn a blind eye to "diminished democracy" after entry. In Hungary, for example, the Orban Government has reversed many of the pledges made on human rights prior to membership, ushering in a new form of "authoritarian populist neo-liberalism" which combines neo-liberal economic policies and neo-liberal understandings of welfare as a burden with anti-market, anti-capitalist and anti-democratic measures in the service of building an ethnicised, nationalistic state[75]. Similarly, after joining the EU, Croatian politics also took a sharp turn to a populist-driven right-wing authoritarian nationalism, underpinned by a successful referendum defining marriage constitutionally as a union of a man and a woman and through continued protests by Veteran's groups against any potential erosion of their rights or perceived equality between Veteran's rights and the rights of so-called "aggressors."[76]

The EU, as evident in annual Progress Reports and other disciplinary practices, considers the region as "a repository of ethnic conflicts, . . . corruption, and . . . violence that requires containment and external tutelage."[77] It is true that political elites in the countries of the region have been able, largely with impunity, to turn a neo-liberal paradigm of privatisation, deregulation and a residual social welfare system into a predatory project of resource capture and wealth distribution within elite networks often misrepresented within liberal democratic discourse as a problem of "corruption" in the periphery. Hence, the EU disciplinary frame understands this not as a particular, problematic, mode of insertion into capitalist accumulation but, rather, as a pathology of democracy and human rights. Each group of countries entering or hoping to enter, Bulgaria and Romania, then Croatia, now the Western Balkans, faces a wider range of disciplinary techniques than their predecessors in this regard. At the same time, of course, the Greek crisis means that, after Bosnia and Herzegovina and Kosovo/a, "the EU has . . . created its third protectorate in the Balkans"[78] with harsh economic conditionalities enforced rigorously by the European Commission, the European Central Bank and the IMF.

Inevitably, in this multiplex assemblage of a disciplinary EU, along with "fictions" come "frictions" as hegemonic schemes are "enacted in the sticky materiality of practical encounters."[79] In recent years, within and beyond the EU, the politics of austerity has been met by a widening repertoire of "scepticism about dominant tendencies and strategies."[80] It is not only that dominant disciplinary practices have their contradictions but that there has been an articulation of "other imaginaries, other solidarities and other possible futures."[81] Another EU may be possible, much as "another world is possible," beyond the actor animation of liberal NGOs "jumping scale," moving from the location in which they are embedded to a more global scale[82]. It will be another EU, however, which is engaged critically with the EU's "soft" "social dimension," not content to merely complain that the current economistic neo-liberal core ignores it.

TRANSLATING THE SOCIAL: WELFARE ASSEMBLAGES AND THE POLITICS OF WELL-BEING AND AUSTERITY

It would be far too easy to conclude that the conjuncture of imperial governance throughout the accession and enlargement process as well as the crisis-driven neo-liberalism, coercive retrenchment and permanent austerity has further marginalised the Eastern European periphery. There are no shortage of concerned voices. In their influential book, Bohle and Greskovits (2012) conclude that Eastern European countries have lost their capacity to prevent social disintegration, face the crisis or post-crisis period with significantly weakened institutional capabilities, with some in real danger of democratic breakdown. Favell, reflecting on East-West migration in the EU, warns that mobility and freedom of movement may further reinforce the asymmetry between East and West, amplify structural inequalities and contribute to exclusion and exploitation[83]. He argues that new European fault lines emerge where "ambitious 'new Europeans' are in danger of becoming a new Victorian servant class for a West European aristocracy of creative-class professionals and university educated working mums."[84] Similarly, Meardi argues that with no available "voice," exit is the dominant response to the ongoing and persistent marginalisation of social rights in the European project[85].

Indeed, some of these scenarios are very real. Yet, we hold on to the performative, affective and improvised aspects of the postcolonial encounter. No matter how coercive the current hegemonic EU governance framework might be, countries and their denizens will subvert, mobilise and divert the "interference" and "intrusion." The entangled frictions of an EU project which is both "utopian" and "disciplinary" create multiple modes of adaptation, recalcitrance and resistance. Viewed through a lens of translation, then, Europeanisation implies "*productions* of the original and not mere interpretations."[86] Multiple EUs are being actively produced in this process rather than a copy of a singular structure, grammar and syntax. Translation implies precisely the kind of agency which is often completely silenced or ignored by mainstream scholarship. As Saurugger argues, "[i]n this top-down Europeanization literature, resistance to the implementation of policies is mechanically analysed as dysfunctional behaviour and not as a widespread and general phenomenon in politics."[87] Translation involves complex and contested folded negotiations and resistances in terms of both writing the scripts and performing them. Petrović, for example, shows how narratives or metaphors of "family," "home" and of "journeys" ahead serve to place the post-Yugoslav states on a symbolic map of Europe, in which "choosing the European course" becomes "the only option for the Western Balkan countries to rid themselves of the burden of the past and destructive nationalisms."[88] At the same time, nuances of "no progress," "little progress," "some progress" and, on rare occasions, "significant progress" in the appropriately named "progress reports" of the Commission reveal how long and treacherous the journeys may be. In terms of resistance, as an example, the Hungarian Government's reference to "family mainstreaming" rather than the accepted EU concept of "gender mainstreaming," alongside a nuancing of "social inclusion" as "social closeness," is far more than linguistic semantics, revealing deep political contestations regarding the EU's strategic frameworks and priorities[89].

Importantly, subversive resistances tend to tell us more about the EU than the mass of strategic documents produced by the EU itself. Many of these strategic frameworks are largely fictions corresponding to the vagueness, paradoxes and chaos of the European integration project itself. Coercion might, paradoxically, produce more "voice" rather than exit, and might move the fault lines in terms of renegotiating conditions, actions and sanctions. It is very noticeable for example how for the first time, in the 2014 National Reform Programme for Hungary, a number of EU recommendations are explicitly rejected rather than "responded to." Within the functionalist and rationalist assumptions of the Europeanisation literature, new member states are often labelled as "laggards" in terms of implementing EU policy frameworks, with domestic difficulties attributed to "poor implementation capacity." Setting aside, for now, considerations that this behaviour might represent "rational choice" by the new member states, it is worth noting the resonances invoked by these strictures amongst the first wave of post-communist new member states. As Kovacs puts it:

> Ambiguity mobilises routine coping strategies on the part of governments in ex-communist countries. Paying lip-service to a foreign dominant ideology while trying to do what they had anyway wanted/had to do (at home) – this is exactly what the governments in the region were trained for under Soviet rule. Their response is, therefore, pre-programmed: it is an amalgam of avoiding making spectacular mistakes on the surface and the pursuit of autonomous policies, as far as in-depth reforms (or the lack of these reforms) are concerned[90].

As postcolonial studies remind us, crucial to the postcolonial project is the heteroglossia of resistances, which makes Europeanisation a "relational rather than essential"[91] process, as well as a discursive encounter of power and interruption, always displacing and unsettling the colonisers' intentions, even assuming these are monolithic, as they rarely are. Conceptualising the translations of the Utopian modernist project of the EU, a range of subversive resistances are mobilised by new member states and the disciplined older member states of the periphery. Fictions, we argue, are a crucial component of these strategies. Member states are called upon to "transplant" legislation, comply with standards, reproduce strategic policy frameworks, produce and convincingly present strategic priorities and take part in soft governance. All of these can, more or less, be performed as staged fictions, a discursive dance.

Most welfare users, however, appear not to have received their invitations to the dance. In contrast to EU policy texts, a new wave of ethnographic and anthropological studies, enriching a rather small critical literature which explores the development of social work and social welfare in South East Europe across different conjunctures[92], reveals a rather different picture. Well-developed, if contradictory, socialist welfare arrangements have been undermined and replaced by uneven, hybrid, highly residualised and increasingly punitive forms of welfare. Complex reconfigurations have occurred in conflict and post-conflict conditions, including a rapid de- and re-territorialisation of welfare, in which changing relationships between the formal and the informal, the public and the private, and between state and non-state actors co-exist with a range of diverse diaspora, migrant, cross-border and enclave welfare claims and entitlements[93]. Welfare assemblages are emerging, and these are marked by multiple and asymmetric citizenship rights, reproducing, but never reducible to, power relations of class, gender, ethnicity, age, disability, sexuality and geographic location, as welfare is "layered" and overdetermined by clientelistic capture[94].

Azra Hromadžić has described the "semi-absence" of both the family and the state in the context of post-war and post-socialist reconfigurations in Bosnia and Herzegovina, inducing a crisis of care in which mere survival and the reproduction of the self and the management of intimate relationships of kin is a seemingly constant, never ending, struggle[95]. Likewise, in her study of mothers of children with disability, Čarna Brković argues that "the ambiguous ground of social protection," experienced as "erratic, unpredictable and mysterious," requires extreme flexibility, to mobilise whatever resources they can, including any possible informal contacts, just to get a fraction of the services needed[96]. Welfare users in both studies invoke a seemingly lost logic of welfare as a right and a duty of the state in the face of the realities of a system which is limited, discretionary and largely lacking in compassion. Survival depends on a constant struggle to find and gain access to the right people who, with enough luck, when "all the pieces fall into place," might support "humanitarian actions" allowing one to get by, at least for a while.

These emerging unstable assemblages of welfare and care in contemporary South East Europe are not merely a product of neo-liberal injunctions for the state to retreat. They also appear to have little to do with the "fiction" of the EU social. Ideologies, modalities and practices of care that are "fraught, uncertain and provisional"[97] create new chains of meaning, new hierarchies of power and agency, new forms of inclusion and exclusion, new regimes of blame and of virtue, recalibrations of what Andrea Muehlebach has termed "moral citizenship," and new marginalisations, subordinations and silences[98].

CONCLUSION: FOR A "SOCIAL EUROPE OTHERWISE?"

A crucial dilemma for social policy scholars witnessing the folding and unfolding of the EU's social dimension is that in some sense all three elements of the current critical conjuncture: the imperial governance of enlargement, or the imperial promise of future enlargement; the variegated austerity and coercive retrenchment concomitant on the economic and financial crisis and its reframing in terms of "debt reduction" (aka "fiscal consolidation"); and the performative and affective policy responses from "new periphery" member states, all contribute to the marginalisation of the "social" and the weakening of "social Europe." The imperial governance during enlargements has consistently privileged the economic and subordinated and silenced the "social." The economic crisis has reified "fiscal consolidation" and sharpened economic and financial instruments, putting public spending under tremendous strain, whilst protecting those groups that exercise clientelistic state and local state capture. Finally, the performative policy responses through fiction writing has also made social consensus more difficult. As a strategic document prepared by the Friends of Europe argues, "Social inclusion rhetoric by the European Union without delivery is counterproductive in terms of the EU's own legitimacy."[99] Responding discursively to the vagueness of EU social policy may not help to discuss, promote or further social rights, or reduce social inequalities in domestic contexts. "Social Europe otherwise" therefore needs to be much more multi-lingual beyond the Eurospeak, much more based on voice rather than exit, and recoupled with economic policy, bringing social policy back from its "elsewheres."

As Ladi and Tsarouhas argue, a useful starting point would be to reconsider the politics of extreme austerity and develop policy tools that would be able to go beyond the current institutional set-up that is able to think only in terms of "growth and employment."[100] It is striking how the meta-theory of policy learning seems to feature incessantly in the European integration literature[101]. If anything, a postcolonial perspective, a call for "social Europe otherwise," requires unlearning in terms of "stopping oneself from always wanting to correct, teach, theorise, develop, colonise, appropriate, use, record, inscribe, enlighten: the impetus to always be the speaker and speak in all situations must be seen for what it is: a desire for mastery and domination."[102]

A call for "social Europe otherwise" offers an entry point to the full potentiality of a view of translation as a site of struggle, of a multiplication of the possible policy assemblages that a reflexive translation may bring into being, above all responsive to multiple voices and diverse trajectories[103]. In searching for a connection to that which is "beyond," a sociology and social policy of the "not yet,"[104] requires a commitment to a "double orientation" to the movements of policy and power: to recognise hegemonic plans and projects; but to be attentive to their interruptions, disjunctures and challenges, a search for what Judith Butler has termed "collective disidentification."[105] A "social Europe otherwise" requires a commitment to politics as interruption more than politics as grand narrative, a "methodological reflexivity" sensitive to multiple positionalities and standpoints, whilst privileging those voices that tend to be marginalised or silenced in policy processes. Where might we look for new "loci of enunciation,"[106] for a new politics of rights, recognition, representation and redistribution?

In and beyond South East and Southern Europe, a new wave of social movements and struggles has emerged, in which the idea of the "commons" resonates quite strongly. The practice of "commoning," the active making and claiming of commons, and the protection of public space against enclosures, appropriations and commodifications seem to offer a kind of unity in diversity, offering a new narrative for escaping the logic of austerity and envisioning more humane alternatives. These movements, then, are central to a new politics otherwise, opening up meaningful spaces for contestation, resistance and alternatives, a kind of talking and acting back to power. Some elements of this are visible in a "third wave" of activism in Croatia and beyond, including student protests, particularly around the demand for free higher education, and various "Right to the City" campaigns[107], contributing to a wider "new left" sensibility across the post-Yugoslav space[108].

These movements and anti-austerity protests provide glimpses of "policies and practices otherwise" not least in terms of an "interruption" of hegemonic structures and processes and, crucially, are evidence of precisely the kind of creative expressions of the new, the unthought and the unexpected as Gibson-Graham has called them[109]. A view from the Balkans, as Étienne Balibar remarked over a decade ago, still provides a somewhat privileged vantage point for exploring the contradictions, problems and possibilities of another Europe, another EU and, above all, a more socially just Europe:

> The fate of European identity as a whole is being played out in Yugoslavia and more generally in the Balkans (even if this is not the only site of its trial). Either Europe will recognize in the Balkan situation not a monstrosity grafted to its breast, a pathological "after-effect" of under-development or of communism, but rather an image and effect of its own history and will undertake to confront it and resolve it and thus to put itself into question and transform itself. Only then will Europe probably begin to become *possible* again. Or else it will refuse to come face-to-face with itself and will continue to treat the problem as an exterior obstacle to be overcome through exterior means, including colonisation[110].

The spread of direct democracy through peoples' Plenums, across Bosnia and Herzegovina in February 2014, in the wake of street protests in a number of cities, was an important moment, not least in terms of the translation of a model of decision-making from student activism and university blockades across the region. Such events provide glimpses "of the possibility of demands for equality, justice, dignity and fairness being able to be translated into winnable claims and sustainable social platforms."[111] Much work is needed, at all levels, of course, before these glimpses or moments of resistance can contribute, meaningfully, to new narratives of social justice and welfare and a more humane ethics of care, recognising what Fiona Williams has termed "interdependence, mutuality, and human frailty."[112] There is an urgent need to raise the social, economic and political value of welfare and care and to connect struggles for social justice across and beyond the region.

NOTES

1. Email to members of the European Social Policy Network (ESPN) from the Network Core Team, December 23, 2014. For more on the ESPN, see http://ec.europa.eu/social/main.jsp?catId=1135&langId=en, accessed February 16, 2015.

2. IFRC–International Federation of Red Cross and Red Crescent Societies *Think Differently: Humanitarian Impacts of the Economic Crisis in Europe* (Geneva: IFRC, 2013), https://www.ifrc.org/PageFiles/134339/1260300-Economic%20crisis%20Report_EN_LR.pdf, accessed May 28, 2015.

3. Noémi Lendvai and Paul Stubbs, "Europeanisation, Welfare and Variegated Austerity Capitalisms: Hungary and Croatia," *Social Policy and Administration* 49, no. 4 (2015): 445–65.

4. Noémi Lendvai and Paul Stubbs, "Assemblages, Translation and Intermediaries in South East Europe: Rethinking Transnationalism and Social Policy," *European Societies* 11, no. 5 (2009a): 673–95.

5. Jean-Claude Barbier, "Languages of 'Social Policy' at 'the EU level'," in *Analysing Social Policy Concepts and Language: Comparative and Transnational Perspectives,* Daniel Béland and Klaus Petersen, eds. (Bristol: Policy Press, 2014), 66.

6. Stuart Hall, Doreen Massey and Michael Rustin, "After Neoliberalism: Analysing the Present," *Soundings* 53 (2013):13.

7. Jean-Claude Barbier and Fabrice Colomb, "The Unbearable Foreignness of EU Law in Social Policy, a Sociological Approach to Law Making," *CES Working Papers* 2011, 65, ftp://mse.univ-paris1.fr/pub/mse/CES2011/11065.pdf, accessed May 30, 2015

8. Nicholas Ostler, *The Last Lingua Franca: English Until the Return of Babel* (London: Penguin, 2011).

9. Noémi Lendvai, "Soft Governance, Policy Fictions and Translation Zones: European Policy Spaces and Their Making," in John Clarke, Dave Bainton, Noémi Lendvai and Paul Stubbs, *Making Policy Move: Towards a Politics of Translation and Assemblage* (Bristol: Policy Press, 2015), 131–56.

10. Lewis Carroll, *Alice's Adventures in Wonderland and Through the Looking Glass* (New York: Kosimo, 2010), 57.

11. Mary Louise Pratt, *Imperial Eyes: Travel Writing and Transculturation* (London: Routledge, 1992), 6.

12. John Clarke, Dave Bainton, Noémi Lendvai, and Paul Stubbs, *Making Policy Move: Towards a Politics of Translation and Assemblage* (Bristol: Policy Press, 2015), 55–56.

13. Lendvai, "Soft Governance," 145, 150.

14. Anna Tsing, *Friction: An Ethnography of Global Connection* (Princeton, NJ: Princeton University Press, 2005), 4.

15. Rolando Vazquez, "Translation as Erasure: Thoughts on Modernity's Epistemic Violence," *Journal of Historical Sociology* 24, no. 1 (2011): 27.

16. See Ilan Kapoor, "Capitalism, Culture, Agency: Dependency Versus Postcolonial Theory," *Third World Quarterly* 23, no. 4 (2002): 647–64.

17. Noémi Lendvai and Paul Stubbs, "Globale Sozialpolitik und Governance: Standpunkte, Politik und Postkolonialismus," in *Nord-Süd-Beziehungen im Umbruch*, ed., Hans-Jürgen Burchardt (Frankfurt: Verlag, 2009b), 219–44.

18. Cf. Clarke, et al., *Making Policy Move.*

19. Noémi Lendvai and Paul Stubbs, "Policies as Translation: Situating Transnational Social Policies," in *Policy Reconsidered: Meanings, Politics and Practices*, Susan Hodgson and Zoë Irving, eds. (Bristol: Policy Press, 2007), 173–89; Lendvai and Stubbs, "Assemblages"; Paul Stubbs, "Translating Welfare Assemblages in the 'New' Eastern Europe: Re-domaining the Social?," in *Lost and Found in Translation: Circulating Ideas of Policy and Legal Decision Processes in Korea and Germany*, Eun-Jeung Lee and Hannes Mossler, eds. (Frankfurt am Main: Peter Lang, 2015), 31–54.

20. Francesca Orsini and Neelam Srivastava, "Translation and the Postcolonial," *Interventions: International Journal of Postcolonial Studies* 15, no. 3 (2013): 323–31.

21. Jacqueline Best, "Bureaucratic Ambiguity," *Economy and Society* 41, no. 1 (2012): 86.

22. József Böröcz and Mahua Sarkar, "What Is the EU?" *International Sociology* 20, no. 2 (2005): 153–73, 164, 154.

23. Ibid., 162, 163.

24. Ibid., 167.

25. József Böröcz, *The European Union and Global Social Change* (Routledge: London, 2010), 168.

26. Ibid., 164.

27. Ibid., 158.

28. József Böröcz and Melinda Kovács, *The Empire's New Clothes: Unveiling EU Enlargement* (Telford: Central Europe Review, 2001).

29. József Böröcz, "The Fox and the Raven: the European Union and Hungary Renegotiate the Margins of 'Europe'," in *The Empire's New Clothes: Unveiling EU Enlargement*, József Böröcz and Melinda Kovács, eds. (Telford: Central Europe Review, 2001), 108, emphasis in original.

30. Jan Zielonka, *Europe as Empire: The Nature of the Enlarged European Union* (Oxford: Oxford University Press, 2006).

31. Ibid., 13.

32. Burca and Scott 2000, quoted by Zielonka, *Europe as Empire*, 56.

33. Zielonka, *Europe as Empire*, 57.

34. Ibid., 59.

35. Magali Gravier, "The Next European Empire?" *European Societies* 11, no. 5 (2009): 633.

36. Böröcz, *The European Union and Global Social Change*, 166, 165.

37. Ibid., 166, 167.

38. William Walters and Jens Haar, *Governing Europe: Discourse, Governmentality and European Integration* (London: Routledge, 2005), 138.

39. Noémi Lendvai, "Europeanization of Social Policy? Prospects and challenges for South East Europe," in *Social Policy and International Interventions in South East Europe*, Bob Deacon and Paul Stubbs, eds. (Cheltenham: Edward Elgar, 2007), 26.

40. Walters and Haar, *Governing Europe*, 139.

41. Ibid.

42. Lendvai, "Europeanization of Social Policy?," 27, 35.

43. Lendvai, "Soft Governance," 134.

44. Janet Newman, "Performing New Worlds? Policy, Politics and Creative Labour in Hard Times," *Policy and Politics* 41, no. 4 (2013): 527.

45. Pratt, *Imperial Eyes*.

46. Emily Apter, *The Translation Zone: A New Comparative Literature* (Princeton, NJ: Princeton University Press, 2006).

47. Pratt, *Imperial Eyes*, 7.

48. David Mosse, "Introduction: The Anthropology of Expertise and Professionals in International Development," in *Adventures in Aidland: The Anthropology of Professionals in International Development*, ed., David Mosse (New York: Berghahn, 2011), 4.

49. Lendvai, "Soft Governance," 136.

50. David Lewis and David Mosse, "Encountering Order and Disjuncture: Contemporary Anthropological Perspectives on the Organization of Development," *Oxford Development Studies* 34, no. 1 (2006): 1–13.

51. Lendvai and Stubbs, "Europeanisation," 446.

52. Maarten Hajer, "Rebuilding Ground Zero: The Politics of Performance," *Planning Theory and Practice* 6, no. 4 (2005): 446.

53. Lendvai, "Soft Governance," 134.

54. Ibid.

55. Lendvai and Stubbs, "Europeanisation," 448.

56. Best, "Bureaucratic Ambiguity," 90.

57. Lendvai, "Soft Governance," 136.

58. Best, "Bureaucratic Ambiguity," 90.

59. Lendvai and Stubbs, "Europeanisation," 447.

60. Sabine Saurugger, "Europeanisation in Times of Crisis," *Political Studies Review* 12, (2014): 185.

61. Harry Lambert, "Exclusive: Yanis Varoufakis Opens Up about His Five Month Battle to Save Greece," *New Statesman* July 13, 2015, http://www.new-statesman.com/world-affairs/2015/07/exclusive-yanis-varoufakis-opens-about-his-five-month-battle-save-greece, accessed September 3, 2015

62. European Commission, *Europe 2020: A Strategy for Smart, Sustainable and Inclusive Growth* COM(2010)2020 final, 2010, http://eur-lex.europa.eu/LexUriServ/LexUriServ.do?uri=COM:2010:2020:FIN:EN:PDF.

63. Lendvai and Stubbs, "Europeanisation".

64. Susanne Lutz and Matthias Kranke, "The European Rescue of the Washington Consensus? IMF and EU Lending to Central and Eastern European Countries," *LSE Working paper, LEQS* 22/2010, http://www2.lse.ac.uk/europeanInstitute/LEQS/LEQSPaper22.pdf, accessed June 2, 2015

65. Guglielmo Meardi, *Social Failures of EU Enlargement: A Case of Workers Voting with Their Feet* (London: Routledge, 2012).

66. John Clarke, "Of Crises and Conjunctures: The Problem of the Present," *Journal of Communication Inquiry* 34, no. 4 (2010): 337–54; John Clarke, "What

Crisis Is This?," in Jonathan Rutherford and Sally Dawson, eds., *The Neoliberal Crisis* (London: Lawrence and Wishart, 2012), 44–54.

67. Mark Blyth, *Austerity: The History of a Dangerous Idea* (Oxford: Oxford University Press, 2013), 73.

68. Mark Blyth, "The SPD Has to Do More than Enforce a Creditor's Paradise in Europe," *Social Europe* 3, March (2015), http://www.socialeurope.eu/2015/03/creditors-paradise/, accessed May 28, 2015

69. Caroline De la Porte and Elke Heins, "Game Change in EU Social Policy: Towards More European Integration," in *The Eurozone Crisis and the Transformation of EU Governance: Internal and External Implications*, Maria João Rodrigues and Eleni Xiarchogiannopoulou, eds. (Farnham: Ashgate, 2014), 157–71.

70. Stella Ladi and Dimitris Tsarouhas, "The Politics of Austerity and Public Policy Reform in the EU," *Political Studies Review* 12 (2014): 171–80.

71. Zielonka, *Europe as Empire*.

72. Noémi Lendvai, *Critical Dialogues: EU Accession and the Transformation of Post-communist Welfare* (Saarbrucken: VDM Verlag, 2009).

73. Lendvai and Stubbs, "Europeanisation".

74. Igor Štiks and Srećko Horvat, "Introduction: Radical Politics in the Desert of Transition," in *Welcome to the Desert of Post-Socialism: Radical Politics after Yugoslavia* Srećko Horvat and Igor Štiks, eds. (London: Verso, 2015), 2.

75. Lendvai and Stubbs, "Europeanisation".

76. There are approximately 500,000 registered war veterans in Croatia, entitled to a number of benefits for themselves and family members, with many of them organised into associations which fight not only to protect these rights but to advocate for their permanent incorporation into the Croatian constitution and, above all, to resist ideas of "'relativising' the suffering of Croatian war veterans with civilians or those fighting on the other side", see Stubbs, Paul and Siniša Zrinščak, "Citizenship and Social Welfare in Croatia: Clientelism and the Limits of 'Europeanisation'," *European Politics and Society* 16, no. 3 (2015): 395–410, 406.

77. Ibid., 3.

78. Jan Zielonka, "Greece Has Become the EU's Third Protectorate," *Open Democracy* August 14, 2015, https://www.opendemocracy.net/can-europe-make-it/jan-zielonka/greece-has-become-eu's-third-protectorate, accessed June 2, 2015.

79. Tsing, *Frictions*, 2.

80. John Clarke, *Changing Welfare, Changing States: New Directions in Social Policy* (Bristol: Policy Press, 2004), 158.

81. Ibid., 159. See also chapter 11 in this volume on possible Europe's futures.

82. Willem van Schendel, "Geographies of knowing, geographies of ignorance: jumping scale in Southeast Asia," *Environment and Planning D: Society and Space* 20 (2002), 647–68.

83. Adrian Favell, "The New Face of East-West Migration in Europe," *Journal of Ethnic and Migration Studies* 34, no. 5 (2008): 701–16.

84. Ibid., 711.

85. Meardi, Guglielmo. *Social Failures of EU Enlargement: A Case of Workers Voting with Their Feet* (London: Routledge, 2012). The concepts of 'voice' and 'exit' derive from Hirschman, Albert, *Exit, Voice and Loyalty* (Cambridge: Harvard

University Press, 1970), seeing 'voice' as "general protest" and 'exit' as "leav(ing) the organization," 4.

86. Orsini and Srivastava, "Translation and the Postcolonial," 324, emphasis in original.

87. Saurugger, "Europeanisation in Times of Crisis," 183.

88. Tanja Petrović, "On the Way to Europe: EU Metaphors and Political Imagination of the Western Balkans," in *Welcome to the Desert of Post-Socialism: Radical Politics after Yugoslavia*, Srećko Horvat and Igor Štiks, eds. (London: Verso, 2015), 103–21.

89. Lendvai and Stubbs, "Europeanisation," 455–6.

90. Janos Kovacs, "Approaching the EU and Reaching the US? Rival Narratives on Transforming Welfare Regimes in East-Central Europe," *West European Politics* 25, no. 2 (2002): 200.

91. Malreddy Pavan Kumar, "Postcolonialism: Interdisciplinary or Interdiscursive?" *Third World Quarterly* 32, no. 4 (2011): 653–72.

92. Paul Stubbs and Reima Ana Maglajlić, "Negotiating the Transnational Politics of Social Work in Post-conflict and Transition Contexts: Reflections from South-East Europe," *British Journal of Social Work* 42, no. 6 (2012): 1174–91; Darja Zaviršek, "Engendering Social Work Education Under State Socialism in Yugoslavia," *British Journal of Social Work* 38, no. 4 (2008): 734–50.

93. Paul Stubbs and Siniša Zrinščak, "Rescaling Emergent Social Policies in South East Europe," in *Social Policy Review 21*, Kirstein Rummery, Ian Greener, and Chris Holden, eds. (Bristol: Policy Press, 2009): 283–305.

94. Paul Stubbs and Siniša Zrinščak, "Citizenship and Social Welfare in Croatia: Clientelism and the Limits of 'Europeanisation'," *European Politics and Society* 16, no. 3 (2015): 395–410.

95. Azra Hromadžić, "Where Were They until Now? Aging, Care and Abandonment in a Bosnian Town," *Etnološka tribina*, forthcoming.

96. Brković, Čarna, "Flexibility of veze/štele: Negotiating Social Protection in a Bosnian Town," in *Negotiating Social Relations in Bosnia and Herzegovina* Čarna Brković, Vanja Čelebičić and Stef Jansen, eds. (Farnham: Ashgate, forthcoming, July 2016).

97. Ibid.

98. Andrea Muehlebach, *The Moral Neoliberal: Welfare and Citizenship in Italy* (Chicago: University Press, 2012).

99. Friends of Europe, *Unequal Europe: Recommendations for a More Caring EU*. Report published February 2015, http://www.friendsofeurope.org/quality-europe/unequal-europe-recommendations-caring-eu/, accessed June 2, 2015

100. Ladi and Tsarouhas, "The Politics of Austerity," 177.

101. Claudio Radaelli and Claire Dunlop, "Learning in the European Union: Theoretical Lenses and Meta-theory," *Journal of European Public Policy* 20, no. 6 (2013): 923–40.

102. Ilan Kapoor, "Hyper-self-reflexive Development? Spivak on Representing the Third World 'Other'," *Third World Quarterly* 4 (2004): 642.

103. Clarke et al., *Making Policy Move*. See also chapter 8 in this volume.

104. Bonaventura de Sousa Santos, *The World Social Forum: A User's Manual* (Madison: University of Wisconsin-Madison, 2004), 24, http://www.ces.uc.pt/bss/documentos/fsm_eng.pdf, accessed June 4, 2015
105. Judith Butler, *Bodies That Matter: On the Discursive Limits of "Sex"* (New York: Routledge, 1993), 4.
106. Cristina Rojas, "International Political Economy/Development Otherwise," *Globalizations* 4, no. 4 (2007): 584.
107. Paul Stubbs, "Networks, Organisations, Movements: Narratives and Shapes of Three Waves of Activism in Croatia," *Polemos: Journal of Interdisciplinary Research on War and Peace* 15, no. 30 (2013): 11–32; Bilić, Bojan and Stubbs, Paul. "Unsettling 'The Urban' in Post-Yugoslav Activisms: 'Right to the City' and Pride Parades in Serbia and Croatia," in *Urban Grassroots Movements in Central and Eastern Europe*, Kerstin Jacobsson, ed. (Farnham: Ashgate, 2015), 119–38.
108. Igor Štiks, "'New Left' in the Post-Yugoslav Space: Issues, Sites and Forms," *Socialism and Democracy,* 29, no. 3 (2015): 135–46.
109. J. K. Gibson-Graham, *A Postcapitalist Politics* (Minneapolis, MN: University of Minnesota Press, 2006), 60.
110. Étienne Balibar, *We, The People of Europe?* (Princeton: University Press, 2003), 6.
111. Clarke et al, *Making Policy Move,* 208. See also chapter 5 in this volume.
112. Fiona Williams, "Global Social Justice, Ethics and the Crisis of Care," in Alexandra Kaasch and Paul Stubbs, eds. *Transformations in Global and Regional Social Policies.* (Basingstoke: Palgrave Macmillan, 2014): 101.

BIBLIOGRAPHY

Apter, Emily. *The Translation Zone: a new comparative literature.* Princeton, NJ: Princeton University Press, 2006.
Balibar, Étienne. *We, The People of Europe?* Princeton, NJ: Princeton University Press, 2003.
Barbier, Jean-Claude. "Languages of 'social policy' at 'the EU level'." In *Analysing Social Policy Concepts and Language: comparative and transnational perspectives* Daniel Béland and Klaus Petersen, eds., 59–79. Bristol: Policy Press, 2014.
Barbier, Jean-Claude and Colomb, Fabrice "The Unbearable Foreignness of EU Law in Social Policy, a Sociological Approach to Law Making." *CES Working Papers* 2011, 65, ftp://mse.univ-paris1.fr/pub/mse/CES2011/11065.pdf.
Best, Jacqueline. "Bureaucratic Ambiguity." *Economy and Society* 41, no. 1 (2012): 84–106.
Bilić, Bojan and Stubbs, Paul. "Unsettling 'The Urban' in Post-Yugoslav Activisms: 'Right to the City' and pride parades in Serbia and Croatia." In *Urban Grassroots Movements in Central and Eastern Europe*, Kerstin Jacobsson, ed., 119–138. Farnham: Ashgate, 2015.
Blyth, Mark. *Austerity: The History of a Dangerous Idea.* Oxford: Oxford University Press, 2013.

Blyth, Mark. "The SPD Has to Do More than Enforce a Creditor's Paradise in Europe." *Social Europe* 3, March (2015), http://www.socialeurope.eu/2015/03/creditors-paradise/, accessed May 28, 2015

Bohle, Dorothee and Greskovits, Béla. *Capitalist Diversity on Europe's Periphery.* Ithaca: Cornell University Press, 2012.

Böröcz, József. "The Fox and the Raven: the European Union and Hungary renegotiate the margins of 'Europe'." In *The Empire's New Clothes: unveiling EU enlargement*, József Böröcz and Melinda Kovács, eds., 51–100. Telford: Central Europe Review, 2001.

Böröcz, József and Kovács, Melinda. *The Empire's New Clothes: unveiling EU enlargement.* Telford: Central Europe Review, 2001.

Böröcz, József and Sarkar, Mahua. "What is the EU?" *International Sociology* 20, no. 2 (2005): 153–73.

Böröcz, József. *The European Union and Global Social Change.* London: Routledge, 2010.

Butler, Judith. *Bodies That Matter: On the Discursive Limits of "Sex."* New York: Routledge, 1993.

Čarna, Brković. "Flexibility of veze/štele: negotiating social protection in a Bosnian town." In *Negotiating Social Relations in Bosnia and Herzegovina* Čarna Brković, Vanja Čelebičić and Stef Jansen, eds., Farnham: Ashgate, forthcoming, July 2016.

Butler, J. *Bodies that Matter: on the discursive limits of 'sex'.* London: Routledge, 1993

Carroll, Lewis. *Alice's Adventures in Wonderland and Through the Looking Glass.* New York: Kosimo, 2010.

Clarke, John. *Changing Welfare, Changing States: new directions in social policy.* Bristol: Policy Press, 2004.

Clarke, John. "Of Crises and Conjunctures: the problem of the present." *Journal of Communication Inquiry* 34, no. 4 (2010): 337–54.

Clarke, John. "What crisis is this?" In *The Neoliberal Crisis*, Jonathan Rutherford and Sally Dawson, eds., 44–54 (London: Lawrence and Wishart, 2012).

Clarke, John, Bainton, Dave, Lendvai, Noémi and Stubbs, Paul. *Making Policy Move: towards a politics of translation and assemblage.* Bristol: Policy Press, 2015.

De Burca, Grainne and Scott, Joanne. "Introduction" In *Constitutional Change in the EU: from uniformity to flexibility,* Grainne de Burca and Joanne Scott, eds., 1–9. Oxford: Hart Publishing, 2000.

de la Porte, Caroline and Heins, Elke. "Game Change in EU Social Policy: towards more european integration." In *The Eurozone Crisis and the Transformation of EU Governance: internal and external implications*, Rodrigues, Maria João and Xiarchogiannopoulou, Eleni, eds., 157–71. Farnham: Ashgate, 2014.

de Sousa Santos, Bonaventura. *The World Social Forum: a user's manual* http://www.ces.uc.pt/bss/documentos/fsm_eng.pdf, Madison: University of Wisconsin-Madison, 2004, accessed June 4, 2015.

European Commission. *Europe 2020: a strategy for smart, sustainable and inclusive growth* COM(2010)2020 final. 2010, http://eur-lex.europa.eu/LexUriServ/LexUriServ.do?uri=COM:2010:2020:FIN:EN:PDF, accessed June 4, 2015.

Favell, Adrian. "The New Face of East-West Migration in Europe." *Journal of Ethnic and Migration Studies* 34, no. 5 (2008): 701–16.

Friends of Europe. *Unequal Europe: recommendations for a more caring EU.* Report published February 2015, http://www.friendsofeurope.org/quality-europe/unequal-europe-recommendations-caring-eu/, accessed June 2, 2015.

Gibson-Graham, J. K. *A Postcapitalist Politics.* Minneapolis, MN: University of Minnesota Press, 2006.

Gravier, Magali. "The Next European Empire?" *European Societies* 11, no. 5 (2009): 627–47.

Hall, Stuart, Massey, Doreen, and Rustin, Michael. "After Neoliberalism: analysing the present." *Soundings* 53 (2013): 8–22.

Hajer, Maarten. "Rebuilding Ground Zero: the politics of performance." *Planning Theory and Practice* 6, no. 4 (2005): 445–64.

Hirschman, Albert. *Exit, Voice and Loyalty.* Cambridge: Harvard University Press, 1970.

Hromadžić, Azra. "Where were they until now? Aging, care and abandonment in a Bosnian town." *Etnološka tribina*, forthcoming.

IFRC–International Federation of Red Cross and Red Crescent Societies. *Think Differently: humanitarian impacts of the economic crisis in Europe.* Accessed May 28, 2015, https://www.ifrc.org/PageFiles/134339/1260300-Economic%20crisis%20Report_EN_LR.pdf. Geneva: IFRC, 2013, accessed June 2, 2015.

Kapoor, Ilan. "Capitalism, Culture, Agency: Dependency Versus Postcolonial Theory." *Third World Quarterly* 23, no. 4 (2002): 647–664.

Kapoor, Ilan. "Hyper-self-reflexive Development? Spivak on Representing the Third World 'Other'." *Third World Quarterly* 4 (2004): 627–47.

Kovacs, Janos. "Approaching the EU and Reaching the US? Rival Narratives on Transforming Welfare Regimes in East-Central Europe." *West European Politics* 25, no. 2 (2002): 175–204.

Kumar, Malreddy Pavan. "Postcolonialism: interdisciplinary or interdiscursive?" *Third World Quarterly* 32, no. 4 (2011): 653–72.

Ladi, Stella and Tsarouhas, Dimitris. "The Politics of Austerity and Public Policy Reform in the EU." *Political Studies Review* 12 (2014): 171–80.

Lambert, Harry. "Exclusive: Yanis Varoufakis opens up about his five month battle to save Greece." *New Statesman* July 13, 2015, http://www.newstatesman.com/world-affairs/2015/07/exclusive-yanis-varoufakis-opens-about-his-five-month-battle-save-greece, accessed September 3, 2015

Lendvai, Noémi. "Europeanization of Social Policy? Prospects and challenges for South East Europe." In *Social Policy and International Interventions in South East Europe*, Bob Deacon and Paul Stubbs, eds., 22–44. Cheltenham: Edward Elgar, 2007.

Lendvai, Noémi. *Critical Dialogues: EU Accession and the transformation of post-communist welfare.* Saarbrucken: VDM Verlag, 2009.

Lendvai, Noémi. "Soft Governance, Policy Fictions and Translation Zones: European policy spaces and their making." In John Clarke, Dave Bainton, Noémi Lendvai, and Paul Stubbs, eds., *Making Policy Move: towards a politics of translation and assemblage*, 131–56. Bristol: Policy Press, 2015.

Lendvai, Noémi and Stubbs, Paul. "Policies as Translation: situating transnational social policies." In *Policy Reconsidered: meanings, politics and practices*, Susan Hodgson and Zoë Irving, eds., 173–89. Bristol: Policy Press, 2007.

Lendvai, Noémi and Stubbs, Paul. "Assemblages, Translation and Intermediaries in South East Europe: rethinking transnationalism and social policy." *European Societies* 11, no. 5 (2009a): 673–95.

Lendvai, Noémi and Stubbs, Paul. "Globale Sozialpolitik und Governance: Standpunkte, Politik und Postkolonialismus." In *Nord-Süd-Beziehungen im Umbruch*, ed., Hans-Jürgen Burchardt, 219–44. Frankfurt: Verlag, 2009b.

Lendvai, Noémi and Stubbs, Paul. "Europeanisation, Welfare and Variegated Austerity Capitalisms: Hungary and Croatia." *Social Policy and Administration* 49, no. 4 (2015): 445–65.

Lewis, David and Mosse, David. "Encountering Order and Disjuncture: contemporary anthropological perspectives on the organization of development." *Oxford Development Studies* 34, no. 1 (2006): 1–13.

Lutz, Susanne and Kranke, Matthias. "The European Rescue of the Washington Consensus? IMF and EU Lending to Central and Eastern European Countries." *LSE Working paper, LEQS* 22/2010, http://www2.lse.ac.uk/europeanInstitute/LEQS/LEQSPaper22.pdf, accessed June 2, 2015.

Meardi, Guglielmo. *Social Failures of EU Enlargement: A Case of Workers Voting with their Feet*. London: Routledge, 2012.

Mosse, David. "Introduction: the anthropology of expertise and professionals in international development." In *Adventures in Aidland: the anthropology of professionals in international development*, ed., David Mosse, 1–31. New York: Berghahn, 2011.

Muehlebach, Andrea. *The Moral Neoliberal: welfare and citizenship in Italy*. Chicago: University Press, 2012.

Newman, Janet. "Performing New Worlds? Policy, politics and creative labour in hard times." *Policy and Politics* 41, no. 4 (2013): 515–32.

Ostler, Nicholas. *The Last Lingua Franca: English until the return of Babel*. London: Penguin, 2011.

Orsini, Francesca and Srivastava, Neelam. "Translation and the Postcolonial." *Interventions: International Journal of Postcolonial Studies* 15, no. 3 (2013): 323–31.

Petrović, Tanja. "On the Way to Europe: EU metaphors and political imagination of the Western Balkans." In *Welcome to the Desert of Post-Socialism: radical politics after Yugoslavia*, Srećko Horvat and Igor Štiks, eds., 103–21. London: Verso, 2015.

Pratt, Mary Louise. *Imperial Eyes: travel writing and transculturation*. London: Routledge, 1992.

Radaelli, Claudio and Dunlop, Claire. "Learning in the European Union: theoretical lenses and meta-theory." *Journal of European Public Policy* 20, no. 6 (2013): 923–40.

Rojas, Cristina. "International Political Economy/Development Otherwise." *Globalizations* 4, no. 4 (2007): 573–87.

Saurugger, Sabine. "Europeanisation in Times of Crisis." *Political Studies Review* 12, (2014): 181–92.

Stubbs, Paul. "Networks, Organisations, Movements: narratives and shapes of three waves of activism in Croatia." *Polemos: Journal of Interdisciplinary Research on War and Peace* 15, no. 30 (2013): 11–32.

Stubbs, Paul. "Translating Welfare Assemblages in the 'New' Eastern Europe: re-domaining the social?" In *Lost and Found in Translation: circulating ideas of policy and legal decision processes in Korea and Germany*, Eun-Jeung Lee and Hannes Mossler, eds., 31–54. Frankfurt am Main: Peter Lang, 2015.

Stubbs, Paul and Maglajlić, Reima Ana. "Negotiating the Transnational Politics of Social Work in Post-conflict and Transition Contexts: reflections from South-East Europe." *British Journal of Social Work* 42, no. 6 (2012): 1174–91.

Stubbs, Paul and Zrinščak, Siniša. "Rescaling Emergent Social Policies in South East Europe." In *Social Policy Review 21*, Kirstein Rummery, Ian Greener, and Chris Holden, eds., 283–305. Bristol: Policy Press, 2009.

Stubbs, Paul and Zrinščak, Siniša. "Citizenship and Social Welfare in Croatia: Clientelism and the limits of 'Europeanisation'." *European Politics and Society* 16, no. 3 (2015): 395–410.

Štiks, Igor. "'New Left' in the Post-Yugoslav Space: issues, sites and forms." *Socialism and Democracy* 29, no. 3 (2015): 135–46.

Štiks, Igor and Horvat, Srećko. "Introduction: radical politics in the desert of transition." In *Welcome to the Desert of Post-Socialism: radical politics after Yugoslavia* Srećko Horvat and Igor Štiks, eds., 1–19. London: Verso, 2015.

Tsing, Anna. *Friction: an ethnography of global connection*. Princeton, NJ: Princeton University Press, 2005.

Vazquez, Rolando. "Translation as Erasure: thoughts on modernity's epistemic violence." *Journal of Historical Sociology* 24, no. 1 (2011): 27–44.

Van Schendel, Willem. "Geographies of Knowing, Geographies of Ignorance: jumping scale in Southeast Asia." *Environment and Planning D: Society and Space*, 20 (2002): 647–668.

Walters, William and Haar, Jens. *Governing Europe: discourse, governmentality and European integration*. London: Routledge, 2005.

Williams, Fiona. "Global Social Justice, Ethics and the Crisis of Care." In Alexandra Kaasch and Paul Stubbs, eds., *Transformations in Global and Regional Social Policies,* 85–107. Basingstoke: Palgrave MacMillan, 2014.

Zaviršek, Darja. "Engendering Social Work Education under State Socialism in Yugoslavia." *British Journal of Social Work* 38, no. 4 (2008): 734–50.

Zielonka, Jan. *Europe as Empire: the nature of the enlarged European union*. Oxford: Oxford University Press, 2006.

Zielonka, Jan. "Greece Has become the EU's Third Protectorate." *Open Democracy,* August 14, 2015, https://www.opendemocracy.net/can-europe-make-it/jan-zielonka/greece-has-become-eu's-third-protectorate, accessed June 2, 2015.

Chapter 2

Limitations of European Media Policy in the Balkans

Observations on TV Pink BH

Monika Metykova

The tenth anniversary of the first eastward enlargement of the European Union, celebrated in 2014, was marked by a number of speeches by EU representatives, which stressed the primacy of the Union's symbolic dimension, but said little about the actual success of Europeanization. To illustrate, it is worth quoting from the then President of the European Commission José Manuel Barroso's central address:

> The 1st of May, we celebrate the 10th anniversary of the reunification of Europe. This is a moment to remember how important the accession of these 10 member states has been, not only for them but for us in Europe, because we were able to share stability and security and also contributed to prosperity in our era. This enlargement reunited Europe after many years of artificial division. It was also a way to anchor democracy, freedom and the rule of law for many millions of people who were living before behind the Iron Curtain[1].

Celebratory events and political speeches are, clearly, not occasions for a critical reflection on complex issues – particularly not at times of economic crises – but those following developments in the ten 'new' EU member states from behind the Iron Curtain may have wondered about the limits of the democratizing influence of EU membership, or what Stubbs and Lendvai, in the previous chapter, refer to as democracy 'diminished . . . after entry'.

In this chapter, I reflect on the constrained impact of EU membership on media policy, particularly in those member states that joined in the most recent waves of enlargement[2]. I draw partly on my interviews with select EU civil servants and on my case study of TV Pink BH, a popular commercial television station in Bosnia and Herzegovina, which has been known for promoting 'turbofolk'[3]. I argue that EU interventions related to the securing of the democratic roles of media, such as the adequate representation of cultural diversity in member states, are considerably limited. Though central to the European project, cultural pluralism is outside the radar of European media policy makers for whom culture is too 'messy' to be translated into easy-to-define and ready-to-implement policy criteria. A civil servant I interviewed at the European Commission expressed this problem succinctly, 'I find culture a really infuriating area because it is not hard and well defined but there's something there and it's just a shame that people have no window into what is happening in other member states'[4]. Interestingly, the latter part of this statement is in line with the expectations related to the first wave of east-ward EU enlargement in 2004 when 82% of EU15 respondents thought the enlargement will be highly beneficial from a cultural point of view[5]. In order to highlight inherent shortcomings in EU media policy conceptualizations, I draw on the case of the highly controversial commercial television station in the Balkans, TV Pink BH, that broadcasts in both, previously warring entities of this former Yugoslav country, the Bosniak-Croat Federation of Bosnia and Herzegovina and the Bosnian Serb Republic.

In April 2015, the City of Belgrade awarded TV Pink's owner Željko Mitrović a Golden Ring for his permanent contribution to culture, a deci-sion that prompted the artist Veljko Mihajlović to return his award received 16 years previously as a protest against such a promotion of 'barbarism and kitsch'[6]. Critics of TV Pink object to its churning out of low-quality programmes with high ratings as well as to Mitrović's (past) political allegiances (he managed to amass a fortune under the regime of Slobodan Milošević). This chapter introduces a different side to debates on Balkan media phenomena such as TV Pink BH. It looks beyond the conventional dichotomy of 'good' (empowering, inclusive) culturally pluralist broadcast-ing provided by public service broadcasters and 'shallow' (exploitative, kitsch) but possibly culturally pluralist broadcasting of commercial media. By doing so, this chapter also demonstrates that public service broadcast-ing, which in European countries has the role of representing the society's cultural diversity, is – as a media policy tool – limited in capturing everyday transnational cultural links that continue to exist in countries that 'broke up' recently (not only former Yugoslavia but also my country of origin – former Czechoslovakia) as its remit is closely related to narrow conceptualizations of national culture[7].

MEDIA AND DEMOCRACY: THE EU AS A SAVIOUR?

Media reform formed part of the wide-ranging transition from state socialism to liberal democracy in what later became the 'new' EU member states.

However, shortly after the fall of the Iron Curtain, during the 1990s, governments interfered with the newly established independence of media extensively and this applies to East/Central European countries as well as former Yugoslav republics. The term 'media wars' has been used to describe this situation in a number of post-socialist countries. In Hungary, for example, it was characterized as 'a bitter dispute along party lines over the degree of government presence in Hungarian broadcasting that ended in a legislative debacle'[8]. In the Czech Republic in December 2000 and January 2001, a crisis ensued at the public service Czech Television (CT) following political pressures that resulted in changes of staff (including the dismissal of CT's director general) and consequently demonstrations were held all over the country with the aim of preventing political intervention in the running of the station[9]. In Slovakia, 'in 1997 the news coverage on STV [public service television] was yet again the tool for the ruling movement's, the Movement for Democratic Slovakia, propaganda'[10] and the country's track record in press freedom was less than outstanding[11]. The awarding of broadcast licences to persons close to the government has also taken place, the case of the private Slovak television channel Markíza being one such example[12].

Similar developments characterize the media in countries that have joined the EU most recently. In her study on Bulgarian journalists' perceptions of the functioning of media in their country, Lada Trifonova Price concludes that 'the consensus among participants is that most Bulgarian media outlets were bought specifically to serve certain agendas and to represent particular political and business interests. Ownership of a media outlet is perceived as an important tool for exerting undue influence on politics, business and society'[13]. Similarly, the diversity of ownership in Croatia and its relationship to media independence have been the subject of debate prior to its accession to the EU[14], and although new legislation had been introduced in the early 2010s, its implementation remains somewhat problematic[15]. The popular expectation in those countries that a supranational European political entity will somehow 'right' the 'wrongs' of their national political elites may have been unfounded in terms of the accession process, which was mainly about the adoption of certain common EU laws and procedures, but can be situated and interpreted within the narrative that dominated the pre-accession period in those countries, of a 'return to Europe', where 'some things [like bad governance] just cannot happen'. As we have seen, the impact of EU membership on the development and implementation of policies linked to good democratic, social and cultural performances of the media has been limited. This applies to the widely publicized case of Hungary which in 2010 adopted extensive media legislation that has been seen as undermining press freedom[16] and also to the continuing concerns over media ownership transparency in Bulgaria and in Croatia.

MARKET VERSUS CULTURE: THE
ISSUE OF EU COMPETENCES

It has been widely acknowledged that the impact of the EU on its member states is more pronounced with regard to economic policy than the political conditions of liberal democracies[17]. In terms of media policy, the effect of EU membership has been very limited not merely because the accession process does not involve a concrete body of laws related to media, democracy and cultural rights that are transposed into the candidate country's legislation[18] but exactly due to the fact that media 'is not an area where European Commission competences are very strong. . . . It is not an area like competition or electronic communication where there is a fully harmonized European Commission law based on an article of a Treaty or a set of directives'[19]. Media – as related to minority cultural or language rights – could also fall under minority rights policies. However, in this area the EU's impact is limited as well. There seems to be general agreement that the limitations of the EU's influence on minority rights in 'new' member states are largely due to a lack of internal minority rights standards and the overarching emphasis on the *acquis communautaire* (or – as the EU legislation glossary explains – the body of common rights and obligations that binds all the member states together within the EU). In relation to Bulgaria, Rechel argues that other limiting factors include a lack of concern for human rights and a failure in addressing public attitudes towards minorities[20].

At the heart of the principles that guide EU media policy lies a distinction between market/economic justifications and goals and cultural/diversity ones. Given the emphasis of the EU integration on the creation of a single market, it is perhaps not surprising that EU media policy is mainly driven by economic interventions and goals[21]. The market versus culture interplay was described to me by a European Commission civil servant:

> You could argue that the underlying reason for that fault line is that the high watermark of the integration strand came with the Maastricht Treaty in the sense that it was the Maastricht Treaty that created the articles on cultural policy, education, vocational training. But if you look at those articles they all say the same thing, they say these are the prerogatives of the member states, this is a quintessential part of national sovereignty like fiscal policy or health, these are things that are really specific to member states and the EU should only become involved to the extent that it can prove that there is an added value. That division is there because it is in the Treaties, it is the dividing line between national identity and national sovereignty and the European level[22].

The significance of public service broadcasting which is 'directly related to the democratic, social and cultural needs of each society and to the need to preserve media pluralism'[23] is recognized in the *Protocol on the System of Public Service Broadcasting in Member States*, which forms part of the

Treaty of Amsterdam. However, each member state is responsible for conferring, defining and organizing the public service remit and, importantly, public service broadcasting is subject to EU competition law. In other words, there are no straightforward EU mechanisms that could be invoked if the democratic/cultural/social roles and independence of public service media are threatened in member states.

MEDIA INTERVENTIONS IN BOSNIA AND HERZEGOVINA FOLLOWING THE DAYTON AGREEMENT

The above examples from 'new' EU member states make it clear that national governments are not necessarily the best guardians of the public interest in relation to media. While this applies also to 'old' EU member states (for example, in the case of the British Broadcasting Corporation – BBC, concerning political intervention in editorial policy[24]), it is particularly pronounced in East/Central Europe as well as the Balkans. Moreover, it seems that European policy makers associate specific desirable democratic, social and cultural roles of media only with public service broadcasting and specifically with news and current affairs programming. The case of TV Pink BH – a privately run television station in Bosnia and Herzegovina that forms part of Željko Mitrović's TV Pink group (a major media player in the Balkans) – illustrates the shortcomings of such an assumption well. It is also one of the rare cases when the EU played a major role in shaping media policy and the country's media system (as part of democratizing reforms).

In 1995, following a three-year war which accompanied the break-up of Yugoslavia, the Dayton Peace Agreement set up a complex and often dysfunctional system of two entities: a Bosniak-Croat Federation of Bosnia and Herzegovina and the Bosnian Serb Republic (or Republika Srpska), each with its own president, government, parliament, police and other bodies. A central Bosnian government and rotating presidency overarches the two entities and the Office of the High Representative (appointed by the UN and EU) has been in place as an ad hoc international institution tasked with overseeing the implementation of the so-called Dayton Peace Agreement (the General Framework Agreement for Peace in Bosnia and Herzegovina negotiated in Dayton, Ohio, and signed in Paris on 14 December 1995) that ended the war in Bosnia and Herzegovina. The official website describes the role of the High Representative as 'working with the people and institutions of Bosnia and Herzegovina and the international community to ensure that Bosnia and Herzegovina evolves into a peaceful and viable democracy on course for integration in Euro-Atlantic institutions. The OHR is working towards the point where Bosnia and Herzegovina is able to take full responsibility for its own affairs'[25].

The failure of the international community – represented by the Office of High Representative, the Organization for Security and Co-operation in Europe and the European Commission – in reforming media and establishing a public service broadcasting system has been discussed in great detail[26] and the reform of public service broadcasting remained a contested issue[27] under the conditions of the Stabilization and Association Agreement with the EU until 1 June 2015. The significance of the intervention needs to be spelt out clearly:

> Intervention into the Bosnian media has been the most ambitious incursion into journalistic practices and institutions by the international community in any post-conflict society thus far. . . . [It] has been focused on the creation of alternative media outlets to the prevailing nationalist press and TV stations – initially by fostering independent media and then, later on, by creating regulatory bodies and transforming the existing state-TV stations into a single public broadcasting service for entire Bosnia and Herzegovina[28]. The greatest failure – and the most expensive experiment – of the international effort was the creation of the independent TV channel OBN, envisioned in 1996 as the network of independent stations from all over Bosnia and as the replacement for state-wide TV. Twenty million US dollars of international aid later, and with almost 70 per cent of coverage of the territory of Bosnia and Herzegovina, OBN was forced to shut down as it never found its audience[29].

In her analysis of media democratization in Bosnia and Herzegovina, Aida Hozic focusses on three aspects of the international community's intervention[30]. She discusses how the conflict between European and US models of media systems that were to be imposed combined with tensions and distrust between local journalists and international advisers and the political neutralization of media, all of which 'have helped create an incredibly complex, fragmented and diverse media system, which is a far cry from ideals of public service and unsustainable by market forces alone'[31]. In terms of the conflicting policy goals and media models that guided the international community's interventions, I would like to stress again that the EU does not have competences related to public service broadcasting (other than ensuring competition) as these fall under the jurisdiction of the individual member states. This perhaps provides an additional layer to explanations about the failure of public service broadcasting in Bosnia and Herzegovina. It was supervised by an entity that has its hands tied on its own turf.

TV PINK BH: 'THE SUCCESS STORY'

TV Pink BH was founded in 2003 and it quickly established itself on the market and continues to be the broadcaster with the highest ratings. According to Tanja Vojtehovska-Stevanov[32], 'Pink BH is the only channel that connects both administrative entities in Bosnia – The Federation and Republika Srpska, which means we accomplished what the international community attempted for the past 10 years . . . We are particularly proud of this project because we have the same news program for both entities'[33]. She goes on to explain how TV Pink BH managed to achieve highest ratings in both administrative entities within six months of setting up there.

> We play Bajaga [Serbian pop musician], we get phone calls that say 'you chet- niks [irregular Serbian army fighting for ultranationalist goals], we'll throw a bomb at you'. We play Severina [Croatian singer], they say 'you ustashas [Croatian fascist movement], we'll throw a bomb at you'. And then we started paying attention, three Serbian clips, three Croatian, three Bosniak. I mean that was . . . almost tragicomic, when we talk about video clips and their distribu- tion according to national divisions, it could almost be tragicomic, I mean, if it wasn't tragic it would have been very funny[34].

The strategy that Mitrović chose for his expansion into Bosnia and Herzegovina could not have differed more from that pursued by the inter- national community. Teofil Pančić[35] argues that for Mitrović to become a transnational player – that is, to cover Bosnia and Herzegovina as well as Republika Srpska – he had to make clear that he distanced himself from his past, he changed since the times when he supported Milošević.

> He does something excellent for himself. They have this press conference in Sarajevo, where some of the participants include Sonja Biserko[36] and Petar Luković[37]. . . . From the perspective of someone from Sarajevo, there aren't more respected names than Sonja and Petar, as those were the people who consistently fought every sign of Serbian nationalism, who spoke against every- thing, not only Milošević, but against the war, and accusing everything that was going on in Bosnia, they were outspoken critics of ethnic cleansing, simply, they are people who represent something good over there[38].

And indeed Petar Luković was charged with running current affairs at Pink BH when it began broadcasting. In 2006, Radenko Udovičić claimed that 'although there was a lot of repulsion for this TV station [TV Pink BH] in Sarajevo before it started broadcasting because of its owner's ties with Slobodan Milošević, the station's programming has proven to be diverse, entertaining, good quality and all-Bosnian with particular emphasis on events in Banja Luka and Sarajevo'[39]. Or, in Teofil Pančić's description:

> Now, those who watch Pink BH say that it really was a novelty in this Bosnian ether, specifically because everything was Bosnian – it was not acknowledging

the separate entities, Serbs, Croats and Muslims, it simply reported what was
going on and wasn't interested in anything else. According to some books, this
would be the responsibility of a public service, but I think that you cannot really
have a public service in a country that has a problem to prove that it exists in the
first place. . . . So they [TV Pink BH] tell you, this is what happened, these guys
fired, those were killed, and that's all, everybody else can use this information
as they please. In a way, this is how they positioned themselves[40].

This is in contrast with the already described international community's
interventions that attempted to de-ethnify and de-politicize the media by
setting up rules on the use of local languages, which are all perfectly understandable to all ethnic groups, election coverage and so on[41]. The popularity
of TV Pink BH shows that the representatives of the international community
behind the media reforms in Bosnia and Herzegovina 'have failed, however,
to recognize the persistently important link between entertainment and politics in former Yugoslavia, and infused a fear of politics to such a degree that
news and even election coverage has become "politically neutered"'[42].

ENTERTAINMENT, TRANSNATIONAL TIES
AND PUBLIC SERVICE BROADCASTING

Hozic goes on to argue that TV Pink BH and OBN (following its resuscitation
as a commercial channel) 'also reveal, along with a few Bosnian counterparts,
the degree to which commercial interests can eventually trump ethnic loyal-
ties, and the strange ways in which the slide into entertainment has been, perhaps unintentionally, entwined and helped by the presence of the international
community in Bosnia and Herzegovina and the region'[43]. While I agree with
Hozic's assessment of the role of entertainment in overcoming ethnic divides,
I think that there are additional layers that need to be taken into account. First
of all, as she points out, the link between politics and entertainment is one that
tends to be omitted by policy makers in general and by those involved in public service broadcasting in particular. Entertainment genres, however, are not
exempt from de-ethnicization. Reality TV shows that TV Pink BH has been
known for are particularly well suited (or cost efficient – after all, it is profits
that commercial broadcasters are after) to attracting audiences of different
ethnic backgrounds (and indeed transnational, post-Yugoslav audiences and
participants). This move towards entertainment programming is demonstrated
not only by commercial media like TV Pink BH but also by independent
media with a long track record of opposition to Slobodan Milošević's regime,
such as the Serbian B92 that was the first to broadcast *Big Brother* (its Serbian
version). This trend has actually characterized public service broadcasting all

over Europe too. Thus, as Hozic importantly points out, the assessment of the failure of public service broadcasting in Bosnia and Herzegovina should not be based on the ideals of public service broadcasting but rather on its actually existing forms[44].

When it comes to the post-Yugoslav region, however, linguistic closeness is crucial in mapping how locally produced programmes move across borders (a number of television programmes have been popular across former war enemies Croatia and Serbia, e.g. *Ljubav u zaledju* [Love in Ambush], *Vratice se rode* [The Storks Will Return]) and how they become transnationalized also in terms of cast, production teams etc. For example, reality shows broadcast on TV Pink BH make regular use of contestants from a variety of former Yugoslav republics, illustrating Pančić's observation that 'the most important thing is to find something that is metanational, and something that everyone can equally be involved in, which is not local, and which does not cause any traumas. If you fill in those conditions, everything goes. *Big Brother* goes, *Triumph* goes, *Grand Show* goes, whatever you want goes'[45]. Public service broadcasting – as a policy tool – is ill suited to produce transnational programmes that are clearly in demand, particularly in countries that were 'dismantled' recently.

I have argued in this chapter that the EU has – and indeed can – played a very limited role when it comes to the democratic, social and cultural roles associated with the media. This applies to member states and also to interventions that were overseen by the EU in Bosnia and Herzegovina in the aftermath of the Dayton Agreement. Some of the assumptions of media policy (and particularly what constitutes public interest in communication) are arguably unsuited to dealing with the complex media-related needs of European citizens, and the underlying assumption that public service broadcasters should be the sole (main) guardians of the public interest needs considerable rethinking. This, however, is unlikely to originate from politicians. As one of my interviewees at the European Commission put it,

> I think that cultural ministries and media policy makers in the member states are some of the most conservative people that I've ever come across. It's not an area of policy where change comes easily because it covers areas like identity, language, language is an important area . . . it's very political in the sense of not being completely rational. . . . There is less and less scope for a completely independent approach because you're constrained by wider media developments and the fact that within the single market member states do rub up against each other[46].

As the case of TV Pink BH suggests, entertainment and its links to politics should be paid more attention and the importance of the transnational cultural roles of media should not be underestimated. The fact that Željko Mitrović arguably managed to build a broadcaster that fulfilled – at least to a greater extent than its competitors – roles traditionally associated with public service broadcasting in a post-war situation should not be dismissed as a coincidence, rather – as I suggested above – policy makers can learn important lessons from this case.

NOTES

1. "Statement by President Barroso on the 10th Anniversary of the Reunification of Europe," *European Commission*, April 30, 2014. http://europa.eu/rapid/press-release_STATEMENT-14–142_en.htm (accessed July 10, 2016).
2. The chapter provides examples from "new" EU member states which are intended as symptomatic of key issues in post-socialist media policy. The examples are not intended to suggest that similar issues are non-existent in 'old' EU member states and they are by no means supposed to suggest that 'new' member states are in an earlier stage of linear development in respect of their media policies.
3. On "turbofolk," a specific mixture of Balkan ethnic and dance music presented in various forms of kitsch, see chapter 4 in this volume.
4. Anonymous A, interview by Monika Metykova, May 27, 2009.
5. "Flash Eurobarometer 140: Enlargement of the European Union." *European Union Open Data Portal*, Last modified July 27, 2015, https://open-data.europa.eu/ en/data/dataset/S299_140 (accessed July 10, 2016).
6. "Culture Honour for Pink TV Boss Draws Protest." *Balkan Insight*, April 9, 2015, http://www.balkaninsight.com/en/article/serbian-artist-protests-against-award-to-pink-tv-owner (accessed July 10, 2016).
7. I leave aside the question of the quality of programming, the case for paying more attention to the links between popular television programmes and political culture has been made convincingly, for example, by Lisbet van Zoonen in *Entertaining the Citizen: When Politics and Popular Culture Converge*. My interest in some of these programmes (the local versions of "wife swaps" or singing contests) was sparked by the inclusion of participants from different countries of former Yugoslavia. It is not my intention to discuss the complex politics of representation in these programmes, in that respect see Aniko Imre's *Identity Games: Globalization and the Transformation of Media Cultures in the New Europe* and also Gordana Đerić's *Intima Javnosti*.
8. Peter Molnar, "Transforming Hungarian Broadcasting," *Media Studies Journal* 13, no. 3 (1999): 90–7.
9. For more details, see Monika Metykova, "Regulating Public Service Broadcasting: The Cases of the Czech Republic, Slovakia and Ireland" (PhD diss., Masaryk University, 2005), 90.
10. Jan Füle, "Médiá" ["The Media"], in *Slovensko 1997: Súhrnná správa o stave spoločnosti a trendoch na rok 1998* [*A Global Report on the State of Society with Trends for 1998*], eds., Martin Bútora and Michal Ivantyšyn (Bratislava: Inštitút pre verejné otázky, 1998), my translation.

11. See, for example, reports by Human Rights Watch and also Monika Metykova, "Establishing Public Service Broadcasting in the Slovak Republic (1993–2004): From State Control to the European Single Market," *Trends in Communication* 12, no. 4 (2004): 223–32.

12. See Metykova, "Regulating" 2005, 100 and Sharon Fisher, "A Year of Dramatic Change," in *EastWest Institute Annual Survey of Eastern Europe and the Former Soviet Union: Holding the Course 1998*, ed., Rutland Peter (Armonk, NY: EastWest Institute, 2000), 86–87.

13. Lada Trifonova Price, "Journalists' Perceptions of Nomenklatura Networks and Media Ownership in Post-Communist Bulgaria," *Medijske Studije/Media Studies* 6, no. 11 (2015): 19–34. Cf. Barbara Pfetsch and Katrin Voltmer, "Negotiating Control: Political Communication Cultures in Bulgaria and Poland," *The International Journal of Press/Politics* 17, no. 4 (2012): 388–406; On investigative journalism in Bulgaria see Vaclav Stetka and Henrik Örnebring, "Investigative Journalism in Central and Eastern Europe: Autonomy, Business Models, and Democratic Roles," *The International Journal of Press/Politics* 18, no. 4 (2013): 413–35.

14. On developments in the early 2000s which were characterized by a lack of transparency in media ownership and when some media owners were subjected to physical attacks see Stjepan Malović, "Croatia," in *Media Ownership and Its Impact on Media Independence and Pluralism*, ed., Brankica Petković (Ljubljana: Peace Institute, 2004).

15. See, for example, a report by South East European Media Observatory from 2014 on Croatian media legislation, Cf. Helena Popović et al., "Background Information Report: Media Policies and Regulatory Practices in a Selected Set of European Countries, the EU and the Council of Europe: The Case of Croatia," *Media Observatory*, 2010, http://mediaobservatory.net/sites/default/files/Croatia.pdf (accessed July 10, 2016).

16. "European Parliament Resolution of March 10, 2011 on Media Law in Hungary," *European Parliament*, March 10, 2011, http://www.europarl.europa.eu/sides/getDoc.do?pubRef=-//EP//TEXT+TA+P7-TA-2011–0094+0+DOC+XML+V0//EN (accessed July 10, 2016).

17. Specifically in relation to "new" member states, see, for example, Milada Anna Vachudova, "The Leverage of International Institutions on Democratizing States: Eastern Europe and the European Union," *European University Institute,* October 2001, http://cadmus.eui.eu/bitstream/handle/1814/1742/01_33.pdf?sequence=1 (accessed July 10, 2016). See also Ulrich Sedelmeier, "Anchoring Democracy from Above? The European Union and Democratic Backsliding in Hungary and Romania after Accession," *Journal of Common Market Studies* 52, no. 1 (2014): 105–21, doi: 10.1111/jcms.12082.

18. Issues of freedom of expression and media freedom are to some extent part of the accession process particularly following the introduction of the EU Enlargement Strategy 2013–2014, see European Commission 2013. I believe that it is a telling sign that the 134-page document entitled Agenda 2000 – Commission Opinion on the Czech Republic's Application for Membership of the European Union (from 1997) mentions media only once (see "Agenda 2000 – Commission Opinion on

the Czech Republic's Application for Membership of the European Union," *European Commission,* July 15, 1997, http://ec.europa.eu/enlargement/archives/pdf/dwn/opinions/czech/cz-op_en.pdf [accessed July 10, 2016].) and the equivalent – much shorter – 4-page document on the application of Croatia from 2011 ("Commission Opinion on the Application for Accession to the European Union by the Republic of Croatia," *European Commission,* October 12, 2011, http://ec.europa.eu/enlargement/pdf/key_documents/2011/package/hr_opinion_2011_en.pdf [accessed July 10, 2016].) does not mention media at all. Issues of competition, however, are a different concern, ensuring the viability and competitiveness of media markets has been a major EU concern, see, for example, Directorate General Competition's information on the media sector available at http://ec.europa.eu/competition/sectors/media/overview_en.html (accessed July 10, 2016).

19. Anonymous A, interview by Monika Metykova, May 27, 2009.

20. Bernd Rechel, "What Has Limited the EU's Impact on Minority Rights in Accession Countries?," *East European Politics and Societies* 22, no. 1 (2008): 171–91. doi: 10.1177/0888325407311796.

21. On more general issues, see, for example, the following: Peter Humphreys, "The Principal Axes of the European Union's Audiovisual Policy," in *Communication and Cultural Policies in Europe,* ed., Isabel Fernandez Alonso and Miguel de Moragas i Spa (Barcelona: Generalitat de Catalunya, 2008); Jan van Cuilenburg and Denis McQuail, "Media Policy Paradigm Shifts: Towards a New Communications Policy Paradigm," *European Journal of Communication* 18, no. 2. (2003): 181–207; Peter Lunt and Sonia Livingstone, *Media Regulation: Governance and the Interests of Citizens and Consumers* (London: Sage, 2012).

22. Anonymous B, interview by Monika Metykova, May 27, 2009.

23. "Protocol on the System of Public Service Broadcasting in the Member States," *The Lisbon Treaty,* http://www.lisbon-treaty.org/wcm/the-lisbon-treaty/protocols-annexed-to-the-treaties/680-protocol-on-the-system-of-public-service-broadcasting-in-the-member-states.html (accessed July 10, 2016).

24. See, for example, Peter Goodwin, "Low Conspiracy? Government Interference in the BBC," *Westminster Papers in Communication and Culture* 2, no.1 (2005): 96–118.

25. "General Information," *Office of the High Representative,* 2015, http://www.ohr.int/?page_id=1139&lang=en (accessed July 10, 2016). Although it is not the purpose of this chapter to discuss the overall impact of the international governance arrangement, I should point out that it has been criticized widely for the consequences of non-accountable law making, see e.g. Hozic, "Democratizing," 2008 and also David Chandler, "State-Building in Bosnia: The Limits of 'Informal Trusteeship'," *International Journal of Peace Studies* 11, no. 1 (2006): 17–38.

26. See, for example, Hozic, "Democratizing," 2008; Mark Thompson and Dan De Luce, "Escalating to Success: Media Intervention in Bosnia and Herzegovina," in *Forging Peace: Intervention, Human Rights, and the Management of Media Space,* ed., Monroe Price and Mark Thompson (Edinburgh: Edinburgh University Press, 2002). There are also reports by international agencies such as USAID and OSCE and by local civil society actors such as the South East European Media Observatory.

27. See, for example, Salena Hodžić, "Flash Report: Bosnia and Herzegovina," *South East European Media Observatory,* July 31, 2013, http://mediaobservatory.net/ radar/flash-report-bosnia-and-herzegovina (accessed July 10, 2016).

28. Tarik Jusić and Nidzara Ahmetašević argue that "between 1998 and 2002, the two government-controlled entity broadcasters – the Radio-Television of federation BiH (RTVBiH) and the Radio-Television of Republika Srpska (RTRS) – were pressed by OHR to become public service broadcasters. A third, state-wide, cross-ethnic public service broadcaster, the Bosnia-Herzegovina Radio and Television (BHRT), was established. The three broadcasters were ambitiously supposed to establish a joint public service broadcasting service . . ." ("Media Reforms through Intervention: International Media Assistance in Bosnia and Herzegovina," *Analitika Center for Social Research,* 2013, http://www.analitika.ba/sites/default/files/publikacije/jusic_ and_ahmetasevic_-_rrpp_bih_medassistance_31dec2013_final.pdf, 35 [accessed July 10, 2016]).

29. Aida Hozic, "Democratizing Media, Welcoming Big Brother: Media in Bosnia and Herzegovina," in *Finding the Right Place on the Map*, eds., Karol Jakubowicz and Miklos Sükösd (Bristol: Intellect, 2008), 151.

30. Ibid.

31. Ibid. The state of the media market has been an ongoing concern, a 2005 Open Society Institute report – *Television Across Europe: Regulation, Policy and Independence* (Budapest: Open Society Institute, 2005), 195 – characterized the situation this way:

> BH broadcasting sector is ethnically segregated, oversaturated, complex, and financially poor. It is a puzzle how such a large number of outlets survive in such a limited and underdeveloped market. Market dynamics are not the only forces driving the broadcasting sector; donor funding and political subventions still do much to distort it. The multiplicity of outlets does not therefore reflect a vibrant market, with potential for development and capable of offering a diversity of voices and opinions.

In the 2015 IREX Media Sustainability Index – "Media Sustainability Index 2015: The Development of Sustainable Independent Media in Europe and Eurasia," *IREX,* 2015, https://www.irex.org/projects/msi/europe-eurasia – business management scored the lowest in Bosnia Herzegovina (again),

> The media sector is stagnating due to a highly unfriendly business environment. Media companies generally welcome the entrance of foreign capital through regional television stations, but those business operations stand in stark contrast to the grim conditions at most domestic media. There were no indicators that stood out as performing significantly better than the rest; all indicators scored within half a point of the objective score. Only a few larger media outlets are truly self-sustainable enterprises, while the majority of media are on the brink of bankruptcy. This is a result of structural shortfalls that individual workmanship can hardly overcome, but some

media suffer additionally from a lack of human capacity and expertise in business planning, marketing, and financing. The overall picture on business operations is somewhat improved by the founding of new television broadcaster N1 (a regional partner of CNN, with offices in Zagreb, Sarajevo, and Belgrade) as well as Al Jazeera Balkans.

32. Managing Director of Media System; Head of Public Relations; formerly journalist and talk show host.
33. Vana Goblot, *Pink TV Report* (London: Goldsmiths College, 2009), 23.
34. Ibid., 24. A similar approach to broadcasting for Croats and Serbs and representatives of twenty other national minorities living in Vukovar was in place on a local radio (Radio Vukovar) station before the war thanks largely to the efforts of a local journalist Siniša Glavašević. Glavašević was killed by Serb paramilitaries at the end of the siege of Vukovar in November 1991, see Alan Little, "Croatia Vukovar War: Overcoming a Legacy of War," *BBC News,* June 23, 2011, http://www.bbc.co.uk/news/world-europe-13887103 (accessed July 10, 2016).
35. Independent journalist and columnist, social commentator.
36. A leading Serbian human rights activist, Chairperson of the Helsinki Committee for Human Rights in Serbia (HCHRS).
37. A leading left-wing Serbian journalist, former executive editor of the political weekly Vreme, known for his critical stance on Milošević's regime.
38. Ibid., 25.
39. As quoted in Hozic, "Democratizing," 156.
40. Goblot, *Pink TV*, 25.
41. See Hozic, "Democratizing".
42. Ibid., 151.
43. Ibid., 155.
44. Ibid.
45. Goblot, *Pink TV*, 19.
46. Anonymous A, interview by Monika Metykova, May 27, 2009.

BIBLIOGRAPHY

"Agenda 2000 - Commission Opinion on the Czech Republic's Application for Membership of the European Union." *European Commission.* July 15, 1997. http://ec.europa.eu/enlargement/archives/pdf/dwn/opinions/czech/cz-op_en.pdf.
"Commission Opinion on the Application for Accession to the European Union by the Republic of Croatia." *European Commission.* October 12, 2011. http://ec.europa.eu/enlargement/pdf/key_documents/2011/package/hr_opinion_2011_en.pdf (accessed July 10, 2016).
"Communication from the Commission to the European Parliament and the Council: Enlargement Strategy and Main Challenges 2013–2014." *European Commission.* October 16, 2013. http://ec.europa.eu/enlargement/pdf/key_documents/2013/package/strategy_paper_2013_en.pdf (accessed July 10, 2016).

"Culture Honour for Pink TV Boss Draws Protest." *Balkan Insight.* April 9, 2015. http://www.balkaninsight.com/en/article/serbian-artist-protests-against-award-to-pink-tv-owner (accessed July 10, 2016).

"European Parliament Resolution of 10 March 2011 on Media Law in Hungary." *European Parliament.* March 10, 2011. http://www.europarl.europa.eu/sides/getDoc.do?pubRef=-//EP//TEXT+TA+P7-TA-2011–0094+0+DOC+XML+V0//EN (accessed July 10, 2016).

"Flash Eurobarometer 140: Enlargement of the European Union." *European Union Open Data Portal.* Last modified July 27, 2015. https://open-data.europa.eu/en/data/dataset/S299_140 (accessed July 10, 2016).

"General Information." *Office of the High Representative.* 2015. http://www.ohr.int/?page_id=1139&lang=en (accessed July 10, 2016).

"Media Integrity Research: Croatia." *South East European Media Observatory.* March 2, 2014. http://mediaobservatory.net/radar/media-integrity-research-croatia (accessed July 10, 2016).

"Media Sustainability Index 2015: The Development of Sustainable Independent Media in Europe and Eurasia." *IREX.* 2015. https://www.irex.org/projects/msi/europe-eurasia (accessed July 10, 2016).

"Protocol on the System of Public Service Broadcasting in the Member States." *The Lisbon Treaty.* http://www.lisbon-treaty.org/wcm/the-lisbon-treaty/protocols-annexed-to-the-treaties/680-protocol-on-the-system-of-public-service-broadcasting-in-the-member-states.html (accessed July 10, 2016).

"Statement by President Barroso on the 10th Anniversary of the Reunification of Europe." *European Commission.* April 30, 2014. http://europa.eu/rapid/press-release_STATEMENT-14–142_en.htm (accessed July 10, 2016).

Brunner, Roland. "How to Build Public Broadcast in Post-Socialist Countries: Experiences and Lessons Learned in the Former Yugoslav Area." *Medien Hilfe.* June 2002. http://archiv2.medienhilfe.ch/topics/PBS/pbs-1st.pdf (accessed July 10, 2016).

Chandler, David. "State-Building in Bosnia: The Limits of 'Informal Trusteeship'." *International Journal of Peace Studies* 11, no. 1 (2006): 17–38.

Đerić, Gordana, ed. *Intima Javnosti.* Belgrade: Fabrika Knjiga, 2008.

Fisher, Sharon. "A Year of Dramatic Change." In *EastWest Institute Annual Survey of Eastern Europe and the Former Soviet Union: Holding the Course 1998*, edited by Peter Rutland, 84–90. Armonk, NY: EastWest Institute, 2000.

Füle, Jan. "Médiá." ["The Media."] In *Slovensko 1997: Súhrnná správa o stave spoločnosti a trendoch na rok 1998. [A Global Report on the State of Society with Trends for 1998.]* edited by Martin Bútora and Michal Ivantyšyn. Bratislava: Inštitút pre verejné otázky, 1998.

Goblot, Vana. *Pink TV Report.* London: Goldsmiths College, 2009.

Goodwin, Peter. "Low Conspiracy? Government Interference in the BBC." *Westminster Papers in Communication and Culture* 2, no.1 (2005): 96–118.

Hirsch, Mario and Petersen, Vibeke. "Enlargement of the Arena: European Media Policy." In *Power, Performance and Politics: Media Policy in Europe*, edited by Werner A. Meier and Josef Trappel, 21–39. Baden-Baden: Nomos, 2007.

Hodžić, Salena. "Flash Report: Bosnia and Herzegovina." *South East European Media Observatory*. July 31, 2013. http://mediaobservatory.net/radar/flash-report-bosnia-and-herzegovina (accessed July 10, 2016).

Hozic, Aida. "Democratizing Media, Welcoming Big Brother: Media in Bosnia and Herzegovina." In *Finding the Right Place on the Map*, edited by Karol Jakubowicz and Miklos Sükösd, 145–63. Bristol: *Intellect*, 2008.

Humphreys, Peter. "The Principal Axes of the European Union's Audiovisual Policy." In *Communication and Cultural Policies in Europe*, edited by Isabel Fernandez Alonso and Miguel de Moragas i Spa, 151–82. Barcelona: Generalitat de Catalunya, 2008.

Imre, Aniko. *Identity Games: Globalization and the Transformation of Media Cultures in the New Europe*. Cambridge, MA and London: MIT Press, 2009.

Imre, Aniko. "Love to Hate: National Celebrity and Racial Intimacy on Reality TV in the New Europe." *Television and New Media* 16, no. 2 (2015): 103–30.

Jusić, Tarik and Ahmetašević, Nidzara. "Media Reforms through Intervention: International Media Assistance in Bosnia and Herzegovina." *Analitika Center for Social Research*. 2013. http://www.analitika.ba/sites/default/files/publikacije/jusic_and_ahmetasevic_-_rrpp_bih_medassistance_31dec2013_final.pdf (accessed July 10, 2016).

Little, Alan. "Croatia Vukovar War: Overcoming a Legacy of War." *BBC News*. June 23, 2011. http://www.bbc.co.uk/news/world-europe-13887103 (accessed July 10, 2016).

Lunt, Peter and Livingstone, Sonia. *Media Regulation: Governance and the Interests of Citizens and Consumers*. London: Sage, 2012.

Malović, Stjepan. "Croatia." In *Media Ownership and its Impact on Media Independence and Pluralism,* edited by Brankica Petković, 119–40. Ljubljana: Peace Institute, 2004.

Metykova, Monika. "Establishing Public Service Broadcasting in the Slovak Republic (1993–2004): From State Control to the European Single Market." *Trends in Communication* 12, no. 4 (2004): 223–32.

Metykova, Monika. "Regulating Public Service Broadcasting: The Cases of the Czech Republic, Slovakia and Ireland" (PhD diss., Masaryk University, 2005).

Molnar, Peter. "Transforming Hungarian Broadcasting." *Media Studies Journal* 13, no. 3 (1999): 90–7.

Open Society Institute. *Television Across Europe: Regulation, Policy and Independence*. Budapest: Open Society Institute, 2005.

Pfetsch, Barbara and Voltmer, Katrin. "Negotiating Control: Political Communication Cultures in Bulgaria and Poland." *The International Journal of Press/Politics* 17, no. 4 (2012): 388–406.

Popović, Helena, Bilić, Pasko, Jelić, Tomislav and Švob-Đokić, Nada. "Background Information Report: Media Policies and Regulatory Practices in a Selected Set of European Countries, the EU and the Council of Europe: The Case of Croatia." *Media Observatory*. 2010. http://mediaobservatory.net/sites/default/files/Croatia.pdf (accessed July 10, 2016).

Rechel, Bernd. "What Has Limited the EU's Impact on Minority Rights in Accession Countries?" *East European Politics and Societies* 22, no. 1 (2008): 171–91. doi: 10.1177/0888325407311796.

Sedelmeier, Ulrich. "Anchoring Democracy from Above? The European Union and Democratic Backsliding in Hungary and Romania after Accession." *Journal of Common Market Studies* 52, no. 1 (2014): 105–121. doi: 10.1111/jcms.12082.

Stetka, Vaclav and Örnebring, Henrik "Investigative Journalism in Central and Eastern Europe: Autonomy, Business Models, and Democratic Roles." *The International Journal of Press/Politics* 18, no. 4 (2013): 413–35.

Thompson, Mark and De Luce, Dan. "Escalating to Success: Media Intervention in Bosnia and Herzegovina." In *Forging Peace: Intervention, Human Rights, and the Management of Media* Space, edited by Monroe Price and Mark Thompson, 201–35. Edinburgh: Edinburgh University Press, 2002.

Trifonova Price, Lada. "Journalists' Perceptions of Nomenklatura Networks and Media Ownership in Post-Communist Bulgaria." *Medijske Studije/Media Studies* 6, no. 11 (2015): 19–34.

Vachudova, Milada. Anna. "The Leverage of International Institutions on Democratizing States: Eastern Europe and the European Union." *European University Institute.* October 2001. http://cadmus.eui.eu/bitstream/handle/1814/1742/01_33. pdf?sequence=1 (accessed July 10, 2016).

van Cuilenburg, Jan and McQuail, Denis. "Media Policy Paradigm Shifts: Towards a New Communications Policy Paradigm." *European Journal of Communication* 18, no. 2 (2003): 181–207.

van Zoonen, Lisbet. *Entertaining the Citizen: When Politics and Popular Culture Converge.* Lanham, MD and Oxford: Rowman and Littlefield, 2005.

Part III

RENAMING

Chapter 3

The Renaming Machine in the Balkans as a Strategy of "Accumulation by Dispossession"

Suzana Milevska

In this chapter, I analyse the contemporary transformations of the Balkans through the phenomenon of renaming, where one can clearly observe how both Europe and the Balkans operate as referential political platforms, rather than merely geographical territories. Recalling Gilles Deleuze and Félix Guattari's famous distinction between social, visible machines and desiring, invisible machines[1], I ponder the use of the particular strategy of renaming I call "the renaming machine". I argue that observing the Balkans through the optics of "the renaming machine" offers us a useful insight into matters of the post-1989 transition, collective memory and identity politics in the region. These issues are specifically relevant in the understanding of the Balkans because they tend to remain outside the scope of more conventional historical, economic or political analyses.

Renaming affects visual culture and shapes cultural identities and politics most obviously through the array of symbolism it produces. Moreover, it cuts through the visual to inform both political maps and practical "common sense". I take a close look at such complex entanglements of culture and politics involved in the processes of renaming in the Balkans, which I find to be specific in the wider European context, because it has acquired the relevance of a constitutive political force. Assessing an array of renaming practices, I propose that renaming in the Balkans is yet another political means for "accumulation by dispossession" in David Hervey's terms. However, while Harvey refers to wealth and territory, one can reliably assume that no less power has been acquired through the "accumulation by dispossession" of names[2]. Renaming does not necessarily involve physical or military aggression; instead, it relies on violence by signification.

Overburdened with frequent changes of state borders as part of turbulent and inward-looking nation-building, the Balkan region possesses a history

abounding in the politics of renaming that can be traced back long before
the Second World War and the formation of the Soviet bloc and Yugoslavia
as the Socialist Federal Republic of Yugoslavia (SFRY). In order to better understand the ways in which certain renaming processes have shaped
national, cultural and personal identities in the Balkans, I find it important
to examine renaming at a variety of macro- and micro-levels. I first look
at renaming at the level of geopolitics, then focus on cases of urban design
projects and finally examine politically motivated (self)renaming within the
arts and everyday life. Connecting these seemingly quite diverse contexts in
this survey will be my predominant focus on cases of renaming in Macedonia.
This former Yugoslav republic, situated between two different parts of the
Balkans (post-Soviet Bulgaria to the north and Greece to the south) provides
an explicit demonstration of how renaming can simultaneously shape relations between different nations in the region, the hegemonic narration of a
country's own history, as well as various attempts at subversion.

GEOPOLITICAL RENAMING:
FIRST AS AN EXCEPTION, THEN AS A RULE

The generations succeeding the dissolution of Yugoslavia in 1991 in all of the
newly independent states have witnessed profound and numerous changes in
the names of institutions[3], individuals[4], languages[5] and toponyms[6]. Countless
squares and streets, factories and organizations, which carried the names of
Partisan heroes from the Second World War or socialist workers, as well as
international communist figures, were replaced by religious, medieval and
nationalist heroes, to which I return later. The region itself has been called
various names – the Balkans, the Western Balkans, South-Eastern Europe
etc. – depending on the geopolitical interests and attitudes of more powerful
European states regarding the region's integrity or dismemberment[7]. Such
changes, occurring for the most part after severe political upheavals, conflicts and wars, were often the first steps in the process of appropriating or
erasing the inherited national, cultural and personal identities, although those
have also served to protect certain long-term political interests and ensure
continued domination over a territory.

  In any discussion of names and renaming in the Balkans, the most obvious and unresolved, if absurd, conceptual "war of names" remains the one
between the Hellenic Republic (Greece) and the Republic of Macedonia. The
main source of conflict emerged when the first post-Yugoslav government in
Macedonia decided to keep the name of the previously existing "Republic
of Macedonia". The conflict began in 1991 as a bilateral dispute: Greece
objected to the use of the name "Macedonia" by its northern neighbour, which

seceded that year from the SFRY and declared its independence. In 1993, the conflict escalated into an international game of wits, with the United Nations compelling Macedonia and the international community to use the periphrastic description "The Former Yugoslav Republic of Macedonia". This was later replaced by the unrecognizable acronym "F.Y.R.O.M." that completely hid the name "Macedonia", which is also shared by a northern Greek province[8]. Such an unequal exchange with regard to a country's right to declare its own name made it seem as if the name was protected by copyright – one that had previously rarely been claimed by Greece.

The direct consequences of this conflict were more than just the postponement of the admission of the Republic of Macedonia into NATO[9] and the EU. The dispute over the name blocked efforts by the so-called "refugee children from Aegean Macedonia" (evacuated from Greece after the defeat of the communist forces in 1949) to reassert their property rights over the land and houses they had been forced to abandon. This case illustrates how renaming can serve as invisible, yet no less powerful, social and conceptual means of "accumulation by dispossession"[10]. Negotiations with internationally appointed mediators about the name of the republic ensued. During these negotiations, the Greek government proposed names like "Northern Macedonia" and "New Macedonia" for its neighbour to the north[11]. Even though the territory of Ancient Macedonia does not entirely match either contemporary Greece or Macedonia[12], for more than twenty years, the name dispute stranded Macedonia in a political limbo of endless waiting for EU accession; an ongoing, normalized "state of exception".

Such identity politics are not new in Europe, nor exclusive to the Balkans. According to Giorgio Agamben, the emergence of camps in the Nazi period signalled that the "state of exception" had become the rule and transformed society into an unbounded and dislocated biopolitical place[13]. In this respect, the name issue is a precedent that sets a compelling symptom: what was meant to last only two months (the allegedly temporary name "FYROM") became a twenty-year-long "state of exception". A former Yugoslav republic became a state without a proper name, or what Jacques Derrida called a "rogue state" [14]. The latter refers to the possibility that one state declares another state unlawful according to some established international standards. Thus, while the "state of exception" has more to do with the declaration by a sovereign power that the conditions within that country are so far beyond the possibility of governance that exceptional rules need to be applied[15], when a state or regime is proclaimed *rogue* by the international community, that community starts acting as if it gained some unwritten rights to intervene in the proclaimed rogue state's internal affairs and to break the sovereignty of that state.

This double articulation of the name dispute in the Macedonian case shows how much the implied equation of name equals identity was an inadequate

starting point for international negotiations about the issue[16]. This is particularly so given that ancient Macedonian identity does not completely overlap
with the contemporary culture and identity of either Greek or Macedonian
societies. Needless to say, some of the comparable issues of homonymy that
exist elsewhere in Europe were resolved much earlier and with no recurring
conflicts. Such was the case of Luxembourg, the southernmost province of
Wallonia and of Belgium, and the neighbouring Grand Duchy of Luxembourg:
although the initial separation was the consequence of the Belgian Revolution of 1830, the name-war hatchet seems to have been buried in 1839, after
William I, King of the Netherlands and Grand-Duke of Luxembourg, agreed
to hand over the province to the newly created Kingdom of Belgium[17]. However, in the case of the postponement of a resolution of Macedonia's "name
issue", the coupling of the "state of exception" and the "rogue state" created
a long-term vacuum, in which violent post-Yugoslav nationalism could thrive.

Fuel was added to the fire in 1992 when the Macedonian government
decided to use symbols, such as "Vergina Sun", a flag with sixteen sun rays
that were associated with Ancient Macedonia, even though Greece claimed
to have the sole historic right to these symbols. This case became a powerful
mechanism that made visible the means by which an endlessly postponed
closure of renaming can produce a "state of exception"[18], which ultimately
serves to reinforce the political power of "the renaming machine" by either
trivializing or exaggerating it.

URBAN RENAMING: VISUAL AMNESIA
AND "FALSE MEMORIES"

An analogical practice operates in another, related realm of public remembrance and collective memory. This form of the renaming machine is closely
related with the hegemonic performativity of post-Yugoslav nationalisms and
also transitional economies in the Balkans. After the break-up of Yugoslavia,
the renaming "apparatus" erased and overwrote most traces from the Tito
era (including the Yugoslav leader's own name, which had been attached
to many places in the former country) with the names of some celebrated
nationalist events and personalities. The renaming machine thus functioned
as a mechanism for remembering and forgetting and re-forging history.
Acting against the background of the violent dissolution of Yugoslavia, the
renaming machine produced a host of "false memories". Those were analogical to the well-known phenomenon from psychopathology, which refers to
trauma-driven, imagined events that figure as real in the subject's memory
and replace the subject's old, trauma-related, name with a new one, often
bearing no significant historic memory yet still hoping to compensate for the
meaning lost to the future.

The collective fabrication of memories, which Ivaylo Ditchev in the follow-ing chapter rightly aligns, in formal terms, with "kitsch", became particularly evident during the massive urban building project "Skopje 2014". Initiated by Macedonia's ruling nationalist party (VMRO-DPMNE), this undertaking was a major state investment in a city with a population of half a million, which is the capital of a country with a struggling economy and one of Europe's highest unemployment rates[19]. From 2010 to 2014, the project involved the erection of dozens of modernist, heroic monuments and the construction of neoclassicist governmental buildings with the aim of constructing a national identity through a "Disneyfication" of the city's urban landscape.

This newly created abundance of monuments and public sculptures in Skopje can be seen as an attempt to use ultra-nationalism to compensate for the haunting incompleteness of the post-Yugoslav identity of the "rogue" state. This connection between nationalism in the "ill-named" state and its urban rebuilding was particularly evident in the official attempts to explain the purpose behind the "Skopje 2014" project. The mayor of Skopje stated that the project was meant to serve as a 3D history textbook that would correct the supposed lack of nationalist interpretation of past in history books. From the perspective of the "renaming machine", this argument resonated with Viktor Shklovsky's parable about historical monuments in post-revolutionary Russia, which, for him, functioned "as a strange alibi for not telling the whole truth" or even "a quarter of the truth" about the past[20]. In fact, according to Derrida, monuments, like tombs, inevitably announce "the death of the tyrant"[21]. But what kind of void was sought to be filled by the *Warrior on a Horse*, a twenty-five-metre tall ágalma that has "adorned" the main Skopje square since 2011? What were the "renam-ing" politics behind the will to build a monument so obviously dedicated to the ancient Greek leader, Alexander the Great, yet generically named *Warrior on a Horse*?[22]

In the cacophony of voices heard during public debates about the project, the supporters of the "Skopje 2014" project advanced a particularly regres-sive argument, saying "at least they built a lot". From this perspective, Slavoj Žižek's explanation of the constitutional role of enjoyment in the production of excess is particularly useful:

It is this paradox which defines surplus-enjoyment: it is not a surplus which simply attaches itself to some "normal", fundamental enjoyment, because enjoyment as such emerges only in this surplus, because it is constitutively an "excess". If we subtract the surplus, we lose enjoyment itself, just as capitalism, which can survive only by incessantly revolutionizing its own material condi-tions, ceases to exist if it "stays the same", if it achieves an internal balance. This, then, is the homology between surplus-value – the "cause" which sets in motion the capitalist process of production – and surplus-enjoyment, the object-cause of desire[23].

According to Žižek, this dialectical play between lack and surplus creates the main paradox behind forms of "excess" sanctioned by the state. From his psychoanalytical perspective, "excessive power" is a manifestation of "a fundamental impotence", that is, "the Lacanian *objet petit a*, of the leftover that embodies the fundamental, constitutive lack"[24].

The iconoclastic radicalism of such "void" is to be traced in Macedonia's own inferiority complex, as articulated by the "Skopje 2014" project. One of the most symptomatic of all objects built as part of this mega celebration of the country's failed, impotent diplomacy[25] is the triumphal arch titled the "Porta Macedonia". Triumphal arches in cities like Berlin or Paris (built in the late 18th and early 19th centuries) were intended both to commemorate victorious events in the past and to anticipate and enable the celebration of any future victory. In this respect, a triumphal arch is a monument that is supposed to collapse the time after and before the event that is celebrated. In other words, it consists of an open multitude of events whose list can be endlessly re-written[26]. In Skopje, the 21st century triumphal arch attempts to do something quite different: to compensate for non-existing victories. As many other such newly built monuments in the region, this one is also related with the desire of the post-1989 governments in the Balkans to distance themselves from their communist pasts, which has sadly also included forgetting their antifascist legacy.

In an ironic turn, the Triumphal Arch in Skopje is positioned in a way that it rivals another novel installation, a merry-go-round, constructed in the same square. The sculptures of beggars, frivolous women with bare breasts (no women *heroes* were given monumental representation), bulls, fish, dancers and trees turned into human beings are placed side by side with the militant historic figures (mostly riding horses and holding weapons). This anachronism is a particularly telling symptom of the aesthetics adopted in this overall project: it was entirely defined by the ruling, conservative party's taste (shaped by overt ignorance and admiration for "traditional" values, that is, patriarchy, figurative and representational art)[27], while the art scene's criticism was nonchalantly ignored. However, the "renaming machine", operating across different levels of action, has simultaneously offered relevant opportunities for subversion, to which I turn below.

APPROPRIATING THE "RENAMING MACHINE": ARTS AND EVERYDAY LIFE

Though unsystematic, projects and acts of renaming in the realm of cultural production and civic action are useful demonstrations of the possibility of a more inclusive world of names. Artists' performative use of naming and renaming is based on the assumption that any act of renaming, even when done in a minimal or simplistic way, has the power to set in motion the renaming machine and potentially blur the line between art and social reality in any given case. This is why some artists intervene into the realm of the political by making use of renaming with a conscious assumption of its possible societal consequences.

Renaming proposals that were conceived by artists and researchers have, in some cases, gone so far as to initiate public campaigns, such as the one determined to rename a mountain in Switzerland because of the racist legacy behind its current name Agassizhorn (Sasha Huber, *Rentyhorn*, 2008). The feminist thrust of such projects in the Balkans has targeted the domination of male figures in names and sculptures across the region's cities. Such projects included the proposal to name a bridge after two women who protested against wearing the veil in Skopje at the beginning of 20th century (Hristina Ivanoska, *Naming the Bridge: Rosa Plaveva and Nakie Bajram*, 2004–2006). In Slovenia, a series of public art interventions temporarily renamed sixteen streets in Ljubljana after monument-worthy Slovene women (Tadej Pogačar, *Attention: Women in the City!*, 2010). Another relevant example is Sanja Iveković's artistic investigation into a rare feminine naming of a street – in a quarter in Zagreb that commemorates Croatia's historical figures – as the Street of the Unknown Heroine, referring to a female warrior against the Ottomans (*The Unknown Heroine*, 2009)[28]. Those projects clearly point to the relevance of taking concrete actions – even if they are ultimately doomed in the battle with dominant regimes of signification[29].

One rare example of a project that unravelled the ultimate power of the renaming agency in the post-Yugoslav part of the Balkans is the Belgrade Monument Group's long-term work, aimed against an initiative by the Belgrade Municipality to erect a monument "dedicated to the wars fought on the territory of the former Yugoslavia". The Group saw the Municipality's initiative as a monument that through its name would devour the very people it was supposedly honouring. Of no lesser, comparable importance are the respective research projects *Rudi Dutschke Street*, 2010 by Tanja Ostojić and David Rych and *The Renamed Times*, 2008 by Alexander Vaindorf. In these two projects the artists tried to "correct" the "working memory" of Berlin's public space that had been compromised by the state's fear of the political and mnemonic power of individuals and events it deemed inappropriate. The iconic figures of Rudi Dutschke, the spokesperson for German students in the 1960s, and the unresolved assassination of Prime Minister Olof Palme of Sweden in 1986 have in common the "political incorrectness" of the conundrums surrounding their names. Thus, to rename relevant streets after them turned out being a long and complicated process accompanied by conflicts. The fact that a number of these projects have been discussed in front of parliamentary committees, municipal officials, mayor's councils and directors of major art biennials, speaks volumes about the power of renaming as an agent of sociopolitical and cultural change.

Within contemporary art history, the use of multiple names, pseudonyms and imaginary personas has been a familiar way of gaining, and regaining, certain cultural territories[30]. For some Eastern European artists specifically, seemingly minor mistakes in writing the artist's name, such as ignoring or changing diacritics or other particularities that indicate ethnic, cultural or gender background, are not held to be simply naïve: they are interrogated as constituent elements of hegemonic strategies of representation. Besides offering much-needed criticism, the artists who address these issues scrutinize such inadvertent mistakes with irony and humour and even offer do it yourself (DIY) kits as aids[31].

Such actions are particularly relevant in the sphere of personal names. According to Deleuze and Guattari, the moment of giving/receiving a name is in itself "the highest point of depersonalization" because that's when we are confronted with an "instantaneous apprehension of the multiplicities" that otherwise belong to us[32]. Frederick Martin, a philosopher of Native American origin who in his culture goes by the name Standing Bear, has written about the violence hidden in such concepts as the acquisition of the proper name in Western culture. According to Martin, "Westerners" are given their names before they have identities, before they are even born. "John Smith" is arbitrary in the sense that it signifies nothing essential about the individual who goes by it, as is true of any other European name. Native Americans, on the other hand, are not named until they have acquired an identity. The name and the identity that a Native American goes by are acquired simultaneously, and the name is sacred and private[33]. With the large refugee crisis in the EU during 2015, a similar challenge arises at a bigger scale, in relation to the integration of those who will be permitted to stay. That this issue can have serious consequences for the identity of the newcomers can be already assumed if we recall one of the biggest earlier waves of migration in the Balkans, which occurred during 1989 in Bulgaria. President Todor Zhivkov's nationalist renaming policy required Turks and other Muslims in Bulgaria to adopt Bulgarian (Christian or traditional Slavic) names and renounce their Muslim customs. As a consequence of this assimilation campaign, 310,000 Turks left Bulgaria. Amnesty International and Turkish Government estimated that, prior to the renaming, 900,000 ethnic Turks were living in Bulgaria, whereas the Bulgarian Government claimed there to be none[34].

If the state's biopolitics can be seen as reactions to the creative power of the multitude, certain civic practices can offer useful means of interrupting dominant identity politics and proposing alternative naming orders. In this context, renaming is used tactically[35] and constructively, not only as a way to speak back to regimes of power but also to produce new meanings. The most obvious case is the attempt to subvert the state regulation of personal/family names that people are allowed to use in daily transactions. In many parts of the remaining non-EU countries in the Balkans, EU border is within walking distance, but can nonetheless remain largely insurmountable for those with incorrect citizenships. As a response to this obstruction to mobility, approximately 50,000 citizens of Macedonia, a country that awaits EU accession, have acquired the passports of the northern neighbour Bulgaria, which had been admitted to the EU in 2007, by changing their surnames and claiming Bulgarian ethnic roots, so as to gain the ability to travel and work freely in the European Union[36]. The use of multiple names by Roma citizens in certain hostile Eastern European milieus is yet another example of how self-renaming, even if it involves a defiance of official regulations, affords better opportunities for those whose minority rights have not been protected by the state. What is needed is further research into how such groups consequently deal with mnemonic fragments and faded nameplates during forced mobility and pressures to integrate themselves in host communities.

Many cases of self-renaming for purposes of overcoming stringent politics in turbulent times point to the relevance of the aforementioned Deleuze and Guattari's argument about symbolic violence built into the imposition of personal/family names. Some obvious examples include the changing of names of endangered Jewish people during the Nazi regime. During the Yugoslav wars in the 1990s, many Serbs in Croatia felt pressured to take Croatian names and surnames, while the Bosnian authorities were forced to change the earlier Yugoslav system of city abbreviations on car plates with arbitrary, unrelated ones, so as to prevent attacks on vehicles arriving from the "wrong" ethnic area. In the post-war period, migrants from the Balkans have benefited from the relaxed policies in Scandinavia on renaming. These were originally introduced as a result of the enormous number of requests received from national citizens for their own change of names, which until 1901 were mainly inherited patrilineally[37]. Even if this renaming policy was originally devised as a marker of status for the socially and politically privileged, it was appropriated as a means of self-empowerment amongst the displaced and disadvantaged minorities. For many of the lucky migrants who have recently made it to the wealthy and inclusive parts of Europe, self-renaming is likely to remain as a subsidiary, symbolic shelter.

CONCLUSION: RENAMING MACHINES BETWEEN APPROPRIATION AND DISPOSSESSION

Different cultures use naming and renaming diversely in their own contexts, but the difficulty of recognizing the biopolitical methods of one's own society remains, especially when these are used as a kind of cunning strategy of control, and when its consequences are not visible immediately. As I sought to show in this chapter, the renaming machine in the Balkans has operated in parallel with, and as an extension of, the post-1989 political upheavals. With a particular focus on Macedonia, I demonstrated that the transitional nation-building in the Balkans draws abundantly on the symbolic power of renaming, which can range from the level of personal to the level of state names. Renaming has been a focus of various state policies, as a means for the nationalist rewriting of memory, specifically through a wide-ranging and exhaustive erasure of the Yugoslav legacy[38]. However, renaming has also been the language of artistic interrogations of local dominant systems of meaning like illiberal transition and patriarchy, and a civic tactic of circumventing the imposed limits to trans-European mobility. Those cases together demonstrated the constitutive power of renaming in the Balkans, whereby renaming operates as a source of political legitimacy and a basis for negotiating identity.

The intrinsically multi-ethnic space of the Balkans, where people drew on their diverse roots to adopt more favourable personal names, is a particularly useful demonstration of the fact that the realm of names remains to be a continuous battlefield. This aspect alone reminds us of Deleuze's powerful argument that our lives are always the sum of little "becomings" which inform and shape our identities and which ultimately create idiosyncrasies that might not fit with inherited identities forever. As Gilbert Simondon put it, the process of individuation is never concluded, since the multiplicity of the pre-individual can never be fully translated into singularity: the subject is a continuous interweaving of pre-individual elements and individuated characteristics[39]. Thus one effective way to overwrite an identity imposed through the act of naming, particularly for those still arriving at Europe's gates, whether from the non-EU Balkans or beyond, will be to combine one's own sub-individualities with others to form possible multitudes. Multiplicities thus formed will always be greater than any strategy of control, in that each of us is greater than any individual or collective label or name that might be assigned to us ("man", "woman", "student", "lesbian", "white", "Roma"), because we are, each of us, more than the names we are given.

NOTES

1. Gilles Deleuze and Félix Guattari, *A Thousand Plateaus*, trans. Brian Massumi (Minneapolis: University of Minnesota Press, 1996).

2. See David Harvey, "The 'New' Imperialism: Accumulation by Dispossession," in Leo Panitch and Colin Leys, eds., *Socialist Register 2004: The New Imperial Challenge* (London: Merlin Press, 2003), 63–87.

3. Institutions such as the Yugoslav Academy of Arts and Sciences or the Yugoslav People's Army were transformed into national ones in each of the former republics.

4. Individuals bearing the names of well-known politicians, the Yugoslav state or obviously Yugoslav nationalities frequently changed their names in the 1990s, such as Bosnian scholar *Jugoslav* Vlaisavljević who now goes by the name *Ugo* Vlaisavljević.

5. A well-known example is the publication of a Croatian-Serbian "distinguishing" dictionary that emphasizes the differences of the two mutually understandable languages.

6. Each republic had a city bearing the name of Tito, such as Montenegro's capital Titograd (Tito's Town), which reverted to Podgorica after the dissolution of the SFRY.

7. See the general introduction to this volume for further information about the background of those names.

8. The adoption of the name "Macedonia" for the names of different institutions proliferated in Greece almost simultaneously. For example, Thessaloniki's international airport (located in the nearby Mikra area) was called Mikra since it opened in 1930 until 1993, when it was renamed into "Makedonia".

9. The main "retaliation" for the allegedly *rogue* behaviour happened when, at the NATO Summit in Bucharest in April 2008, the veto used by the Greek delegation prevented Macedonia from becoming a NATO member.

10. The total number of people who were evacuated from Greece during the Civil War is difficult to estimate: while the Greek government claims there were 52,000–72,000 refugees, including the Greeks, Macedonian sources claim that up to 213,000 Slavic-speaking people fled Greece at the end of the Civil War. See: *Human Rights Violations against Ethnic Macedonians-Report 1996*, Macedonian Human Rights Movement of Canada (Toronto, 1996), 111–12.

11. For extensive research into the political arguments involved in the dispute between Macedonia and Greece, see Zlatko Kovach, "Macedonia: Reaching Out to Win L. American Hearts," *Scoop World*, February 26, 2008. http://www.scoop.co.nz/stories/WO0802/S00363.htm. Accessed 10 August, 2015.

12. For a discussion of the theoretical and philosophical interpretations of this dispute, see *The Renaming Machine: The Book,* ed. Suzana Milevska (Ljubljana: P.A.R.A.S.I.T.E. Institute, 2010). This book is based on a cross-disciplinary curatorial project comprised of ten different events (exhibitions, conferences and seminars) that took place in Ljubljana, Skopje, Pristina, Zagreb and Vienna 2008–2010. The book examines the arbitrariness of names, the problematic issue of equating names with identity and the implications of the erasure of memory through renaming.

13. Giorgio Agamben, *Homo Sacer: Sovereign Power and Bare Life,* trans. Daniel Heller-Roazen (Stanford: Stanford UP, 1998), 166.

14. Jacques Derrida, *Rogues: Two Essays on Reason,* trans. Pascale-Anne Brault and Michael Naas (Stanford, CA: Stanford University Press, 2005), 97. Derrida points out several authors who have examined the use of the expression "rogue state" in foreign policy, including Noam Chomsky, *Rogue States: The Rule of Force in World*

Affairs (Cambridge, MA: Sound End Press, 2000); Robert S. Litwak, *Rogue State and U.S. Foreign Policy* (Baltimore, MD: Johns Hopkins University Press, 2000); William Blum, *Rogue States: A Guide to the World's Only Superpower* (Monroe, ME: Common Courage Press, 2000).

15. Giorgio Agamben, *State of Exception,* trans. Kevin Attell (Chicago, IL: University of Chicago Press, 2005), 23.

16. For the philosophical dispute around names and descriptions, see Bertrand Russell's and Gotlib Frege's descriptivist theory of names and the counterarguments from the causal theory of Saul Kripke, Hilary Putnam and others.

17. The problem with the Macedonian minority of Slavic origin in Greece was first mentioned during the negotiations of the name, in the last few sessions of the NATO summit of June 2008. The refugees of Slavic and Greek origin (communists' children at the time of the civil war in Greece in 1946 who now mostly live in the Republic of Macedonia) were sent away from Greece to communist countries by their parents who thus wanted to protect them from the Greek government. The children of Slavic origin were never admitted back to Greece and that caused many issues with the appropriation of the property of these refugees and their human and citizenship rights.

18. Agamben, *State of Exception*, 23.

19. Figures concerning costs vary depending on the sources: between 80 million euros according to the government, and 560 million euros according to the Balkan Investigative Reporting Network's report. See http://birn.eu.com/en/news-and-events/birn-macedonia-launches-skopje-2014-uncovered-database. Accessed 10 July, 2016.

20. Viktor Shklovsky, *The Knight's Move* (Champaign, IL: Dalkey Archive Press, 2005), originally written 1919–21, quoted in Svetlana Boym, "Tatlin, or Ruinophilia," *Cabinet* 28 (Winter 2007–08), http://www.cabinetmagazine.org/issues/28/boym2.php. Accessed 10 July, 2016.

21. Jacques Derrida, *Margins of Philosophy,* trans. Alan Bass (London: Prentice Hall, 1982), 4.

22. See Jasna Koteska, "Troubles with History: Skopje 2014," *ARTMargins Online,* http://www.artmargins.com/index.php/2-articles/655-troubles-with-history-skopje-2014. Accessed 10 July, 2016.

23. Slavoj Žižek, *The Sublime Object of Ideology* (New York; Verso, 1989), 54. Žižek explains the *objet petit a* in relation to such phenomena as the *lack*; the remainder of the Real that sets in motion the symbolic movement of interpretation; a hole at the centre of the symbolic order; the mere appearance of some secret to be explained, interpreted, etc. Ibid.

24. Ibid.

25. Amongst many embarrassing diplomatic blunders, the most famous one became the gaffe by the former Minister of Foreign Affairs Antonio Milososki. His statement from 2010, given in an interview for *the Guardian* (quoted also in Koteska, "Troubles with History"), that the equestrian statue was meant to be "saying [up yours] to them!" (that is, the Greeks) provoked ridicule in parts of the local press, calling for a new sculpture of the Minister's middle finger (digitus impudicus). Helena Smith, "Macedonian statue: Alexander the Great or a Warrior on a Horse?," *Guardian*, 14 August 2011. http://www.theguardian.com/world/2011/aug/14/alexander-great-macedonia-warrior-horse. Accessed 20 May, 2014.

26. Ironically, the few events, which have initiated public gatherings under the triumphal arch "Gate Macedonia", were not so glorious themselves: in 2011, the mass celebrations of the Macedonian national basketball team's victory over Greece and the winning of the 4th place in the European Championship; and, in 2012, the protests, initiated by the organization "Aman", against high electricity bills for the lighting of the "Gate".

27. Suzana Milevska, "The Internalisation of the Discourse of Institutional Critique and the 'Unhappy Consciousness'," in *Evaluating and Formative Goals of Art Criticism in Recent (De)territorialized Contexts,* AICA press, The International Press of the Association of the Art Critics, 2009, 2–6.

28. Strategies of naming and renaming have been present in the work of Sanja Iveković at least since 1997, starting with her critical comments in the 1990s on the impact of the then process of transition on the change of women's roles in Croatian society from war heroines to objectified bodies (*Gen XX,* 1997–2001). She has also dealt with the overwriting of the communist economic and political past in public space. In the installations *Nada Dimić File* (2000–2001) and *Lost & Found* (2003–2004), for example, she addressed the issue of changing the names of the factories in the former Yugoslavia (specifically, from the Nada Dimić Factory to Endi International), as a direct means of signifying the transition from collective to private ownership. For a wider, comparative perspective of negotiating the past in the field of cultural practice, see Vjeran Pavlaković, Pauković, Davor, Raos, Višeslav (eds.) *Confronting the Past: European Experiences* (Zagreb: Centar za politološka istraživanja, 2012).

29. An unusual example of a successful renaming campaign was the long, but positively concluded, battle for the renaming of a street called the Miškec Passage in Zagreb (until 2009, named after an unknown local man) into the Passage of Sisters Baković, who were the acclaimed local antifascist fighters and were killed by the then Croatian Nazi puppet state's regime.

30. Consider Marcel Duchamp's pseudonym Rrose Selavy; the multiple names Cantsin, Karen Eliot, Mario Rossi, Bob Jones; the multiple name Klaos Oldanburg and the well-known Luther Blissett Project in mail art; Blinky Palermo (born Peter Schwarze, aka Peter Heisterkamp); and the intentional anonymity of individual artists who signed works under group names such as Fluxus, Gutai, Irwin, Monument, etc. – to mention only a few examples of such artistic renaming. See the entry "Multiple name" in Sztuka Fabryka Mail-Art Encyclopedia, http://www.sztuka-fabryka.be/encyclopaedia/items/multiple_name.htm. Accessed 16 November, 2012.

31. Oliver Musovik̃, for example, described his work Ć≠Ќ, 2002 (video, 8') as an "educational" video about the genealogy, orthography and phonetic differences in writing his surname, while Sašo Stanojkovik̃ defined his workshop/performance *To Whom It May Concern,* 2005 (60', ICA-London) as an "instruction workshop" for Western artists, teaching them how to write the names of their Eastern European colleagues without mistaking any diacritical signs.

32. Gilles Deleuze and Félix Guattari, *A Thousand Plateaus,* trans. Brian Massumi (Minneapolis: University of Minnesota Press, 1996), 40.

33. Martin, Frederick. "Derrida(da)ism: Note 4: (Un)covering Identity." White-crow Borderland: Native American Cultural Philosophy. http://www.mayanastro.

freeservers.com/derrida4.html. Accessed 16 November, 2012. In this respect, one could also examine certain moral and ideological implications of renaming with regard to proper names in community and gender politics across Europe. Patriarchal marriage contract has traditionally dictated that a woman assumes her husband's family name and thus overwrites her premarital identity. In this context, feminism and the feminist political project view naming and renaming as an important struggle, not only in the concrete issue of patrimony but also in the kinship chain, and the issue of naming remains an important area of battle against patriarchy in general.

34. See also chapter 11 in this volume.

35. Cf. De Certeau, Michel, *The Practice of Everyday Life* (Berkley and Los Angeles, CA: University of California Press, 1984).

36. See "Bulgarian Citizenship: The Latest Numbers," *Sofia Echo*, 23 April 2010, http://sofiaecho.com/2010/04/23/891995_bulgarian-citizenship-the-latest-numbers. Accessed 10 July, 2016.

37. The renaming procedure in countries like Sweden was made widely accessible (simple and cheap) because it was recognized as a response to the limited choice of surnames. Yet, gender-wise the renaming rules are more restrictive: a male child cannot take a female name and vice versa, which reflects negatively on the legal and social position of LGBT persons and creates new hierarchies regarding the access to procedures of renaming.

38. I gesture here to Sigmund Freud's brief discussion of an early 20th century mechanical toy (the "mystic writing pad") which allows anything written to be erased at the flip of the switch.

39. Gilbert Simondon's views are discussed in Paolo Virno, *A Grammar of the Multitude: For an Analysis of Contemporary Forms of Life* (New York: Semiotext(e), 2004), 78–79.

BIBLIOGRAPHY

Agamben, Giorgio. *Homo Sacer: Sovereign Power and Bare Life,* trans. Daniel Heller-Roazen. Stanford: Stanford UP, 1998.

Agamben, Giorgio. *State of Exception,* trans. Kevin Attell. Chicago, IL: University of Chicago Press, 2005.

Blum, William. *Rogue States: A Guide to the World's Only Superpower*. Monroe, ME: Common Courage Press, 2000.

Boym, Svetlana. "Tatlin, or Ruinophilia." *Cabinet* 28, Winter 2007–08, http://www.cabinetmagazine.org/issues/28/boym2.php. Accessed 10 July, 2016.

"Bulgaria: A Country Study," ed., Glenn E. Curtis. Research Completed June 1992, Federal Research Division Library of Congress, https://cdn.loc.gov/master/frd/frdcstdy/bu/bulgariacountrys00curt_0/bulgariacountrys00curt_0.pdf. Accessed 10 July, 2016.

"Bulgarian Citizenship: The Latest Numbers." *Sofia Echo*, 23 April 2010, http://sofiaecho.com/2010/04/23/891995_bulgarian-citizenship-the-latest-numbers. Accessed 10 July, 2016.

Chomsky, Noam. *Rogue States: The Rule of Force in World Affairs*. Cambridge, MA: Sound End Press, 2000.

Deleuze Gilles and Guattari Félix. *A Thousand Plateaus*, trans. Brian Massumi. Minneapolis: University of Minnesota Press, 1996.

De Certeau, Michel. *The Practice of Everyday Life*. Berkley and Los Angeles, CA: University of California Press, 1984.

Derrida, Jacques. *Margins of Philosophy,* trans. Alan Bass. London: Prentice Hall, 1982.

Derrida, Jacques. *On the Name*, ed., Thomas Dutoit. Stanford, CA: Stanford University Press, 1995.

Derrida, Jacques. *Rogues: Two Essays on Reason,* trans. Pascale-Anne Brault and Michael Naas. Stanford, CA: Stanford University Press, 2005.

Freud, Sigmund. "A Note Upon the 'Mystic Writing-Pad." In *The Standard Edition of the Complete Psychological Works of Sigmund Freud*, ed., James Strachey. *Volume XIX (1923–1925): The Ego and the Id and Other Works*, 225–32. London: The Hogarth Press and the Institute of Psycho-Analysis, 1978/1925.

Harvey, David. "The 'New' Imperialism: Accumulation by Dispossession." In Leo Panitch and Colin Leys, eds., *Socialist Register 2004: The New Imperial Challenge*, 63-87. London: Merlin Press, 2003.

Human Rights Violations Against Ethnic Macedonians-Report 1996, Toronto: Macedonian Human Rights Movement of Canada, 1996.

Koteska, Jasna. "Troubles with History: Skopje 2014," *ARTMargins Online*. http://www.artmargins.com/index.php/2-articles/655-troubles-with-history-skopje-2014

Kovach, Zlatko. "Macedonia: Reaching Out To Win L. American Hearts." *Scoop World,* February 26, 2008, http://www.scoop.co.nz/stories/WO0802/S00363.htm. Accessed 10 August, 2015.

Large, Will. "The Multitude." *Dave Harris (& Colleagues): Essays, Papers, Courses*, http://www.arasite.org/WLnew/empire/multi.html. Accessed 10 July, 2016.

Litwak, Robert S. *Rogue State and U.S. Foreign Policy*. Baltimore, MD: Johns Hopkins University Press, 2000.

Martin, Frederick. "Derrida(da)ism: Note 4: (Un)covering Identity." *Whitecrow Borderland: Native American Cultural Philosophy*. http://www.mayanastro.freeservers.com/derrida4.html. Accessed 10 July, 2016.

Milevska, Suzana. "The Internalisation of the Discourse of Institutional Critique and the 'Unhappy Consciousness'." In *Evaluating and Formative Goals of Art Criticism in Recent (De)territorialized Contexts*. Paris, France: The International Press of the Association of the Art Critics, 2009, 2–6.

Milevska, Suzana, ed. *The Renaming Machine: The Book*. Ljubljana: P.A.R.A.S.I.T.E. Institute, 2010.

"Multiple Name." In *Sztuka Fabryka Mail-Art Encyclopedia*, http://www.sztuka-fabryka.be/encyclopaedia/items/multiple_name.htm. Accessed 10 July, 2016.

Pavlaković, Vjeran, Pauković, Davor, and Raos, Višeslav (eds.) *Confronting the Past: European Experiences*. Zagreb: Centar za politološka istraživanja, 2012.

Shklovsky, Viktor. *The Knight's Move*. Champaign, IL: Dalkey Archive Press, 2005.

Smith, Helena. "Macedonian Statue: Alexander the Great or a Warrior on a Horse?" *The Guardian,* 14 August 2011. http://www.theguardian.com/world/2011/aug/14/alexander-great-macedonia-warrior-horse, Accessed 20 May 2014.

Spivak, Gayatri Chakravorty. *Outside in the Teaching Machine*. London: Routledge, 1993.

Virno, Paolo. *A Grammar of the Multitude: For an Analysis of Contemporary Forms of Life*. New York: Semiotext(e), 2004.

Žižek, Slavoj. *The Sublime Object of Ideology*. New York: Verso, 1989.

Chapter 4

Balkan Mimesis

Kitsch as a Geographic Concept

Ivaylo Ditchev

The Europeanisation of the Balkans has been a much longer plight than is usually assumed in debates about EU enlargement, which focus mainly on the post-1989 developments. The Europeanisation of the region, which I will define loosely as the cultural space of two major fallen empires, the Byzantine and the Ottoman, has been underway for a much longer time, that is, at least since the Balkans lost its former centres. Balkan cities like Sofia, Skopje, Tirana and even Athens were boroughs of the above empires until the late 19th century and they subsequently became capitals of nation states (in this case, Bulgaria, Macedonia, Albania and Greece) for symbolic reasons. These small and somewhat artificially created (from the outside) nation states have been trying to find their place on the wider geopolitical map of Europe ever since their constitution, by opposing each other, not merely through a variety of "renaming", as Suzana Milevska showed in the preceding chapter, but also, as I show in this chapter, through a wider array of material and symbolic cultural production. Whether through architecture or public art, I argue that the top-down nation-state building has been specific in the Balkans in that it has relied abundantly on a curious production of kitsch, servicing primarily a catch-up modernisation, but also, as I show later, the post-industrial growth of tourism industry in the region.

As has been demonstrated across this volume, the Balkans are not a clear entity; some writers like Maria Todorova[1] take it as an ideological label created from outside, then interiorised by the locals. I would add that the Balkans have never been singular either, given that it has been created from various remote outside power centres: Bulgaria from Moscow, Romania from Paris and Macedonia from Belgrade[2]. The region's subsequent Europeanisation has once again been a ritual of allegiance with Western European geopolitical sponsors, and there is thus no reason to assume that this process will have any less relevance in the field of aesthetics than, say, in policy, as shown in chapter 1 in this volume. There is no brand or product as successful as the artistic work by Emil Cioran, Marina Abramović or Christo (Vladimirov Javacheff) that the Balkans have exported to the West, and to this day intellectual events in the Balkans, such as the Subversive Festival in Zagreb, where the former Greek finance minister Varoufakis famously showed his middle finger to the Germans, delight the Western European eye more than politics.

However, I won't use the term "kitsch" as a highbrow mockery of common people's bad taste. Though it emerged as a marker of class difference[3], in the context of the post-1989 Balkans, kitsch very much became a form of trans-border imitation and as such a motor for negotiating geographic proximity to Western Europe. In other words, forms of kitsch I discuss below are not necessarily a resource of the central-European *Bürger*, a figure who tries to look cultivated for himself, but of the Balkan periphery in its aspirations to become recognised as European.

TRACING KITSCH IN THE BALKANS

Kitsch is the result of an increasingly intense cultural exchange in the modern era. It is easy to produce, cheap to distribute and relatively unambiguous to interpret, as it usually stands for some absolute value or noble emotion. According to Herman Broch[4], it dissociates ethic content from the aesthetic form, instrumentalised and consumed without much effort or risk, and largely outside historical time and space: the masterpiece of troubled artistic epochs becomes immortalised as a tapestry in the kitchen.

The belated appearance of the Balkan nation states on the international scene – from the first half of the 19th to the late 20th centuries – gave rise to a hasty, catch-up modernisation, where the symbolic tended to outstrip political or economic developments. Thus, in many cities across the Balkans, constructions like monuments, opera houses and neoclassical parliaments have tended to be prioritised over services and infrastructures like administration, roads or factories. Even today, this time in the context of tourism industry, fancy restaurants and bars are run in Priština or along the Bulgarian Black Sea coast before a proper sewage system has been constructed (in 2015, the Bulgarian Prime Minister Boyko Borissov promised to build one in 2016, "so that we no longer get sick when going on holidays"). Such places may look the same as in the "civilised" West, but the ease and speed of their cultural transfer from the West give them a touch of kitsch.

Romania's Triumphal Arch of 1922, for example, commemorates the victory in the First World War and is a smaller and cheaper version of Napoleon's arch built in honour of Austerlitz. "So what?", one could say, during the establishment of Western European nation states the French imitated the Romans, the Germans drew from ancient Greeks and so on. But then, when Skopje decided to build its Porta Macedonia in 2012, even smaller and cheaper than the one in Bucharest, the practice acquires an amplitude of banality. The essence of kitsch, as I said, is in dissociating form from content: the recently constructed emblem of absolute glory and pride in Macedonia can no longer refer to some collective memory of the group, as Alexander the Great's victories took place quite a while ago, but to other prestigious models of "triumph" around the world (just as the China statuette of the Dying Swan on the piano refers to other such stylised statuettes).

A notorious example for the dissemination of prestigious emblems are national theatres and opera houses built during the "Belle époque" (from the late 19th to the mid-20th centuries), designed by the Viennese architectural studio of Fellner and Helmer that adorned urban spaces across the Austro-Hungarian Empire, including its Balkan cities like Ljubljana in Slovenia, Zagreb in Croatia and Sarajevo in Bosnia and Herzegovina, with dozens of rather uniform neo-baroque and eclectic structures. Those were considered, at the time, to be an essential attribute of the culture of modernity. The buildings constructed in the Balkan, or South-Western part of the Empire, were often supplied with an additional pediment that evokes the idea of Hellenic/Byzantine belonging. As a result, some of the buildings from that period in Sofia (Bulgaria), Rijeka (Croatia) and Iasi and Oradea (Romania) give the impression of batch production, designed for poorer clients. There were even outbursts of discontent in the Bulgarian media, when it was discovered that the proudly erected National Theatre building had replicas elsewhere. A fundamental question arises here whether certain architecture should be a unique sign of place (such as the Eiffel Tower or the Empire State Building), or whether it should be part of a paradigm like the Fellner and Helmer theatre houses that the global audience could easily situate and interpret as a former Empire's imprint on its provinces. The former strategy was more suitable for the more wealthier centres of power and culture; and the latter turned out as "convenient" for the peripheries, where no time had been left for seeking "deeper meanings" of their built environment.

Of course, when we think of kitsch in the Balkans, we usually have in mind more regional phenomena, such as "turbo-capitalism" in Serbia, turbo-folk music in Bosnia and Herzegovina, Chalga in Bulgaria and Manele in Romania. This culture, identified mainly through the particular ready-made blend of ethno-dance music, but also speedy cars, silicon beauties and the arrogant exaggeration in the display of wealth, is, so to say, "down-market" kitsch, where the new rich imitate each other by adopting easy emblems of status[5]. Images of such performances, which circulate the web, ordinarily evoke sneer and indignation, showing such sites as pompous Roma mansions in Romania, or the allegedly golden toilets in the new palace of the Turkish President Erdoğan. The amount of wider public attention the "turbo-folk" culture attracted went as far as inspiring certain Bulgarian connoisseurs to start collecting what they considered as tasteless songs of the 1990s in archival projects such as online "museums of chalga", thus gesturing to the work of Jeff Koons or Pierre et Gilles, who pushed kitsch a step further, transforming it into art.

The "upmarket" version of Balkan kitsch is usually taken rather seriously. Consider the transfer of Stalinist symbolism to the Balkan countries that fell under the Soviet zone (Bulgaria and Romania). For one single decade[6], Bulgaria was hastily covered with replicas of Soviet ideological art in order to signify the ideological change. The cake-like Party house in the centre of Sofia repeats almost literally similar "stamps" of Stalin's hand on several occupied capitals. Numerous naively realist monuments (strangely contrasting with the predominant aesthetic taste of the 1930s) served to articulate the symbolic transfer to Bulgaria of heroic battles, grateful populations and optimistic gazes towards the future. Needless to say, there had been no battles whatsoever on Bulgarian soil, as the country capitulated before the Soviets had crossed the Danube and the Soviets were welcomed by the new government. Thus, in order to make their monuments to the Soviet liberators more persuasive, the Bulgarian authorities buried beneath the monuments some remnants of their soldiers, those who had been wounded in Romania and had died in hospital long afterwards. The imitation of Lenin's mausoleum for the lesser Bulgarian leader Georgi Dimitrov adopted not only the architectural (pseudo-classical) outlook, but also the technology of preserving the body and the rituals it was used for: silent adoration, wreath laying, parade reviewing by the Politburo standing on top of it and so on. Rather than mocking such mega-kitsch, the anti-Communists who came into power after 1989 also took those emblems very seriously, the culmination of this being a triumphal dynamiting of Dimitrov's mausoleum in 1999, with the entire (right-wing) government spectating the event from the neighbouring buildings[7]. Unfortunately, the construction proved to be rather solid and it took four days to perform the democratic ritual of purification, which brought in a tinge of ridicule. And it is not that such "inadequate" passions had been invested only in dealing with the sole existence an empty kitsch-shell itself. Such acts – triumphant destructions of statues and symbols – were supposed to magically make up for the considerable delay in reforms on the road to liberal democracy.

CATCHING UP WITH EUROPE

All young Balkan nation states (except Turkey[8]) faced a major symbolic problem during the 20th century: they emerged after centuries of non-existence and badly needed to bridge the gap, separating their modest modern condition from the supposed glory of some prestigious ancestors. Thus the major problem confronting identity builders was creating a sense of *continuity*. Konstantinos Paparigopoulos, a professor of history at Athens University, was the first to develop, in the mid-19th century, the interpretation of Greek history as a single continuum: ancient, medieval and modern. The founding text of the national revival is the "Slav-Bulgarian History" written by the Athos monk Paisii in 1762, which begins with Adam, and then proceeds to put together scattered accounts about the "very glorious deeds of the first in our race", whereby his principal enemies were not the Ottomans, but rather the Greeks, and to some extent the Serbs, who were said to mock Bulgarians for not having a history of their own[9]. It was even more difficult for the intellectuals in Macedonia, which appeared on the map only in 1945; they undertook the difficult task of bridging the gaps between the ancient kingdom of Alexander the Great in the 4th century BCE, the short rule of the Bulgarian king Samuel from the 10th to the 11th centuries and the Socialist Republic of Macedonia that was part of Tito's Yugoslavia in the 20th century.

Modernity is an era when European nations start to choose their ancestors: Aristotle or Plato? Christianity or local folklore? Medieval kings or ancient heroes? The Balkan nation states, facing many centuries of non-existence, were among the most eager ones to dig up forgotten ancestors. The race was started by the Greek national revival, which rediscovered antiquity in order to capture the desire of the West that was supposed to help the national liberation cause (in the process, Orthodox symbolism was strangely mingled with the reinvented pagan heritage, e.g. Christian names competed with Zeus or Achilles). One may well wonder what a provincial Ottoman borough like Athens could have had in common with the idea of the ancient "cradle of democracy". Nevertheless, at least language seems to be an obvious link: the sheer effort of modern Greece to have every child study the Iliad remains remarkable.

The "progomoplexia" (worship of ancestors) and "arkhaiolatria" (adoration of antiquity) acquire an important dimension of kitsch, especially when imitated by the neighbouring countries competing for Europe's recognition. The Dacians, gradually adopted as ancestors by the Romanians in the 20th century, were made into a more autochthonous version of Romanian identity, after the first surge of Latinism in the 19th century, when the new nation was hailed as a direct heir of Rome. Nevertheless, the legitimate question arose as to why the brave people of Romania had lost their language after such a short occupation that lasted only a century and a half? Various answers were furnished, such as claims that the Dacians were really quick to learn, they intermarried with Roman soldiers, they used this clever strategy to defeat the enemy and so on. The ultimate theory by the autochthonists was that it was

not Rome that brought culture to Dacia, but vice versa, the Dacians, supposedly much more ancient, had been at the origin of Rome[10]. In the same vein,
Albania set itself on a mission to bridge a thousand years of history, declaring
continuity between its modern state and the "noble" Illyrians. Needless to
say, the Illyrians supplied their own soldiers to the Roman Empire and gradually replaced Rome's population by its own kind. Meanwhile, the "peaceful"
Thracians in Bulgaria were proclaimed an official Bulgarian ancestor in the
1970s, when pacified communist leaders tried to integrate the country into
the West. Like the Dacians, nationalised earlier by their northern neighbours
(the Romanians), the Thracians were declared autochthonous in Bulgaria at
least since the Neolithic period, thus helping the state legitimise its claim to
the territory. Hence, given how "ancient" the Bulgarians in fact were, a patri-
otic Bulgarian scholar could not but conclude that it was not them who were
Hellenised, but vice versa: in this narration, it is the ancient Bulgarians who
were at the origin of ancient Greek culture.

Why would I call such identity formations kitsch? Because of its sheer
speed, scope of imitation and use of ready-made patterns, which are adopted
as form with no content. There is no actual trace of the past presence of
"noble" Dacians, Thracians and Illyrians in the respective contemporary
Romanian, Bulgarian and Albanian societies. Nevertheless, their public urban
spaces are all covered with monuments, theme parks, wine drinking tours,
rituals to ancient deities and countless other re-enactments of this "invented
tradition"[11]. The combination of empty prestigious emblems often leads to
eclectic anachronism, as in the Kazanlak "Rose Festival", where Thracian
girls pluck this symbol of Bulgaria, even if roses came to the Balkans much
later, with the Ottomans. The ancient Macedonians are a very similar case
if one keeps in mind the subtle difference between the Hellenised people
that Athens considered as "theirs", and the autochthonous people of the
Republic of Macedonia, who define themselves counter to the Greeks who
actually conquered them. The case of Macedonians particularly has to do
with the Balkan ancestor pattern. The country's politics of *antiquisation*,
begun in 2009 by the conservative government of Nikola Gruevsky, has
made Skopje the universally acknowledged European capital of kitsch (see
chapter 3 in this volume). The 22-metre-high equestrian statue of *Warrior on
a Horse* resembles Alexander the Great, who was declared as the ancestor
of Macedonia after the post-Yugoslav independence of 1991. He is shown
with a sword in his hand, surrounded by soldiers and water-spitting lions,
wise medieval kings, as well as ardent modern revolutionaries. This melange
offers perhaps the utmost plastic expression of the principle I am describing:
pretentious, imitative, eclectic and mawkish. To get at the scope of the empti-
ness of form at work here, it suffices only to imagine all this in the evening,
with coloured lights projected through the water fountains, throbbing under

the sounds of Beethoven's music, played from hanging speakers, over and over. This ancestor imagery, though initially created during communism for ideological reasons, has now been taken up also by the tourism industry, with no significant changes. Only the popular aspect of the ancients (representing the oppressed, according to the former, communist ideology) has been replaced with a more Hollywood-style look, including big muscles, sexy legs and magical weapons.

DIGGING FOR IDENTITY

To aid the post-1989 revival of nationalism in the Balkans, a newer genre of kitsch science has evolved: identity genetics. If, elsewhere, the tracing of gene mutations is used to study migrations and thus assert the fundamental hybridity of the human kind, for some of the Balkan amateur-biologists, it is a way to prove the purity of race and autochthonous origin of their people by percentages, formulae and maps uploaded on services like "YouTube" for the whole world to see. In the West, there exists a similar usage of this new branch of research, but it is more commonly used for commercial reasons: you send some genetic material of yours, along with 100 or so euros, and they tell you which ancient people you come from. Does that change your life? Will you immigrate to Finland, when you learn that your *haplogroups* are traced back to that part of Europe? Kitsch, as I said, is form dissociated from content: a pure emotion, an absolute fantasy, acquired easily and cheaply, without having to explain yourself or suffer legal consequences, especially concerning authorship. In the Balkans, kitsch genetics creates ancestors not merely for individual but also for collective consumption; they are a pattern and fuel for the rapid production of identity, including artefacts like statuary and souvenirs.

In one way, narratives about Balkan ancestors follow the model of the Celts, which was initially a rather vague term for non-Roman, later non-English and non-French populations, and was even later used as a foundation of modern identities of newcomers like the Irish or the Welsh. The model consists of using confused historical data and the vast territory of the allegedly shared culture for modern constructions of identity, through a vigorous rejection of the imperial centres. Nevertheless, there seems to be an important difference from how the Balkan nations furnish their ancestral identities. Celtic identity is nowadays transnational, it stages itself in music events or pagan festivals all over the world; whereas the Dacians, Thracians or Illyrians are strictly nationalised and no country thinks of sharing them with the neighbour. A useful example was the 2015 collaborative exhibition in the Louvre, "The saga of the Thracian kings", where this ancient people were presented as "a crossroads of influences" and located over several countries in the Balkans. In Bulgaria, the exhibition was hailed as a triumph of the artistic genius of "our ancestors, the Thracians".

Nationalism is a delight for kitsch: not only does it postulate, in its pacifist and thus "banal" articulations[12], a supreme value of kitsch, but it also makes kitsch into a broader framework of comparison and competition between different nations, where the instrumentalisation of form is essential. Thus, the aforementioned *Warrior on the Horse* (or, Alexander the Great) statue in Skopje competes with the monument of the same ancestor in Thessaloniki; Cyril and Methodius are contested between Serbs, Bulgarians and Macedonians; and the new monument to King Samuel in Sofia (featuring big muscles, a big sword and battery-powered shining eyes) was erected in 2015, as an answer to the one in Skopje's central square.

Another pretender to absolute values is, of course, religion. But in order to become kitsch, religious practices and symbols must be removed from the realm of personal or collective contemplation, to become a matter of competition and comparison like narratives about ancestors or the constructions of opera houses. Form needs to be dissociated from content. Thus, the big golden cross on the neck of the Serbian 1990s warlord Arkan, who married turbo-folk singer Ceca while wearing a First World War Serbian uniform, is certainly not a sign of Christian humility. The Romanian priests, who inaugurate the offices of the newly rich by exorcising the Devil with incense, are more a sign of wealth and prestige, rather than of belief. Or take the case of the Bulgarian city of Haskovo, where the local authorities built the tallest statue of the Blessed Virgin Mary with the explicit goal to enter into *Guinness World Records*, which they did. The record of Our Lady is noted today in big letters on a plate at the foot of the 14-metre (plus another 17 metres for the pedestal) construction.

Everything absorbed by the tourist industry tends to become kitsch, of course. National symbols and religious practices, as well as folklore, cuisine and even wedding rituals are regularly staged for tourists along the Black Sea or the Adriatic coasts. The Balkan states, which were industrialised rather slowly, started to increasingly rely on tourism beginning in the 1960s. In an attempt to rectify what they perceive as a historical delay in comparison to France, Italy or Switzerland, they tried to sell nature, local colour and flavour, customs, history, hospitality and so on. Now, the basic ambiguity here is one of communication: do I produce cultural emblems because they are important only for me, or do I do so to convey a message to the Other? The former scenario, referring to the tourism industry, could be seen as ideal-typical kitsch. But tourists do not like being fooled, they always look for "real things" that are "not for tourists" or "off the beaten track". Thus efforts are made to swing to the other extreme: be "natural", that is, imitate the naturalness of the "West"!

But if we put this in a more general perspective, we shall see that the instrumentalisation of empty forms goes way beyond the tourism industry. Quick aesthetic gestures could mark political change, without taking the time for debates about heritage and remembrance: the pseudo-church in front of Sofia Palace of Culture, supposed to commemorate the victims of communism, chose a kitschy design, one that is facile, cheap and without risk. So are the realistic, aesthetically Stalinist monuments to Bill Clinton in Prishtina (Kosovo), or George Bush in Kruje (Albania), personae considered as liberators (due to their support of Kosovo's independence from Milošević's Yugoslavia): the first one holds the files authorising the NATO bombing of Belgrade in 1999 under his arm; the second one has his sleeves rolled up the same way when he was visiting the city in 2007, shaking hands with the population (rumour has it, his watch was stolen while greeting the crowd).

A similar phenomenon can be observed in Bulgaria: the authorities started to rebuild, or actually to build up to the roof, dozens of Roman and medieval fortresses with EU funds designated for local development. The reconstruction is in most cases purely hypothetical, and the cultural minister Vezhdi Rashidov, answering to criticism, said that some degree of "fake" will be good for tourism. The interesting thing is that those dull proto-theme-parks (offering tourists the possibility to take a picture while being beheaded by a medieval henchman) are presented as a matter of national pride and most often there is the national flag waving on top. Pride here is very similar to the one a tourist feels when bringing home a souvenir bought in a faraway land. Within years, Bulgaria acquired a number of fortresses that elsewhere on the planet took centuries to build. Is it not unjust to be conquered and have your castles destroyed? Well, here is how history is redeemed: you rebuild your ruins along archaeological hypotheses, feature films or legends, and mobilise local fans to dress up and re-enact glorious moments of the past to the delight of tourists.

Even more curious, from this perspective, are the so-called "turbo-monuments" in the western Balkans: the statues of Bruce Lee in Mostar, Bosnia and Herzegovina (since destroyed); of Sylvester Stallone in the role of Rocky in Žitište, Serbia; of Bob Marley in the private Rock village near Belgrade; and the unaccomplished project for Tarzan in the hometown of Johnny Weissmuller, who played this role (Tarzan was presented as the typical Serbian who starts from nothing in the jungle and survives). Moreover, a great concentration of such statues is to be found in Durres, Albania: Mick Jagger, Elton John, Tina Turner and John Lennon.

How should we explain this new fashion? Obviously tired from the passions of nationalism, some Balkan residents try to capture the world's attention through a new type of imitation directed no longer towards "high" culture, but towards popular culture: film, rock and Disneyland. There is

the Andrićgrad (referring to the work of Ivo Andrić), Drvengrad (the scen-
eries of Emir Kusturica's films transformed into a tourist site), the village
of goat milk and memories of Bela Rechka (a site where one can learn the
supposed proto-Bulgarian martial arts) and so on. Clearly, kitsch – modern
by definition – seeks to keep the pace with the postmodern epoch too and it
draws abundantly from popular culture. Take for instance the feature film
Monument to Michael Jackson (Darko Lungulov, 2014), in which a God-
forsaken Serbian town tries desperately to attract tourists by replacing the top-
pled communist Partisan monument with a statue of Michael Jackson. Why
him? Well, why not? Doesn't everyone appreciate him? Gradually, the idea is
carried out and the result is so absurd that the town, of course, makes global
headlines. This developed another form of legitimation of the production of
kitsch, articulating the credo: give international visitors "what they want".

What does this Balkan instrumentalisation of certain Western cultural
emblems tell us in the process of world competition of places? The establishment of nation states on the European periphery used to be linked to the
figure of the *Kulturträger*, who studied abroad and came home to implement
the achievements of civilisation. His addressee was at home, and his messages about life abroad were drawn from Western European metropolises.
The post-1989 Balkan kitsch-manager – political, cultural and touristic – does
the opposite. He sells local emblems to international audiences, fighting an
ever harder competition, pushing down expenses, as everything needs to
be cheaper on the periphery[13]. He also romanticises his country's history,
in a quest, impossible from the beginning, for a European recognition,
and a compensation for a history lost to a period of invisibility.

NOTES

1. Maria Todorova, *Imagining the Balkans* (New York and Oxford: Oxford
University Press, 2009).

2. A wider historical excursion is beyond the scope of this chapter. See Ivaylo
Ditchev, "The Eros of Identity," in *Balkan as Metaphor: Between Globalization and
Fragmentation*, eds., Dušan Bjelić and Obrad Savić (Cambridge, MA and London:
The MIT Press, 2002), 235–50.

3. See Pierre Bourdieu, *Distinction: A Social Critique of the Judgement of Taste*
(Cambridge, MA: Harvard University Press, 1984).

4. Hermann Broch, "Evil in the Value-System of Art," in *Geist and Zeitgeist: The
Spirit in an Unspiritual Age: Six Essays*, ed., translated, and with an introduction by
John Hargraves (New York: Counterpoint, 2002), 13–40.

5. For a more comprehensive overview of the various forms of "turbo-folk" culture in the Balkans see Uroš Čvoro, *Turbo-folk Music and Cultural Representations
of National Identity in Former Yugoslavia* (Farnham: Ashgate, 2012).

6. Communists take over in 1948 and Stalin is removed from the mausoleum in 1962, which can be seen as the ultimate end of this period.

7. For a comparative perspective on similar post-Yugoslav development see Vjeran Pavlaković, "Contested Histories and Monumental Pasts: Croatia's Culture of Remembrance," in *Monumenti: The Changing Face of Remembrance*, ed., Daniel Brumund and Christian Pfeifer (Beograd: Forum Ziliver Friedensdienst, 2012), 24–25.

8. The Kemalist revolution erases the immediate imperial heritage and tries to invent pre-Ottoman heritages, proclaiming for instance the ancient Hittites as ancestors of modern Turkey.

9. Paisii Hilendarski, *Slav-Bulgarian History* (Sofia: Bulgarski Pisatel, 1972).

10. Lucian Boia, *History and myth in Romanian consciousness* (Budapest: CEU Press, 1977).

11. Cf. Eric Hobsbawm and Terence Ranger, eds., *The Invention of Tradition* (Cambridge: Cambridge University Press, 1983).

12. Cf. Michael Billig, *Banal Nationalism* (London: Sage Publications, 1995).

13. For a wider perspective on the so-called "commercial nationalism" on a global scale, see Zala Volcic and Mark Andrejevic, "Nation Branding in the Era of Commercial Nationalism," *International Journal of Communication*, 5 (2011): 598–618.

BIBLIOGRAPHY

Billig, Michael. *Banal Nationalism*. London: Sage Publications, 1995.

Boia, Lucian. *History and myth in Romanian consciousness*. Budapest: CEU Press, 1977.

Broch, Hermann. "Evil in the Value-System of Art." In *Geist and Zeitgeist: The Spirit in an Unspiritual Age: Six Essays*, edited, translated, and with an introduction by John Hargraves, 13–40. New York: Counterpoint, 2002.

Bourdieu, Pierre. *Distinction: A Social Critique of the Judgement of Taste*. Cambridge, MA: Harvard University Press, 1984.

Čvoro, Uroš. *Turbo-folk Music and Cultural Representations of National Identity in Former Yugoslavia*. Farnham: Ashgate, 2012.

Daskalov, Rumen. *The Fancy World of the Ancient Bulgarians*. Sofia: Gutenberg, 2011.

Ditchev, Ivaylo. "The Eros of Identity." In *Balkan as Metaphor: Between Globalization and Fragmentation*, edited by Dušan Bjelić and Obrad Savić, 235–250. Cambridge, MA and London: The MIT Press, 2002.

Elias, Norbert. *Kitschstil und Kitschalter*. Münster: LIT Verlag, 2004.

Hilendarski, Paisii. *Slav-Bulgarian History*. Sofia: Bulgarski Pisatel, 1972.

Hobsbawm, Eric and Ranger, Terence, eds., *The Invention of Tradition*. Cambridge: Cambridge University Press, 1983.

Monument to Michael Jackson. A film. Serbia-Germany-Macedonia-Croatia. Director Luganov, Darko, 2014.

Pavlaković, Vjeran. "Contested Histories and Monumental Pasts: Croatia's Culture of Remembrance." In *Monumenti: The Changing Face of Remembrance*, edited

by Daniel Brumund and Christian Pfeifer, 24–25. Beograd: Forum Ziliver
Friedensdienst, 2012.

Todorova, Maria. *Imagining the Balkans*. Updated Edition. New York and Oxford:
Oxford University Press, 2009.

Volcic, Zala and Andrejevic, Mark. "Nation Branding in the Era of Commercial
Nationalism." *International Journal of Communication*, 5 (2011): 598–618.

Part IV

REPRESENTING

Chapter 5

'Europe Unfinished' in Bosnia and Herzegovina

The 2014 Protests in the International Media

Eunice Castro Seixas[1]

Since the General Framework Agreement for Peace (known as the Dayton Peace Agreement) ended the war in 1995, Bosnia and Herzegovina (BH) has been under international regulation and supervision of the 'Office of the High Representative' (OHR). The complex political structure established at Dayton to accommodate the various formerly warring factions of Bosnian Serbs, Croats and Muslims (Bosniaks) has divided this country of 3.8 million residents into two 'entities', the Federation of Bosnia and Herzegovina (FBH) and Republika Srpska (RS). FBH is further divided into ten 'cantons', with their own prime ministers and governments. However, the Dayton Peace Agreement has been criticized for having transformed BH into an informal trusteeship or 'shared sovereignty' with opaque relations of international and internal authority and accountability[2]. This has resulted in an increased dependency on foreign aid and a lack of ownership and accountability, whether in civil society, politics or economy[3].

The liberal peace-building project in BH has failed to create a multi-ethnic society, economically sustainable and capable of self-determination and democratic accountability[4]. Liberal policies have been imposed top-down, in a standardized manner, with no attempt to understand and adjust to the complex realities of a society that was undergoing multiple transitions – from socialism to capitalism, from war to peace and from a contested state to a democratic and functional one[5]. Trapped in this long-lasting state of 'in-between', BH society faces a variety of issues engendered by its post-war transition, including a dependency on external aid, investment and international expertise, a 'shared sovereignty' between the local and the international powers and the resulting lack of accountability of the political elite towards the citizens. As a consequence of those issues there is also the depoliticization of political economy, which entails the popular view of economics as if it were a natural law, that is, largely independent of politics and social values. The latter issue of depoliticization may particularly endanger the processes of democratization by denying any meaningful role in economic decisions to civil society and citizens themselves[6].

In this context, the protests of February 2014, which began in Tuzla and spread to other cities, mostly in the FBH, the Croat-Bosniak entity, represent an important event in the social and political life of the country, expressing the immense frustration of Bosnian citizens, and disrupting social lethargy as the dominant public opinion in the country. These events attracted a lot of international media attention, reviving a Bosnian focus in world headlines. In reporting about such upheavals, everyday media can play an important role in highlighting protesters' demands for social change and construing these as either legitimate or illegitimate to an international audience. Indeed, in this specific context of post-war transition, media can act to help prevent future conflicts or to inform the resolution of present conflicts, or to reinterpret the past in order to justify specific actions in the present[7]. At an international level, media play an important role in constructing images of difference and sameness, and forming a civic and moral space where relations with an 'Other' are played out in any given context. In this sense, as Roger Silverstone proposed, the transnational reach of certain events via media reports has the potential to form a 'mediapolis', or a wider, 'global civic space for connection and compassion'. What this proposal emphasizes is the need for a sustained critical interrogation of both the media and the public's responsibility for a shared civic space, because a responsible and accountable media culture depends on a critical and literate citizenry, one 'which is critical with respect to, and literate in the ways of, mass mediation and media representation'[8].

In this chapter, I analyse how the protests in BH were construed by the international media for their audiences so as to explore whether their reports did anything to tackle the traditional West/East divide on which the usual representation of Otherness in Europe rests[9]. I employ a thematic qualitative approach in conjunction with critical discourse analysis. My findings reveal a highly *ambivalent* construal of the Bosnian protesters as both legitimized in their suffering and demands and as traumatized citizens, who are in permanent need of both assistance and oversight by the West. In general, the international media projected both the fear of losing control of BH, that is, the fear on the part of international powers that BH will fall back on the level of extreme violence existent during the war, and the desire of these powers for completing the promise of building a sustainable multicultural society in BH. The fact that the protesters' actions were depicted as warranted and justified highlights the contradictions of the liberal/neoliberal project that at the same time produces depoliticized subjects and leads to claims of abandonment and exclusion.

ANALYSING THE PROTESTS IN THE INTERNATIONAL
MEDIA: A NOTE ABOUT METHODOLOGY

Media reports were searched and retrieved online through a search engine, using the keywords: 'Bosnia protests 2014'. A selection of eleven news articles resulting from the search was based on the following criteria: (a) news items dated from the period between the onset of the unrest (6 Feb. 2014) and its end (late Feb. 2014); (b) items published in English in the most influential international media; (c) a range of media from different countries and geopolitical regions (US, UK, Russia, and Qatar). Such media represent news differently in their respective national and international markets, but this diversity is also an intrinsic characteristic of international media.

The eleven articles are from *The Guardian* (London), *Euronews*, British Broadcasting Corporation (BBC), Al Jazeera (Qatar), the *New York Times* (*NY Times*), Russia Today (RT, Moscow), and the REUTERS and Associated Press news agencies[10]. The news items were qualitatively analysed and initial codes were developed into themes. The following themes were selected according to criteria suggested by Braun and Clarke[11]: 'A war zone', 'legacies from the war', 'warranted mental states', 'A national discontent', 'Balkan Spring', and 'shared responsibilities'. These themes will be presented in detail subsequently. Working with critical discourse analysis, and following Fairclough[12], I also looked at specific discursive features of the selected news articles regarding the representation of the events, worldviews and the identities of those involved and the relationships between them. I took into account degrees of presence (what is absent, presupposed, backgrounded and foregrounded), categories, vocabulary, metaphors, the mode (direct and indirect discourse) and so on. I begin in the next section by focusing on the headlines. I then move on to examining the major themes, and end with a more general discussion of the main findings.

THE HEADLINES: A 'VIOLENT' BOSNIA RETURNS

Most of the headlines highlighted the violence of the protests and their impact on life in Bosnia. The protests were qualified by the majority of the analysed news items as 'violent' or resulting in 'violence': 'Bosnia-Herzegovina hit by wave of violent protests' (*The Guardian*, 7 Feb. 2014); 'Bosnia-Herzegovina protests break out in violence' (BBC news, 7 Feb. 2014); 'Violent anti-government protests spread across Bosnia' (AP, 7 Feb. 2014), 'More than 130 hurt in anti-government protests in Bosnia' (REUTERS, 6 Feb. 2014), 'Anti-government protests turn violent in Bosnia' (FRANCE 24 with REUTERS AP, 7 Feb. 2014). 'Protests' appeared as a nominalization, concealing the agents of these actions. One exception was Al Jazeera's head-line emphasizing the agency of 'protesters' rather than referring to 'protests' – 'Bosnia protesters attack presidency building' (Al Jazeera, 8 Feb.). This picture of Bosnia as hit by violence, complemented by images and videos of the protesters clashing with the police, attacking and burning government buildings, emphasized an idea of drama and chaos that had resonance with images of the 1992–1995 war and contributed to building a sense of urgency.

The headlines gave the impression that the protests were generalized across BH, although they occurred mainly in the FBH (the Bosniak-Croat area), thus implying an idea of 'national discontent'. Some of the headlines also hinted at a reason for the protests, reconstructing these as 'corruption protests', 'anti-government protests', 'protests over government and econ-omy' and as '[a] people[s] demand for government overhaul'. For example, 'Violent protests across Bosnia injure 150 as people demand government overhaul' (RT, 7 Feb. 2014); 'Violent anti-government protests spread across Bosnia' (AP, 7 Feb. 2014), 'Anti-government protests turn violent in Bosnia' (FRANCE 24 with REUTERS AP, 7 Feb. 2014), 'More than 130 hurt in anti-government protests in Bosnia' (RT, 6 Feb. 2014); 'Protests over Government and Economy Roil Bosnia' (*NY Times*, 7 Feb. 2014). Thus, in general, the headlines were consistent in construing the protests as linked to the difficult economic and political situation in the country.

Towards the end of the month, some of the headlines presented interpreta-tions, explanations and predictions regarding the protests, by establishing a referential link to events known as the Arab Spring, which positioned BH symbolically closer to the Orient than to Western Europe. For example, the idea of a 'Balkan Spring' and a 'potential political spring' appeared in two of the headlines: 'Bosnian protests: A Balkan Spring?' (BBC, 7 Feb. 2014) and 'Bosnia-Herzegovina: Corruption protests fuel a potential political spring' (Euronews, 28 Feb. 2014). In one particular *New York Times* headline, on 14 February, a more analytical, historically informed, explanation was pre-sented: 'Roots of Bosnian protests lie in Peace Accords of 1995'.

In sum, the headlines' emphasis on images of violence and chaos invoked memories of the war and the fear of the return of a 'violent', chaotic and unpredictable BH, related to classical Balkanist representations. At the same time, the headlines presented the protests as 'anti-government' or linked to the economic demands of the working class, thus eliciting at once a sense of transnational solidarity, portraying the protesters as somewhat similar to other working-class citizens in the West. This ambivalence in the construal of the Bosnian Other as different and at the same time similar to 'Western' Self appeared throughout the corpus, and it points to a lasting imprint of Balkanist representation, where the Balkans remain in-between the spheres of barbarity and civility[13].

CONSTRUCTING THE BOSNIAN AS A BALKAN OTHERNESS

Six main themes, relevant to the focus of this research, were identified, all pertaining to the representation of the Bosnian citizens as a Balkan 'Other'. On the whole, the news analysed in the themes presented below performed a narrative function that linked BH's past, present and future. The news in the themes 'war zone' and 'legacies from the war' linked the protests to the past, evoking the war of 1992–1995 and its consequences. The themes 'warranted mental states' and 'A national discontent' focus on the present (but long-lasting) socio-economic and political situation in BH, which serves to justify the protests. The media tend to ascribe 'shared responsibilities' for this situation on the Bosnian political elite and the international community. The theme of 'Balkan Spring' involves a projection into the future as a warning of the unpredictability of the events in case the protesters' demands are not taken seriously either by national or international powers.

'A war zone'

The reference to the 1992–1995 war appeared in most of the news articles, typically foregrounded in the first paragraph, as a comparison and a reminder, thus encoding the violence of the more recent protests by evoking the war. This comparison emerged through the voice of the journalist and through the choice of direct quotes from witnesses and the comments of political analysts. All these voices stressed the sheer size and violence of the protests, presenting them as the worst conflict since the end of the war: 'the worst unrest since the end of the 1992–1995 war'; 'the worst outburst of violence since the regional war ended back in 1995'; 'the worst social unrest the country has seen since the 1992–1995 war that killed over 100,000 people following Yugoslavia's dissolution'; 'the worst violence since the end of the war in 1995'. This representation was typically depicting BH as a renewed 'war zone'.

> Srećko Latal, an analyst at the Social Overview Service, a research organization based in Sarajevo, said in a telephone interview that the capital looked like a 'war zone,' with cars set on fire and overturned, buildings burning, and smoke from tear gas billowing into the sky. He said protesters had attacked the headquarters of the Bosnian presidency on Friday, a potent symbol of the country's chronic dysfunction. 'We haven't seen violent scenes like this since the war in the 1990s,' he said. 'People are fed up with what has become total political chaos in Bosnia, with infighting over power, a dire economic situation and a feeling that there is little hope for the future.'
>
> (*NY Times*, 7 Feb. 2014, 'Protests over government and economy roil Bosnia')

In early February, government buildings were set alight in Sarajevo, Zenica and
Tuzla. It was the worst violence since the end of the war in 1995.

(*Euronews*, 28 Feb. 2014, 'Bosnia-Herzegovina:
Corruption protests fuel a potential political spring')

By emphasizing the image of drama and recalling the war, the news outputs
were naturalizing the effects of the war on the Bosnian citizens, construing
the latter as permanently traumatized subjects. This relates to what is otherwise familiar in journalism studies as the reporters' 'vocalization of trauma'
and more generally, a 'therapeutic model of journalism', which builds from
images of distant suffering (e.g. references to powerlessness, despair, emotional and physical pain and death) to project forms of solidarity based on a
notion of common humanity[14]. In this case, images of suffering are related
more to feelings of anguish and hopelessness of the Bosnian citizens and less
to their physical pain or death. Nevertheless, as in the case of the media's
portrayal of the 2010 Haiti earthquake[15], through emphasizing the urgency
of the event, this 'therapeutic discourse' disregarded alternative sociopolitical
and historical constructions of suffering and of citizenship and contributed to
the construal of BH as a place in permanent need of humanitarian assistance,
which is also a lasting component of Balkanist[16] representation. By doing so,
this form of construal may have also worked to distance some of the international audiences from these images, as is familiar from the Yugoslav wars in
the 1990s, presented both to local and international audiences as happening
'there'[17].

The legacies of the war

Whereas references to the chaos and violence of the protests served to evoke
the idea of a war zone, reports on protesters' actions did not necessarily follow the same logic. Rather than being gratuitous and irrational, as is familiar
in the Balkanist discourse, the protests were depicted as warranted, given
the situation of high unemployment and corruption in the country and the
inability of the politicians to deal with these issues in the post-war period.
In fact, the protests were implicitly construed as positive, as a sign of hope,
as unprecedented and unexpected events that counteracted the 'apathy',
'cynicism' and 'fear' of Bosnian citizens in the post-war era.

This specific form of portraying the protesters as legitimized in their
actions went, to a certain extent, against the grain of stereotypical (Balkanist)
representations of Bosnian citizens as 'naturally' violent or irrational. But
although these interpretations of the protests as positive may have encouraged a sympathetic engagement, even identification, of some of the overseas
audiences with the protesters, in terms of witnessing common people in their

determination to put an end to the country's prevailing sentiment of inertia, at the same time, the media were quick to cloud this image by a sense of fear that protests could descend back into the 'chaos', evoked by memories of earlier, equally mediated, but nonetheless vivid, images of the Yugoslav wars. The ambivalence of this construal was significant because it portrayed the actions of BH people as both proximate to those in the 'West' in their demands for a more just society (as familiar from reports on Occupy movements and Greek anti-austerity protests) and also different and distant, in terms of their location in the symbolic geography of Europe: the 'restless' Balkans.

> The chaos is unprecedented, given the common view that Serbs, Bosnians and Croats would rather risk political stagnation than ever returning to the kind of violence they saw during the Bosnian War of 1992–95.
>
> (RT, 7 Feb. 2014, 'Violent protests across Bosnia injure 150, as people demand govt. overhaul')

> For years, Bosnians have fumed about their politicians – whom they almost universally believe to be corrupt. But the war left people apathetic, frightened and cynical. Indeed, the war years left such deep traumas that anger about the way politicians have prospered while standards of living have declined has been suppressed out of fear of a return to conflict.
>
> (BBC news, 7 Feb. 2014, 'Bosnian protests: A Balkan Spring?')

> With her neatly buttoned blue coat, turquoise scarf and discreetly modish black shoes, Emina Bursuladzic, 58, seems an unlikely rebel. Like many others in this largely rural country, with little tradition of street protest and an abiding horror of bloodshed after the war, she disavows the violence. But over the past seven months, she has fought to preserve the remnants of Dita, once the provider of detergent for all Yugoslavia. She and her co-workers stood vigil outside the local government offices, pursuing a vain quest to sue the owner they say came in 2008–9 and stripped their chemical plant almost bare.
>
> (*NY Times*, 14 Feb. 2014, 'Roots of Bosnian Protests lie in Peace Accords of 1995')

The above description of Emina as a case of an 'unlikely rebel' serves to demonstrate the media's sympathy for protesters' actions. At the same time, the conjunction 'but' initiating the third sentence implies a reservation or a limit to this sympathy, which involves the notion that although protests are seen as reasonable, there is a risk of these degenerating into uncontrollable violence, even if protesters, like Emina, are still deeply traumatized by the bloodshed of the 1990s. Here, one finds at once a distancing sympathy with the disadvantaged and the phantasmatic fear of a renewed war. This configuration was difficult to imagine in international media reports about similar civic protests against the government, the Troika, privatization policies and austerity measures across Western Europe. Observing such developments from Portugal, my home country, I noticed that media reports of the protests of 11 March 2011 against the Troika and precarious employment policies highlighted (generally in a sympathetic manner) the nationwide scope of these protests and also their festive nature. Fears and concerns about violent breakouts were practically non-existent in these reports.

Some of the references to the war emphasized another idea: the fact that the protests again brought BH to the attention of the international community after two decades of 'forgetfulness'.

> For years the best description of the political situation in Bosnia-Hercegovina [*sic*] has been 'stagnant but stable'. Now, with astonishing speed, analysts are already talking about a 'Bosnian Spring'.
>   (BBC news, 7 Feb. 2014, 'Bosnian protests: A Balkan Spring?')

In order to better understand the kind of relationship between the international community and the events in BH suggested by the analysed media reports, one can draw a useful parallel to the idea familiar in postcolonial studies, of the 'return of the oppressed/repressed'. This idea relates to the ambivalent way that the oppressed/colonized were construed and silenced in colonial texts through stereotypical discourse. As argued by Homi Bhabha, although it aims to fix knowledge, colonial stereotypical discourse always also undoes itself, revealing its own ambivalences. Thus, it requires a continuous repetition in order to be effective and prevent the 'return of the oppressed'[18]. This constant risk of the 'return of the oppressed' shows us how power-knowledge relations are always ambivalent and open to different readings, and that stereotypes usually involve a mix of both phobia and fetish. In this case, the protests were reported as the citizens' break from the silence that they had been subjected to. The news implied that Bosnian citizens were silenced either because of their own traumas (the haunting experience of the war, the unresolved war crimes, the bad performance of their governments in times of peace) or by the lack of consistent interest by the international community. In any case, this return of their oppressed/repressed voice – even if dependent on the specific, media grammar of articulation – also highlights the complexity of the power-knowledge relations between BH and the international community.

Warranted mental states

References to the sentiments and mental states of the protesters and the citizens of BH ran through most of the analysed news items. The media emphasized protesters' anger, fury, exasperation and frustration with the

country's political and economic stagnation, reflecting in high unemployment and corruption. Although, at times, the agency of the protesters was
reported (e.g. 'Thousands of protesters took to the streets'; see below), it was
nominalized, as if a force on its own (e.g. when reported in the form: 'fury
at the country's political and economic stagnation spread rapidly around the
country' or 'The anger soon spread to other parts of Bosnia').

> Thousands of Bosnian protesters took to the streets in the centre of Sarajevo on
> Friday, setting fire to the presidency building and hurling rocks and stones at
> police as fury at the country's political and economic stagnation spread rapidly
> around the country.
>
> (*The Guardian*, 7 Feb. 2014, 'Bosnia-Herzegovina
> hit by wave of violent protests')

> The protests started on Tuesday in Tuzla, a former industrial center, when more
> than 10,000 factory workers gathered in front of a regional government building
> to voice their anger over factory closings and unpaid salaries, for which they
> blamed poorly executed state privatizations. The anger soon spread to other
> parts of Bosnia.
>
> (*NY Times*, 7 Feb. 2014, 'Protests over gov-
> ernment and economy roil Bosnia')

The emphasis on mental states served to justify the protests as people's
intuitive reaction to their overall hardship ('the country's political and economic stagnation', 'the years of inertia and incompetence', 'factory closings
and unpaid salaries'), for which the political elite's indifference and insensi-
tivity were held responsible. In particular, a strong feeling of humiliation was
expressed through the voices of some witnesses and protesters, following
frustration accumulated during more than two decades.

> Deep down, it was not just the months of unpaid wages, or the plundering of the
> workplace Ms. Bursuladzic has served for 38 years that stirred her ire, she said.
> It was the humiliation.
> 'People inside this building used to look out the window and laugh at us,'
> she said.
> Her co-worker Snjezana Ostrakovic, 29, in faded jeans and a cheap jacket,
> bitterly recalled standing in temperatures well below freezing and accosting a
> local government worker, who she said simply ridiculed her pleas for help in
> feeding her two sons, 5 and 2.
>
> (*NY Times*, 14 Feb. 2014, 'Roots of Bosnian Pro-
> tests lie in Peace Accords of 1995')

Emin Eminagic, an activist in Tuzla complained: 'We have been lied to for
20 years. We have been oppressed for 20 years, people are hungry, people are

starving. We do not have job prospects here, we will not have a future here unless we change something.'

> (*Euronews*, 28 Feb. 2014, 'Bosnia-Herzegovina:
> Corruption protests fuel a potential political spring')

'It is about time we did something,' said a woman in her 20s who gave her name only as Selma. 'This is the result of years and years of not paying attention to the dissatisfaction of the people.'

> (*The Guardian*, 7 Feb. 2014, 'Bosnia-Herzegovina
> hit by wave of violent protests')

These testimonies construed 'the people' as victims of continued oppression and neglect and at the same time as social actors capable of taking action for themselves. Such depiction of the protesters' justified feelings of anger and determination to provoke change may be interpreted as a sign of crisis within the neoliberal project itself, revealing some of its internal contradictions (even if with reference to a transitional economy). If, on the one hand, neoliberalism has produced sceptical and depoliticized citizens, on the other it has also stirred up widely shared feelings of anger and of being forgotten and marginalized. This discontent has aroused protests everywhere in capitalist societies, although these protests have been perceived as fragmented and relatively disconnected[19]. As I show below, in the context of BH protests, the potential impact of fragmented resistance depends very much on how it is construed by the media.

A 'national discontent'

Although the protests were mostly confined to the Federation (the Croat-Muslim entity of Bosnia), international media tended to depict them as generalized to the whole BH and linked to a 'common cause' and 'national discontent'. Some reports described 'Hundreds of people' gathering in support in the RS capital of Banja Luka and even referred to solidarity demonstrations in Serbia. This construal of the protests as happening across the entire BH served to evoke the idea/phantasy of different, previously warring, ethnic groups coming together, which is a frequently repeated desire of the international community for the future of the country.

> Hundreds of people turned out in solidarity protests in the capital Sarajevo and the towns of Zenica, Bihac and Mostar.
>
> > (FRANCE 24 with REUTERS AP, 7 Feb. 2014, 'Anti-
> > government protests turn violent in Bosnia')

> Demonstrators in other towns, including Mostar, Zenica and Bihac, supported the Tuzla workers and criticised the government for failing to tackle the rampant unemployment.

Hundreds of people also gathered in support in the Bosnian Serb capital, Banja Luka.

> (BBC news, 7 Feb. 2014, 'Bosnia-Hercegovina
> [*sic*] protests break out in violence')

On the whole, the image of national discontent presented by the analysed media projected an idea of a multicultural society, active and united in a common cause for the first time since the war. The fact that this cause was not at all clear was deemed far less relevant. What was given importance was the impression of a new era of ethnic unity in BH, an idea that became pronounced within the following theme.

The Balkan Spring

The interpretation of the protests as a potential 'Balkan Spring'/'Bosnian Spring' appeared in two articles, by RT and Euronews. It appeared mostly as an open question, voiced by journalists, but also through some activist voices, although it was unclear if these activists had mentioned the idea spontaneously or had been fed leading questions on the issue.

> 'I think this is a genuine Bosnian spring. We have nothing to lose. There will be more and more of us in the streets, there are around 550,000 unemployed people in Bosnia,' as Reuters was told by Almir Arnaut, an unemployed economist and activist from Tuzla. Another, a construction worker, told AFP that 'people are hungry.'
>
> (RT, 8 Feb. 2014, 'Violent protests across Bosnia
> injure 150, as people demand govt. overhaul')

> It is too early to call the protests a 'Bosnian Spring'. But without change, there will be one, and possibly a violent one. The message from the EU is clear: clean up corruption and keep ethnic questions out of it. Otherwise you're playing with fire. The Balkans are a powder keg and Bosnia is part of it.
>
> (Euronews, 28 Feb. 2014, 'Bosnia-Herzegovina: cor-
> ruption protests fuel a potential political spring')

The reference to a potential 'Balkan Spring' sought to provide a ready and safe definition of the evolving protests, in relation to which categorization its further developments could be assessed. Though 'domesticating' this strange development in BH by naming it after other familiar events (the revolution-ary 'Arab Spring' that had begun in 2010 and its consequences were still being reported), the news simultaneously warned the audiences of the risk of things getting out of control (drawing on the stereotypical Balkanist notion of the 'powder keg'). Furthermore, given the essential difference between the two kinds of uprisings (the former seeking a better functioning democracy and the latter overthrowing the entire system of governance), the symbolic positioning of the protests in BH (particularly in the entity with a constituent Muslim population) with events in the Arab world, rather than with arguably more comparable social unrests in the West, served to Orientalize BH and fix it in the Balkans. This was evident too in the strategic, supervising role the international community was emphasized in this process.

Shared responsibilities

Several of the news articles credited the Dayton Peace Agreement with being at the root of the political and economic deterioration of BH, and more specifically the 'complex and unwieldy power-sharing system' it had created.

> The political and economic deterioration has its roots in the aftermath of the brutal ethnic war in Bosnia, which ended in 1995 after more than 100,000 people were killed. The Dayton Peace Agreement, brokered by the United States, ended the war. But it also divided Bosnia and Herzegovina, a former Yugoslav republic, into two entities – a Muslim-Croat Federation and a Serbian Republic – and created a complex and unwieldy power-sharing system that has helped engender political infighting and stagnation.
>
> (NY Times, 8 Feb. 2014, 'Protests Over Government and Economy Roil Bosnia')

> Many people point the finger at the 'Dayton Agreement'. The deal ended war, but by dividing power in order to stop fighting between Orthodox Serbs, Catholic Croats and Muslim Bosniaks it created a dysfunctional system unable to steer Bosnia through economic transition.
>
> (Euronews, 28 Feb. 2014, 'Bosnia-Herzegovina: corruption protests fuel a potential political spring')

The media also criticized the wide-ranging post-war privatization as an example of bad governance contributing to the illicit enrichment of a handful of tycoons and to the rise of massive unemployment and poverty[20]. However, more than a critique of privatization itself as a political and economic strategy, the reported testimonies stressed the highly problematic manner in which privatization was conducted, the latter being qualified as 'mafia privatization', as in the following extract:

> There used to be several factories in Tuzla, employing around 3,000 people, including Sakib Kopic, who worked in the chemical plant for 33 years. Now he is one of the protesters and says people want to be governed by experts. Laid-off workers use the expression 'mafia privatisation'. Why? Sakib Kopic explained: 'Someone comes to buy a company for almost nothing, they get one,

two three bank loans, then they destroy the company, they close it down, and
the privatisation-mafia put the money into their own pockets. The people who
invented these privatisation schemes should be sent to prison where they should
be made to crush stones with a rubber mallet.'
        (Euronews, 28 Feb. 2014, 'Bosnia-Herzegovina: corruption protests fuel a
                                                potential political spring')

Thus, the media tended to ascribe part of the responsibility for the political
and economic situation in BH to the country's political elites. For example,
regarding the Sejdić-Finci question[21], in a BBC news item one finds the
journalist arguing that the EU and US officials have struggled to help in vain
against what appears to be resistance by the Bosnian politicians.

European and American officials have tried everything to cajole Bosnia's leaders
to adapt the constitution – but they have had no success.
        (BBC news, 7 Feb. 2014, 'Bosnian protests: A Balkan Spring?')

In sum, the analysed media tended to ascribe responsibilities for the present
difficulties in BH first to the political elites, but also to the international community, especially in relation to its endorsement of the Dayton Peace Agreement. Bosnian citizens were presented as victims of the imposed injustice,
inefficiency and inequality created by bad governance, corruption and 'mafia
privatization'. BH was thus presented as having structural problems created
by the Agreement itself, as well as problems of 'bad governance' that were
mainly associated with the politicians' lack of will to fight corruption. Rather
than a critique of the neoliberal project *per se*, which surfaces in reports about
social and economic protests across the EU (where they tend to be framed
as 'riots' when they involve comparable amounts of injury and damage to
property), media reports about the BH 'protests' were rather a critique of
the transitional and reluctant, that is, incomplete Balkan appropriation of the
neoliberal project by the Bosnian political elite.

CONCLUSION

In general, the international media were remarkably consistent in their
appraisals and construals of the 2014 February uprisings in Bosnia. Collectively, the themes identified in the analysis performed a narrative function that
started from a focus on the present, stressing the scope and violence of these
uprisings, moving on to explaining and legitimizing these with reference to
socio-economic, as well as political factors that highlight the 'shared responsibilities' of the Bosnian political elite and the international community.

Finally, the analysed media discourse entailed a projection into the future that served as a warning of what might happen if protesters' demands were not taken seriously, as well as calling for international (re)action.

There was an assumption, in the analysed media, that the protesters' 'fury' and 'rage' were reasonable given the lasting political and economic stagnation in BH. Such representation sought to encourage a legitimation of and identification with the protesters and was discursively achieved through the interchange of the voices of the protesters and witnesses (through direct address) with the voice of the journalist. The protests were construed as unprecedented and unexpected, but also as a sign of hope for the country, symbolizing a break with Bosnian people's feelings of powerlessness. This particular form of portrayal was reinforced by quotes from local political analysts and NGOs who foregrounded the understanding of the protests as coming from a nationwide discontent and resulting in the much desired union of all citizens of BH regardless of their ethnicities.

Although these were not evoked by the media, the popular protests that rose in the second half of the 1980s in Yugoslavia can be compared to the analysed mobilizations in their scope and motives. Popular uprisings in the former Yugoslavia were motivated by economic and political demands shared by all ethnicities. These entailed demands for better living standards for the working class and called attention to the dysfunctionality of political institutions and the structure of governance. Only subsequently, through the political manipulation of the nationalist elites and their leaders, did these political and socio-economic demands become nationalist struggles that eventually led to the break-up of Yugoslavia[22].

The analysed media construals of the 2014 protests in BH as understandable and warranted also counteracted stereotypical representations of Balkan citizens as inherently violent or irrational[23]. However, the situation was also presented as a 'powder keg' at risk of exploding, and this was often linked to traumas from the war, which had finally found expression, as a 'return of the repressed/oppressed'. These media's construals amounted to a 'therapeutic discourse' that underpinned the international media coverage of the events. It is a discourse that produces a traumatized citizen, who is always at risk and in need of outside (here, Western) surveillance and assistance. At the same time, the media projected a sound, though very simplified, image of an active and critical civil society inspired by ideals of multiculturalism, justice and good governance. It remained unclear, however, whether these protests also rejected any possibilities of fragmentation or 'balkanization' of the country in the future. Thus, the media construed the Bosnian Other as both similar and radically different from the Western Self, as legitimized in their suffering and as permanently traumatized and thus unpredictable. The media did so by projecting the West's fears of losing control of the fragmented space of the Balkans and its desire to create a multicultural and democratic society in BH.

And because the media privileged a 'therapeutic discourse' based on the vocalization of trauma, alternative historical, social, political and economic analyses of suffering and citizenship were disregarded, to the exception of a critique of the Dayton Peace Agreement and of post-war privatization. The dominant image was of a bottom-up, spontaneous movement, expressing a generalized feeling of civic discontent and resentment. The news said little or nothing about the organization of the protests and their potential links with local political parties and interests. Furthermore, very few or no comparisons were established between the protests in BH and relevant events in the EU. Rather, the association was made with the Arab Spring (proposing the name 'Bosnian Spring' for the protests), while the possibility of a future EU accession of the country was passed over in silence.

The few media references to the EU stressed its ambivalence – as a subject claiming moral authority but also sharing responsibility for the failure of the liberal project in BH. At the same time, there was an almost desperate call for the international community not to forget BH and a reminder of the international responsibilities and unfulfilled promises of the Dayton Peace Agreement. This overall sense of uncertainty in the representations of the protests, themselves being incomplete events, suggested that BH remains a permanently unresolved, unfinished question for Europe and the EU.

NOTES

1. Acknowledgements: I owe a great debt to Zlatan Krajina and Nebojša Blanuša for their relevant comments and suggestions. I am grateful to Drazen Simić for his insights on BH politics and the international media, as well as to Michael Pugh for his help copy-editing this chapter. None of the above are responsible for the interpretations and expressions in the chapter.

2. David Chandler, "State-building in Bosnia: The limits of 'informal trusteeship'." *International Journal of Peace Studies* 11, no. 1 (2006): 18.

3. Florian Bieber, "Aid dependency in Bosnian politics and civil society: Failures and successes of post-war peacebuilding in Bosnia-Herzegovina," *Croatian International Relations Review*, January–June (2002): 28. See also David Chandler, *Faking Democracy after Dayton* (London: Pluto Press, 2000) and David Chandler "State-building in Bosnia: The limits of 'informal trusteeship'".

4. Michael C. Pugh, "The political economy of peacebuilding: A critical theory perspective". *International Journal of Peace Studies* 10, no. 2 (2005a): 23–5.

5. Timothy Donais, "The politics of privatization in post-Dayton Bosnia." *Southeast European Politics* 3, no. 1 (2002): 3.

6. Michael C. Pugh, "Liquid transformation in the political economies of BiH and Kosovo" (Draft Paper for TD10 at the 46th Annual International Studies Association

Convention, Honolulu, Hawaii, March 1–5, 2005: 15–16). See also Michael C. Pugh, "Employment, Labour Rights and Social Resistance," in *Whose Peace? Critical Perspectives on the Political Economy of Peacebuilding*, ed., Michael Pugh, Neil Cooper, and Mandy Turner (Basingstoke: Palgrave, 2011), 152–3.

7. Monroe Price, "Memory, the media and NATO: Information intervention in Bosnia-Hercegovina," in *Memory & Power in Post-war Europe: Studies in the Presence of the Past*, ed., J.-W. Müller, 137–54. (Cambridge University Press, 2002), 137–154, http://repository.upenn.edu/asc_papers/54. Accessed April 10, 2016.

8. Roger Silverstone, *Media and Morality on the Rise of the Mediapolis* (Cambridge: Polity Press, 2007), 22.

9. Edward Said, *Orientalism* (London: Penguin, 1977). See also David Morley and Kevin Robins, *Spaces of Identity: Global Media, Electronic Landscapes and Cultural Boundaries* (London and New York: Routledge, 1995).

10. Most of the reports included photos or videos, many of them repeated across different outlets. However, a detailed analysis of the visual semiosis was beyond the scope of this chapter.

11. Virginia Braun and Victoria Clarke, "Using thematic analysis in psychology," *Qualitative Research in Psychology* 3 (2006): 82, doi: 10.1191/1478088706qp063oa.

12. Norman Fairclough, *Media Discourse* (London: Edward Arnold, 1995).

13. Maria Todorova, *Imagining the Balkans* (New York and Oxford: Oxford University Press, 1997).

14. Lilie Chouliaraki, *The Ironic Spectator: Solidarity in the Age of Post-Humanitarianism* (Cambridge: Polity Press, 2013), 168–71.

15. The case of the media's portrayal of the 2010 Haiti earthquake was another example of the dominance of the therapeutic discourse, where 'the urgent temporality of simultaneity' precluded a historicized analysis of the specific political context, including colonial and post-colonial relations that impacted on the outcomes and the aftermath of the catastrophe in the country (Chouliaraki, 2013, pp. 169–70).

16. Todorova, *Imagining the Balkans*.

17. See chapter 11 in this volume.

18. Homi Bhabha, *The Location of Culture* (London and New York: Routledge, 1994), 72.

19. Stuart Hall, "The Neo-liberal Revolution," *Cultural Studies* 25, no. 6 (2011): 727, doi: 10.1080/09502386.2011.619886.

20. In 2015, the unemployment rate in the country was 42.9%, one of the highest in Europe (http://ieconomics.com/bosnia-and-herzegovina-unemployment-rate), with one of the highest rates of unemployed youth (57%) in the world (see http://data.worldbank.org/indicator/SL.UEM.1524.ZS. Accessed April 12, 2016).

21. Under the terms of the Dayton Peace Agreement, certain key jobs, such as being a member of the country's tripartite presidency, are reserved for Serbs, Croats and Bosniaks. This was successfully challenged at the European Court of Human Rights by Jakob Finci and Dervo Sejdić, who are Jewish and Roma, respectively.

22. Nebojša Vladisavljevic, "The Break-up of Yugoslavia: The Role of Popular Politics," in *New Perspectives on Yugoslavia: Key Issues and Controversies*, ed., Dejan Đokić and James Kerr-Lindsay (London: Routledge, 2010), 156–8.

23. Some of these stereotypical representations have been contested within BH too, by some popular local musicians such as the bands Edo Maajka and Dubioza Kolektiv, which have promoted a discourse of peace and tolerance, as well as criticizing nationalism and injustice.

BIBLIOGRAPHY

Bhabha, Homi. *The Location of Culture.* London and New York: Routledge, 1994.

Bieber, Florian. "Aid dependency in Bosnian politics and civil society: Failures and successes of post-war peacebuilding in Bosnia-Herzegovina," *Croatian International Relations Review,* January–June, (2002): 25–9.

Braun, Virginia and Clarke, Victoria. "Using thematic analysis in psychology." *Qualitative Research in Psychology* 3 (2006): 77–101. doi: 10.1191/1478088706 qp063oa

Chandler, David. *Faking Democracy after Dayton*, second edition. London: Pluto Press, 2000.

Chandler, David. "State-building in Bosnia: The limits of 'informal trusteeship'." *International Journal of Peace Studies* 11, no. 1 (2006): 17–22.

Chouliaraki, Lilie. *The Ironic Spectator: Solidarity in the age of Post-Humanitarianism.* Cambridge: Polity Press, 2013.

Donais, Timothy. "The politics of privatization in post-Dayton Bosnia." *Southeast European Politics* 3, no. 1 (2002): 3–19.

Fairclough, Norman. *Media Discourse.* London: Edward Arnold, 1995.

Hall, Stuart. "The neo-liberal revolution." *Cultural Studies* 25, no. 6 (2011): 705–728. doi: 10.1080/09502386.2011.619886.

Bosnia and Herzegovina – Unemployment rate. http://ieconomics.com/bosnia-and-herzegovina-unemployment-rate, Accessed February 15, 2016.

Morley, David, and Kevin Robins, *Spaces of Identity: Global Media, Electronic Landscapes and Cultural Boundaries.* London and New York: Routledge, 1995.

Price, Monroe. "Memory, the media and NATO: Information intervention in Bosnia-Hercegovina." In *Memory & Power in Post-war Europe: Studies in the Presence of the Past*, edited by J.-W. Müller, 137–54. Cambridge University Press, 2002. http:// repository.upenn.edu/asc_papers/54. Accessed April 10, 2016.

Pugh, Michael C. "The political economy of peacebuilding: A critical theory perspective". *International Journal of Peace Studies* 10, no. 2 (2005a), 23–42.

Pugh, Michael C. 2005b. "Liquid Transformation in the Political Economies of BH and Kosovo." Draft Paper for TD10 at the 46th Annual International Studies Association Convention, March 1–5, 2005, Honolulu, Hawaii, 1–21. http://www.brad.ac.uk/acad/twe/publications/. Accessed March 15, 2016.

Pugh, Michael. "Employment, Labour Rights and Social Resistance." In *Whose Peace? Critical Perspectives on the Political Economy of Peacebuilding*, edited by Michael Pugh, Neil Cooper, and Mandy Turner, 141–58. Basingstoke: Palgrave, 2011.

Said, Edward. *Orientalism*. London: Penguin, 1977.
Silverstone, Roger. *Media and Morality on the Rise of the Mediapolis*. Cambridge: Polity Press, 2007.
Todorova, Maria. *Imagining the Balkans*. New York and Oxford: Oxford University Press, 1997.
Unemployment – World Total. World Bank. http://data.worldbank.org/indicator/ SL.UEM.1524.ZS, Accessed February 15, 2016. Accessed April 12, 2016.
Vladisavljevic, Nebojša. "The Break-up of Yugoslavia: The Role of Popular Politics." In New Perspectives on Yugoslavia: Key Issues and Controversies, edited by Dejan Đokić and James Kerr-Lindsay, 143–60. London: Routledge, 2010.

Chapter 6

The Balkans Go Global

Mikhail Veshim's The English Neighbor *and the Post-Socialist Variations on "the Balkan" Theme*

Milena Marinkova

In 2004, an Australian mock travel guidebook, suggestively titled *Molvanĭa: A Land Untouched by Modern Dentistry*, became a worldwide success with its gripping parody of the representational conventions of the travel guide genre. It introduces its (most likely Western) readers to a fictitious country – the eponymous Molvanĭa – a landlocked republic "at the crossroads of Eastern Europe", whose main achievements include being the world's biggest producer of beetroot, parsnip and liquorice, "the birthplace of the whooping cough" and "a country steeped in history" that still operates the world's oldest nuclear reactor[1]. Molvanĭa's multicultural origins and unpronounceable Slavic language are traced back to 5th-century invasions of numerous Asiatic groups – the fictitious but phonologically familiar "Bulgs", "Hungars" and "Molvs"– whereas its chauvinistic political set-up is attributed to the iron-fist rule of the charismatic demagogue and "father of modern Molvanĭa", Szlonko Busjbusj, and to the primitivism of that strange syncretism of regional and religious varieties, Baltic Orthodoxy, which allows its "congregations . . . to smoke in church"[2]. Arguably, references to the country's location – a stone's throw away from Chernobyl – and its membership in "the Balkan 7" regional confederation gesture at its Balkan, as well as Eastern European, credentials. At the same time, the construct "Molvanĭa" relies heavily on, while ridiculing, the ease with which locales and populations are voraciously consumed and regurgitated by the travel and publishing industries, and the ignorance of globe-trotting readers who are all too susceptible to the comfortable familiarity of the stereotype and the cliché.

Undoubtedly, the mock travel guide partakes of the loaded discourses that have circulated in the last couple of centuries about these European peripheries. On the one hand, the quasi-Orientalist sentiments of the Jetlag publication reiterate, even if with a huge dose of humour and parody, the meta-phoricization of a region where numerous encounters and exchanges between Europe and its "others" have taken place: Molvanïa is invariably described as "crossroads", "a land of contrasts" and "a country caught between the old world and the new"[3]. On the other hand, to the panoply of these familiar Balkan clichés, the Australian publication has added another layer – that of Cold War Eastern Europe and its contemporary version: market-driven and democracy-aspiring, though constantly falling short of the mark – post-social-ist "new Europe". Thus, the lampooned antiquity of Molvanïa – going back to the Iron Age, which due to scarcity of the metal locally was experienced as the Age of potatoes and cork – is counterbalanced by the country's disturbing lack of ethnic tolerance, civilizational backwardness and violent machismo[4]. The collapse of the infamous "Lutenblag Wall", which ended Soviet control, is described as "not due so much to democratic reform, but just shoddy con-struction", whereas contemporary social and political life is represented by the likes of Igor Ztubalk, "the Singing Neo-Nazi", the occasional indulgence of the average Molvanïan in legalized witch burnings and the national pride in ethnic tolerance towards the almost entirely expelled or incarcerated "gypsy" population[5]. As the mock guide jokingly warns "us", the Western travellers:

> Of course, for a new arrival it takes a bit of time to work out how you should behave in return – the precise degree of brusqueness required, for example, to catch the attention of a waiter. If you are too meek he will ignore you. If you are too aggressive he may produce a concealed weapon[6].

The allusions to Molvanïa as a former stronghold of communism, which in its economic, social and political inadequacy was totally "out of joint" with the modern world, reinforce the perception of European peripheries as com-promised by external (Asiatic or communist) influences and thus essentially a liability, while asserting the supremacy of Europe – white, Christian and modern – and its tenets of industrial progress, competitive capitalism and liberal democracy[7].

I came across *Molvanïa* while studying postcolonial literature in the UK. An enthusiast for the rhizomatic theories of the self by Gilles Deleuze and Félix Guattari, and fascinated by Homi Bhabha's analysis of the centrality of ambivalence and hybridity for identity formation, I was suspicious of any kind of thinking informed by ancient roots, immutable essences and rigid binaries. So I found myself wondering whether the mock framework of *Molvanïa* did enough to challenge the "mass-mediated objectification of the [Balkan] region"[8], achieving little more than what Sacha Baron Cohen's *Borat* did for Kazakhstan. It may have raised some awareness about the region and drawn flocks of tourists to the sites of the peninsula, but *Molvanïa* ultimately seemed to be a self-indulgent romp with Balkan and East European "othering", which failed to lend "the othered" any agency to represent itself. Was it possible to convey the post-socialist Balkans otherwise now that the "end of history" has been widely proclaimed?[9] Or, was the regional trope on its way of becoming a global metaphor in the age of post- and "corpo-nationalism"?[10] Questions of positionality inevitably followed: Was I overly suspicious of *Molvania* because as a Bulgarian student in the UK, aware of and sensitized to different forms of Western prejudice against a range of "Easts" (European or non-European), I was residing in a country whose media-scape was saturated – and continues to be – with unflattering images of "new Europe" in the aftermath of European Union (EU) enlargement in the East and Eastern European migration to the West? Was my reaction somewhat skewed by my "postcolonial" expectations of Australia, a former colonial margin and a multicultural country of significant Balkan diasporas today, to churn out less crude stereotypes about another European periphery? After all, it could have been all down to my own position, which secured me with the proverbial "stereoscopic vision"[11]: perched on the inside-outside of all contexts concerned, I assumed I had sufficient critical distance to take note of the "blobs and slabs"[12] of the fictions of reality circulating around me.

Arguably, certain socio-economic, political and cultural developments in the UK and Europe have inflected both the public imaginary of the Balkans and my response to such discourses on and mediations of the region. With the deepening of the recession since 2008 and the severity of the austerity measures introduced by successive Conservative/Liberal Democratic and Conservative governments since 2010, Eurosceptic sentiment and anti-immigration rhetoric in the UK have been on the rise, as reflected in the increasing popularity of the United Kingdom Independence Party (UKIP) and the knee-jerk reactions of all mainstream parties to the "problem" of EU immigration. While anxieties about "old Europe" have been prompted by the projected impact of the Eurozone crisis on the UK's economic growth and the alleged loss of national sovereignty to a supranational entity such as the European Commission, anti-immigration feelings have been stoked up by fears about the impact of EU immigration on the UK labour market, housing and welfare.

In all this, "new Europe" plays a special role. The fairly recent media hype around the lifting of the transitional restriction measures on Bulgarians' and Romanians' access to the UK labour market[13], for instance, led to crude comparisons with the 2004 EU enlargement in Eastern Europe (especially with reference to Polish immigration into the UK) when such restrictions were not placed on the eight post-socialist Central and Eastern European countries that joined the union. This slippage from "Bulgarian/Romanian" to "Polish" to "Eastern European" in media and political discourse seems to be marked simultaneously by the lingering effects of a Cold War imaginary (of a European East/West divide) and by the neoliberal valorization of economic worth. Nonetheless, in both the Cold War and neoliberal narratives "Eastern European" is constructed as lacking, inferior and threatening.

This chapter will address the above issues of representation by examining a cultural text that responds to the tenacity of "the Balkan" as a trope in a more contextually grounded and politically aware way than *Molvanĩa* did[14]. Mikhail Veshim's novel *The English Neighbor* was first published in Bulgaria in 2008 to great critical acclaim and has since been turned into an equally popular TV series[15]. Ostensibly written from the point of view of a hapless external (English) observer, *The English Neighbor* also offers a trenchant critique of "the Balkan" from within the Balkans. The multiply refracted positionality of Veshim's text, therefore, makes it an apt choice for consideration in this analysis in order to ascertain to what extent the novel departs from the paradigm on which *Borat* and *Molvanĩa* are premised, and how it deploys its own version of "the Balkan". As the discussion below will demonstrate, not unlike *Molvanĩa*, *The English Neighbor* engages in acts of Balkan exoticization and demonization, whereby excessive alcohol consumption, hostile ethnocentrism and masterful pastry-baking do little to dismantle familiar truisms. However, this heightened sense of Balkanness does not function as a mere caricature of Western, or for that matter local, prejudice. Neither does the novel sentimentalize a particular Balkan authenticity in order to promote a marketable nation brand[16] or regional heritage culture[17]. Rather, I will argue that Veshim's recycling of clichés about the region meditates on almost-already Europeanized Balkans, in which "the Balkan" has less to do with the presumed superiority of "Europe" over its margins than with the tensions and ruptures accompanying the escalating state deregulation, economic liberalization and corporatization of life in a globalizing Europe of which the Balkans are an integral part. In this sense, *The English Neighbor* is an important contribution to the ever more shifting discourse on the Balkans: if the latter's origins lay in the bipolarity of civilizational divisions and the toxicity of the Cold War period, its latest versions – as evinced in the fictional universe of Veshim's novel – have more to do with the advancement of globalization and the increasing boundlessness of neoliberalism.

THE MULTIPLE GUISES OF "THE BALKAN"

The geopolitical and cultural entity known as "the Balkans" has been the subject of scholarly and creative investigations for decades. Originally a designation for the mountain range that cuts across the territory of present-day Bulgaria, the term "Balkan" has subsequently been applied to a diverse geopolitical region and a range of cultural and political phenomena. In 1490, which is, according to historian Maria Todorova, the earliest recorded mention of the word, "Balkan" was a reference to what had been previously known as the Haemus mountain range in the Rumeli provinces of the Ottoman Empire. By the end of the 19th century, when Great Power wrangling about the fate of "the sick man of Europe" peaked, the geographical designation had accrued a range of connotations that were somewhat detached from its original referent. "[A]s much a conceptual designator as a geographic one"[18], "Balkan" came to be associated with the imprint of otherness: from the cultural and political legacy of "foreign" or "less European" empires such as the Byzantine, Ottoman and Habsburg ones to the insurmountable impact of communism and ethnic nationalism.

In his discussion of the evolution of what he calls "the Balkan myth", David Norris argues that the use of "Balkan" as a shorthand for volatility, ethnocentrism and sectarianism is a Western invention[19], which, according to the psychoanalytical framework of Dušan Bjelić, "functioned as the fulcrum for Enlightenment Europe's self-image, or the means by which 'progressive' Europe projects its own anxieties and forbidden desires onto the other"[20]. "The Balkan" in this sense has played a double role: offering reductive representations of the Balkans as well as informing Europe's subjectivation process. Larry Wolff links explicitly the processes of "Balkan" knowledge-production and European subject-formation: Europe's emergence into its identity in the Enlightenment period depended on a process of internal fracturing, which pitted one, desirable, part of Europe ("Europe proper") against another, much less desirable periphery ("Eastern/Oriental Europe")[21]. In order to perceive the former as enlightened and civilized, it was necessary to construct the latter as backward, irrational and barbarian. While European peripheries were crucial for retaining and exercising control over zones of geopolitical significance such as the Straits, Europe's preoccupation with its limits was not driven by economic, military or political considerations only, but also by the desire to "sutur[e] [a] cultural identity" that was coherent and exclusive[22]. In the process of securing this European identity, the physical-geographical proximity of the Balkans was neutralized by creating a cultural-symbolical distance between "Europe" and "the Balkan", and producing a Balkan "discourse-geography"[23].

This discourse-geography, which Todorova has called Balkanism, offers simplistic, quasi-Orientalist representations of a real region and its very real people while perpetuating the fallacious binary of a homogeneous "Europe" *versus* an equally uniform "non-Europe". In contrast to Orientalism, however, which is a discourse about imputed differences between "types", Balkanism is a discourse about imputed differences within "one type"[24]. Todorova furthermore argues that within Balkanism, the Balkans are imagined not as the irreducibly different "other" to Europe (which would be "the Orient"), but as "an incomplete European self": almost the same but not quite, almost an anti-world but not yet. Geographically situated on the European landmass, but with a history of political control by a number of "less European" empires, predominantly Christian but with significant Muslim and Jewish admixtures, "the Balkan" is perceived as a culturally compromised, and thus inferior, space given its failure to meet the expectations of a region so proximal to the centres of Europe's classical heritage, Athens and Rome. Even though Europe's "belligerent, imperialistic and colonialist history"[25] has led to a comparable degree of diversity within "Europe proper" as well, it is the heterogeneity of "the Balkan" that has been seen as a vulnerability and threat to Europe's coherence and survival.

At the other end of the spectrum is "complimentary" Balkanism, which has subjected the region to romanticization and exoticization[26]. Unlike the vituperative agenda of "traditional" Balkanism, its complimentary version – prominent during the interwar period in particular – valorizes "Balkan" rusticity, authenticity and simplicity, while bemoaning the moral decay and corruption of "Europe". Nonetheless, even if the content of these two representational paradigms differs, their binary logic is identical: "the Balkan" – be it civilizationally inferior or charmingly authentic – is after all imagined as the opposite of "Europe". Interestingly, the heyday of Cold War détente saw the simultaneous celebration of Balkan pastoralism and modernity, the latter aspect more or less erasing the cultural distance between communist East and democratic West[27]. Despite the semantic variety, these celebratory trends of the interwar and Cold War periods ultimately reinforced the centrality, and superiority, of "Europe". Whereas the emphasis on "the Balkan" as a living museum of all things ancient and spiritual placed the region outside contemporary realities, the praise of Balkan industry, tourism and education during the Cold War period was based on Western European perceptions of what constitutes value, progress and development.

With the collapse of state-supported socialism in Europe, the imagery around "the Balkan" underwent another resignification, constructing a causal link between one kind of "otherness", communism, with an earlier, already familiar one – the ethnocentric nationalism that tore the region apart in the first half of the 20th century. The most notorious term associated with the peninsula, "balkanization", has invoked all the negative attributes of political upheaval – instability, lawlessness, fragmentation – since its first use in the aftermath of the First World War and the disintegration of two of Europe's empires – the Austro-Hungarian and Romanov ones – into a number of small Central and East European nation states. Only a few decades earlier, however, the "balkanization" of a less European empire, that of the Ottomans, and the emergence of a few independent nation states in the Balkans had not been demonized to the same degree. Thus the derogatory meaning ascribed retrospectively to "balkanization" failed to acknowledge the historical phenomenon of decolonization that the term had originally designated[28], nor was it "applied [. . .] to denote that the Balkan nations had been a sort of political vanguard in the denouement of empires that Central and Eastern Europe were emulating" at the end of the First World War[29]. In this sense, the connotations of "balkanization" and "the Balkan" since 1918 did not reflect a civilizational gap between Europe and its "incomplete self" but displaced Europe's anxieties about the ruptures in the power status quo onto the sites where these changes were unfolding.

With the violent dissolution of Yugoslavia in the 1990s, the Balkan region was firmly placed back into the anti-civilizational hinterland, aided by accounts that pathologized the federation's breakup as the inevitable return of repressed nationalisms in the absence of an overarching (quasi)imperial structure[30], or as the recurrent manifestation of "ancient ethnic hatreds"[31]. Somewhat mirroring the border-crossing movements of capital and commodities, "the Balkan" was uprooted from its European moorings and transplanted globally. This is evident in the much bandied term "balkanization", attributed to historical and socio-political processes anywhere: from socio-political disintegration and sectarianism in South Africa[32] to the entrenchment of economic inequalities and escalating ethnic, gender and sexual prejudice in North America[33], so much so that in 2009 *The Financial Times* qualified EU enlargement in the West of the Balkan peninsula as a process of "de-balkanization" of the Balkans[34].

More recently, the government debt crisis across Europe raised the spectre of "the Balkan" in relation to the effects of globalization, corporatization and neoliberalism rather than those of nationalism and identity politics. A country not traditionally deemed "Balkan" due to European civilizational claims, Greece was represented in print media such as *The Guardian* and *The Chicago Tribune* as responsible for the destabilization of the Euro and dangerously teetering over the edge of "Europe" and into "the Balkan" because of its inadequate public funds management, inefficient administration and corrupt political class threatening to undermine the smooth functioning of the European markets[35]. This shows a clear semantic shift in the Balkanist paradigm: if only two decades earlier "the Balkan" inevitably conjured ugly images of prejudice and sectarianism, today it haunts Europe with the prospect of obstructing the free flow of goods and money. Even the debates about the possible "balkanization of Britain" during the 2014 Scottish independence referendum were largely conducted with reference to debt management, control over natural resources and access to international markets[36]. Not unlike identity politics and nationalism, "the Balkan" seems to have been implicated into the current neoliberal agenda that valorizes economic growth, market competitiveness and corporatization of everyday life[37].

While Balkanist stereotypes might be a Western invention, they have also been deployed locally as a way of asserting self-identity and cultural superiority[38]. The identity-formation process within the Balkans is often premised on the "Balkans' European allegiance"[39], which not only eschews the proverbial autochthonous hybridity of the region, but also actively engages in what Milica Bakić-Hayden has called derivative acts of "nesting Orientalisms"[40]. "The Balkan" is thus mobilized in the Balkans themselves as a trope to mark, demonize and expel various "others". This could be observed in the political and media discourse that unleashed during the conflicts in former Yugoslavia, when newly independent states would compete for the position of the least "Balkan". At the same time, as Vesna Goldsworthy comments in the *Writing the Balkans* issue of *Wasafiri*, there is an overwhelming desire within the Balkans to "view themselves as European"[41]. After the end of state-supported socialism in the region, Balkan countries "rushed" to prove their newfound European credentials, even if the two powers typically associated with the presumed non-Europeanness of "the Balkan" – the Ottomans and the Soviets – had been implementing regimes that had descended from or been practised in "Europe proper", that is, imperialism and communism. Similar to the development of European identity outlined by Wolff above, the subjectivation process of post-socialist "new Europe" is simultaneously predicated on smooth integration into "Europe proper" and on clear differentiation from any "Balkan" legacies.

The post-socialist eagerness in Europe's peripheral regions to be recognized as European is reflected in the haste with which terms such as "Balkan" and "Eastern Europe" were discarded for the more appealing *Mitteleuropa*, Central-Eastern and South-Eastern Europe. Meanwhile, "new Europe's" fervour in proving its Europeanness has gone beyond the internalization of "traditional" Balkanism. Keen to restore "the myth of some organic pre-October revolution European unity"[42], governments in the post-socialist Balkans embarked on nation-branding campaigns that fashioned their countries with either Europeanized image-makeovers (for instance, the 2007 "I feel Slovenia" nation brand), or spectacles that glorified folkloric Balkanness (for instance, Romania's 2001 "Dracula Park"), or a combination of the two (see Bulgaria's 2007 "Open Doors to Open Hearts" or Romania's 2009 "Explore the Carpathian Garden" campaigns). While divergent in their treatment of "the Balkan", these campaigns applied marketing principles to the domains of national sentiment, citizenship and public governance. Moreover, not only did they reconstitute the nation into exchange value and collective emotional attachments into commodity[43], but they also tapped into the performative agency of the renaming (rebranding) apparatus in order to rewrite a received version of their histories, as Suzana Milevska powerfully argues in this volume with reference to the "Skopje 2014" campaign in Macedonia. Thus, the erstwhile Balkanness of the Balkans – condensed in the images of

Dracula's castle, bagpipe music, impenetrable forests, ancient ruins and lus-cious rose oil that abound in all of the nation-branding campaigns mentioned above – is not merely an escape into a different (exotic, primitive, authentic) "Europe", but also a profitable investment in the Europeanization of the Balkans. "The Balkan" within the Balkans seems to have received a neolib-eral touch-up: aspects of "traditional" and "complimentary" Balkanism have been repackaged into economically palatable clichés to be consumed within the global circuit of marketable images.

While adding new layers to the well-known trope, these external and internal post-socialist variations on "the Balkan" are structurally homolo-gous, constructing the region as Europe's "incomplete self", irrespective of whether "Europe" is Europe of the nation state or Europe of the multinational corporation. Tomislav Longinović and Slavoj Žižek, however, challenge the explicit and implicit binary between "Europe" and "the Balkan", and suggest instead that what went on in the Western Balkans in the 1990s was nothing short of a repetition of a familiar, if forgotten, nation state building scenario that had already taken place in Western Europe[44], and was symptomatic of the inherent violence of capitalism and implacable advance of globaliza-tion[45]. For Todorova, it was not the "Balkan" spectres of a repressed past that unleashed the ethnocentric violence in the region at the end of the 20th century, but an ongoing process of – and I would add, *pace* Goldsworthy, desire for – "the ultimate Europeanization of the Balkans"[46]. The shorthand "Balkan" and its structural relationship to "Europe" therefore not only obfus-cate the commonality of certain socio-political and historical processes that have unfolded in the Balkans and the rest of Europe, but also gloss over the emergence of new forms of exclusion, marginalization and fragmentation sanctioned by a Europe of neoliberal hegemony, eroded social welfare and weakened public governance. The trope has thus become a metaphorical dumping ground for the ugly scraps of a "face-lifted capitalism"[47]; having recently undergone a corrective "nip and tuck" itself, however, "the Balkan" has also become susceptible to incorporation into the transnational network of capitalist production in a bid to prove the hegemony of the market and inevitability of globalization.

"THE BALKAN" RECALIBRATED

If "ultimate Europeanization" spells the eventual demise of "the Balkan"[48], is this a symptom of Europe's unity or homogenization? And if both Europe and the Balkans are undergoing an inevitable neoliberal "make over", as Žižek and Longinović argue, could we think of "the Balkan" trope as a disruptive pres-ence, which resists capitalist subsumption and therefore constructs a different kind of Europe? I would suggest that in his novel *The English Neighbor*, Veshim does the latter, offering a version of "the Balkan" that undoes the binaries at the heart of "Europe" and its constitution through Balkanism, while cautioning against the appropriative pull of a neoliberal Europeanization project. At the same time, he does not lapse into "Balkan" sentimentalism or socialist nostalgia; more often than not, *The English Neighbor* poses trenchant criticism of Bulgaria's ongoing problems with criminality, corruption and public funds mismanagement[49] irrespective of whether the driving force is Europeanization or nationalism[50]. In this sense, even though he is reliant on the discursive economy of Balkanism, Veshim positions its workings vis-à-vis those of global capitalism-*cum*-Europeanization, revealing in the process the weaknesses and failures of both. Veshim thus recalibrates "the Balkan" into a potentially disruptive counter-discourse that dismantles the constitutive binaries at the heart of "Europe" by foregrounding both Europe's and the Balkans' co-optation in capitalism's global "Empire"[51]. The rest of this chapter will therefore examine in greater detail Veshim's invocation, update and deconstruction of the constitutive binaries upon which "the Balkan" trope is premised, by analysing specific aspects of his representational technique such as setting, plot and characterization, as well as use of humour, irony and parody.

Published in 2008, the year after Bulgaria joined the much coveted European family of nations, at first glance *The English Neighbor* appears to be firmly entrenched in familiar Balkanist territory. Set in the bucolic Bulgarian village of Plodorodno (meaning "fruitful"), it traces the life of the new English arrival John Jones and his interactions with a flock of somewhat dubious Bulgarians, who are desperate to make the most of their financially viable neighbour and newfound access to EU capital flows. The villagers' increasingly surreal enrichment schemes to sell the local rakia drink, build a golf course, run a fox-hunting facility and design a remote cattle-grazing navigation system inevitably fall through, gaining little more than the attention of the local cable channel. These failed business ventures and inability to attract international investment are offset by the Englishman's immersion in all things Bulgarian – from cuisine and farming to voluntary environmental initiatives – and the wry sobriety of his neighbour, baba Mara, who is as keen to help John adjust to Bulgaria's realities as she is to embrace English pie-making and "faif-u-klok" tea.

While maintaining the polarities of "traditional" and "complimentary" Balkanism identified by Todorova and Hammond, *The English Neighbor* updates these representational paradigms against the backdrop of Bulgaria's post-socialist realities. Ostensibly written from the point of view of an external observer, the novel is a comedy of errors, in which the blundering foreigner is introduced to the wily ways of the locals. Veshim thus perpetuates the familiar Balkanist binary between the progress, development and open-mindedness of "Europe", embodied in the Englishman John, and the torpor, prejudice and moral corruption of his Bulgarian neighbours.

Upon his arrival in picturesque Plodorodno, the Mancunian immediately applies himself to restoring the beauty of the semi-dilapidated house he has purchased and the fecundity of the adjoining gardens. His industry and enterprise, however, are met with the scepticism of the villagers; for them, the new Bulgarian realities are not about liberal democracy, fair pay and meritocracy, but about the liberalization of market forces, easy money and immediate gratification. Unlike conventional Balkanist texts, it is the Englishman who looks inadequate in Veshim's fictional Balkan universe. John's neighbour, football fan and lazybones Nottingham Forest Nikolov prefers betting his mother's pension on the football stakes to finding a job[52]; the former school principal Dencho, colonel Shtarbanov and the village skinhead embark on a series of dodgy business enterprises with little regard for ethics; and the lawyer Terziev is more invested in securing his fee than in justice being done[53]. Nominally on the road to Europeanization, these "Balkan" villagers are anything but "European".

Moreover, their nationalism is steeped in irrational anti-European prejudice. Shtarbanov, a former secret service operative, openly declares his distrust of Europe and by extension the new Briton in the village to the mayor, who in his turn sees John and the EU as a strategic – if not necessarily trustworthy – allies to be wooed[54]:

> "I don't like this Brit . . . If he were a Russian, you could trust him, a bratushka . . . But this one . . . Mayor, could he have been sent here by the MI6 to spy on us?"
>
> "What would he spy on us for?"
>
> "The British have always had interests in the Balkans. They are imperialists!"
>
> "Shtarbanov, in theory you are right . . . But the reality is quite different now. We are allies, both in NATO and in the EU . . . It is a United Europe, Shtarbanov!"
>
> "We shouldn't be selling our national interests for the sake of united Europe . . . I have been protecting the national interest all my life"[55].

Operating within a Cold War and pan-Slavic frame of reference, Shtarbanov's paranoiac speech juxtaposes the image of the inherently friendly Russian "bratushka" to the essentially imperialist Brit, who is bound to be an elusive MI6 operative. The deployment of historical-montage as a rhetorical device, as Uroš Čvoro argues elsewhere in this volume, has historically enabled the construction of a particular brand of "transitional aesthetics" by political demagogues in the Balkans. Thus, the former apparatchik Shtarbanov collapses diverse historical realities of colonial and Cold War pasts, on the one hand, and European and neoliberal presents, on the other, in order to effect a nationalist-paranoid response in his audience. The mayor's stance, however, dismisses the colonel's anti-Europeanism as dated, preferring to focus on the financial and political perks of being "European" and thus echoing the recent Balkan "rush to Europe" discussed by Goldsworthy. Arguably, Veshim has clad these characters in a recognizable "Balkan" garb, which fails to dismantle the discourses of both Balkanism and globalization: whereas Shtarbanov's reverse Balkanism simply flips the us/them binary by demonizing ("their") European interests as rapacious, the mayor shrewdly adjusts his allegiance in the Balkanist binary in view of the new, post-Cold War world order: "we" are no longer "them" ("socialist Eastern European" or "Balkan"), "we" are on this side of the binary, "we" are "European".

Yet, the mayor's admission, "in theory you are right", implies awareness that the much coveted Europeanization, with its promise of free-flowing capital and people, might be after all a facile exercise where old divisions still have purchase. His "European" ambitions extend to the construction of a village website and a few cosmetic changes to the roads of Plodorodno – good publicity and infrastructure being the hallmarks of the new European civilization – and overt Balkanism towards his fellow-villagers, whose "Oriental" habit of open-air pepper roasting leads to the mysterious disappearance of a Stop road sign[56]. Veshim's portrayal of this suave character therefore exceeds the Balkanist truism of local inferiority and deviousness in the face of modernity; what is more, the mayor's manipulative use of "Europeanness" troubles assumptions about an imitative if flawed Balkanness desperate for "European" approval. The theft of the road sign presents "the transition", "the return to Europe", as "bumpy" and misguided, with the lack of progress being attributed to European reluctance and inadequacy as much as to local inefficiency. If erstwhile Balkanist binaries and hierarchies persist, despite public declarations of a "united Europe", Veshim's perceptive Balkan character is not overdetermined by some civilizational flaw. Rather, the mayor's simultaneous awareness of Europe's misgivings about its common future with post-socialist Bulgaria and enthusiasm for "European"-style economic reforms demonstrate his ability to assume a "Balkan", as well as a "European" identity. While "Europe" emerges in this identity performance as less liberal than Balkanist discourse would have it, the mayor's "Balkanized" drive for investment blurs the familiar dichotomy between the two. Through the image of the mayor, Veshim constructs Balkanness and Europeanness as strategic identities, responding to current developments in Plodorodno rather than as an inherited trait determined by the character's origins[57]. As Čvoro concludes, such strategic performances of identity foreground the contradictions inherent to the teleological narratives of Europeanization and globalization[58].

The novel's resolution to the deceptively progressive Europeanization process of Plodorodno, however, is not a return to an authentic, pre-modern

Balkanness. Quite the opposite. A drinking establishment serving exclusively non-Bulgarian food and drink to the sound of heavy metal and turbo folk, the bar "London" is the focal point of a village where no one believes in hard work and the setting for a few of the novel's complications. With its English name and Bulgarian staff, the bar is a postmodern pastiche of Western food and entertainment, and socialist-style customer service, making a mockery of the efforts of all-round Bulgarian baba Mara to acculturate her English neighbour to the "authentic" local customs of yogurt-making, cow-milking (by hand) and grass-cutting (with a scythe). "London" is also the headquarters for the main operations of Shtarbanov's gang and the starting point of John's descent into Plodorodno's "Balkan" ways of sloth, misogyny and violence. By the end of the novel, however, the bar has been transformed into a Bulgarian-cuisine bistro run by John's English wife, serving baba Mara's dishes and boasting Bulgarian, Russian, Japanese and English regulars. "London" thus functions as an important site on the global-local nexus, which, not unlike the mayor's investment agenda, collapses the erstwhile Europe/Balkan binary. Its marked foreignness comes to stand for the draining of Plodorodno's human resources and erosion of its cultural traditions – processes that unfold largely under the impact of globalization rather than as a result of an inherent cultural flaw. As a matter of fact, it is the resulting performatively "Balkan" site, with its new foreign owners, global clientele and baba Mara's rustic recipes, that guarantees Plodorodno's cultural survival. Veshim's rejection of a return to "Balkan authenticity" for a Europeanized/globalized "London", however, is not a facile celebration of multicultural syncretism and understanding. On the one hand, the novel's ending foregrounds the inevitable commodifica- tion of "the Balkan" and its reification into "authentic food", which could be the only mode of survival for a palatable, "Europeanized" form of Balkanness. On the other hand, the absence of characters who live through the "Europe- anization" of the village – such as the bar owner and the skinhead, who both emigrate abroad – acts as a silent reminder of the local disillusionment with the promises of both socialism and capitalism.

The counter-discursive stance of *The English Neighbor* in this sense is nei- ther reactionary nor radical. Its ironic take on characters such as Shtarbanov exposes the familiar travesties of ideological mystification performed by Bulgaria's political elites during and after socialism, and thus lends "the Balkan" a degree of agency – something elided in Balkanist discourse, which tends to give the external observer cultural and narrative authority. So when the former secret service agent takes to "the Speakers' Corner" of Bulgaria's "first Hyde Park", he is met with the villagers' scorn:

> "For fifteen years we have been living in a so-called democracy! But is our life any better than before? Back then, there were no beggars or junkies; everyone

had access to free healthcare and education. The state provided everyone with
employment and there was no poverty or hunger. And now there is hunger
everywhere and no one is willing to share their bread!"

"Are *you* one of the hungry ones, Shtarbo," baba Mara sneered from below.
"I've just made some bread – here, have a bite!"

The villagers burst out laughing and heckled . . .

"We've become servants to foreign interests," Shtarbanov went on. "Foreign
agents are all over our country. Americans are opening military bases. We've
sold our sovereignty and become an American state."

"Better than a Soviet republic!" Nottingham interrupted, put two fingers in
his mouth and whistled[59].

The colonel's nostalgia about a false past, that is, the "good old days" of
full employment, welfare and equality, rehearses old socialist clichés while
playing upon the villagers' current anxieties about their impoverishment and
marginalization. Shtarbanov's transfer of past rhetoric onto current circumstances parallels the ease with which global capitalism has absorbed old Cold
War structures. This is reflected at the representational level as well, so that
the colonel's image of old communist-turned-corrupt businessman reiterates
old Balkanisms, albeit within the new framework of globalizing, post-socialist
Balkans. However, he is disrupted by the villagers' reaction, which accentu-
ates the tension between Shtarbanov's combative rhetoric and his reality of
privilege. Nottingham's heckling and baba Mara's sarcasm imply that if anything it is Shtarbanov's clichéd language and life that lack the substance of his
ideas: both under socialism and now he has enjoyed a life of plenty contrary
to his empty, clichéd declarations about wealth redistribution and sympathy
for the underprivileged. Coincidentally, Nottingham's retort is anything but
original. Drawing on counter-hegemonic practices from the days of socialism
when allegory and suggestion were used to condemn political dysfunction,
Nottingham himself recycles a cliché in order to expose the tenuousness of
Shtarbanov's set of clichés. This intervention, therefore, suggests a way in
which "the Balkan" – clichéd yet rooted in historical realities, familiar yet
disruptive – can trouble the platitudes of Balkanism and the reification processes of commodification. As a metaphorical site of resistance, "where the
dreams of global capital meet the flesh and dust of everyday [Balkan] life"[60],
"the Balkan" therefore is simultaneously implicated in and suspicious of the
processes and discourses it calls into question.

CONCLUSION

In a world of ever more intensive globalization, when some of the old
borders collapse and new are erected, the revival of "the Balkan" hardly

seems surprising. Having emerged in a zone of encounters and exchange, it has provided "a screen" for the European desire for coherence, as well as European fears of difference from and within itself[61]. Yet, if the major challenge to Europe today is the recognition of mutual interdependence and responsibility for those beyond "ourselves"[62], a reassessment of the potential of "the Balkan" to help re-imagine "Europe" is warranted. Cultural products such as *Molvanïa* may not necessarily disrupt the navel-gazing stance of traditional Balkanism, which has relegated "the Balkan" to the much despised, and occasionally exoticized, margins of Europe's imaginary. And although Veshim's *The English Neighbor* is certainly reliant on Balkanist truisms as well, the recycled clichés therein enable the constitution of "Balkan" multidimensionality and contextually nuanced agency, which address more adequately the complexity of the challenges facing both Europe and the Balkans today.

NOTES

1. Santo Cilauro, Tom Gleisner, and Rob Sitch, *Molvanïa: A Land Untouched by Modern Dentistry*, Jetlag travel guide (Woodstock, NY: The Overlook Press, 2004), 18, 14, 8.

2. Ibid., 20, 16, 24.

3. Ibid., 18, 15.

4. Ibid., 13.

5. Ibid., 14, 15, 20.

6. Ibid., 21.

7. Elisabeth Cheaure, "Infinite Mirroring: Russia and Eastern Europe as the West's 'Other'," in *Facing the East in the West: Images of Eastern Europe in British Literature, Film and Culture*, eds. Barabra Korte, Eva Ulrike Pirker, and Sissy Helff (Amsterdam: Rodopi, 2010), 25-41.

8. Robert A. Saunders, "Brand Interrupted: The Impact of Alternative Narrators on Nation Branding in the Former Second World," in *Branding Post-Communist Nations: Marketizing National Identities in the "New" Europe*, ed., Nadia Kaneva (London and New York: Routledge, 2012), 70.

9. Francis Fukuyama, "The End of History?" *The National Interest* (1989): 3–18.

10. Paweł Surowiec, "Toward Corpo-nationalism?: Poland as a Brand," in *Branding Post-Communist Nations: Marketizing National Identities in the "New" Europe*, ed., Nadia Kaneva (London and New York: Routledge, 2012), 124–44. See also chapter 4 in this volume.

11. Salman Rushdie, *Imaginary Homelands* (London and New York: Penguin, 1992), 19.

12. Ibid., 13.

13. Migration Observatory, "Bulgarians and Romanians in the British National Press: 1 December 2012–1 December 2013," August 18, 2014, http://www.

migrationobservatory.ox.ac.uk/reports/bulgarians-and-romanians-british-national-press, accessed November 15, 2014.

14. I distinguish between the historical and geopolitical entities located on the Balkan peninsula, which I shall refer to as the Balkans, and the discursive formation whose meaning has shifted, which I shall call "Balkan"/"the Balkan".

15. All quotations used in this article are from the first Bulgarian edition. Translations from the original are mine.

16. Nadia Kaneva, ed., *Branding Post-Communist Nations: Marketizing National Identities in the "New" Europe* (London and New York: Routledge, 2012).

17. David Morley and Kevin Robins, *Spaces of Identity: Global Media, Electronic Landscapes and Cultural Boundaries* (London and New York: Routledge, 1995).

18. Katherine E. Fleming, "Orientalism, the Balkans, and Balkan Historiography," *The American Historical Review* 105, no. 4 (2000): 1230, http://www.jstor.org/stable/2651410, accessed December 19, 2008.

19. David A. Norris, *In the Wake of the Balkan Myth: Questions of Identity and Modernity* (New York: St Martin's, 1999), 11.

20. Dušan I. Bjelić, "Introduction: Blowing up the Bridge," in *Balkan as Metaphor: Between Globalization and Fragmentation*, eds. Dušan I. Bjelić and Obrad Savić (Cambridge, MA: MIT Press, 2005), 3.

21. Larry Wolff, *Inventing Eastern Europe: The Map of Civilization on the Mind of the Enlightenment* (Stanford: Stanford UP, 1994).

22. Morley and Robins, *Spaces of Identity*, 22.

23. Bjelić, "Blowing up the Bridge," 4.

24. Maria Todorova, *Imagining the Balkans*, updated edition (Oxford: OUP, 2009), 19. See also, Edward W. Said, *Orientalism* (London and New York: Penguin, 1978).

25. Morley and Robins, *Spaces of Identity*, 50.

26. Andrew Hammond, *The Debatable Lands: British and American Representations of the Balkans* (Cardiff: University of Wales Press, 2007).

27. Ibid, 206–10.

28. Benyamin Neuberger, "The African Concept of Balkanisation," *The Journal of Modern African Studies* 14, no. 3 (1976): 523.

29. Todorova, *Imagining the Balkans*, 33.

30. Michael Ignatieff, *Blood and Belonging: Journeys into the New Nationalism* (New York: Farrar, Strauss and Giroux, 1993).

31. Robert Kaplan, *Balkan Ghosts: A Journey through History* (New York: Vintage, 1994); Samuel Huntington, *The Clash of Civilizations and the Remaking of World Order* (London: The Free Press, 2002).

32. Nelson Mandela, "Our Common Victory, the Victory of Democracy and Non-racialism, Is within Our Grasp. Address to Parliament (1990)," *Macleans*, December 5, 2013, http://www.macleans.ca/politics/ottawa/nelson-mandela-our-common-victory-the-victory-of-democracy-and-non-racialism-is-within-our-grasp/, accessed November 27, 2014.

33. William Frey, "Immigration and Demographic Balkanization," in *America's Demographic Tapestry: Baseline for the New Millennium*, eds. James W. Hughes and Joseph J. Seneca (New Brunswick, NJ: Rutgers UP, 1999), 78–97.

34. "De-Balkanisation," *Financial Times*, October 15, 2009, http://www.ft.com/cms/s/0/2727cdd2-b9cc-11de-a747-00144feab49a.html#axzz1eY6St7Ob, accessed January 25, 2011.

35. William Pfaff, "Greece's Balkan Inheritance Is Heavy," *Chicago Tribune*, May 15, 2012, http://articles.chicagotribune.com/2012-05-15/opinion/sns-201205151630--tms--wpfafftr--v-a20120515-20120515_1_balkan-peoples-century-greek-civilization, accessed November 4, 2014; "Greek Elections: The Replay Deepens the Divide," *The Guardian*, June 17, 2012, http://www.theguardian.com/commentisfree/2012/jun/17/greek-elections-replay-deepens-divide, accessed July 12, 2014.

36. T.J., "Scottish Independence and the Balkans: The Balkanisation of Britain?" *The Economist*, April 4, 2012, http://www.economist.com/blogs/easternapproaches/2012/04/scottish-independence-and-balkans, accessed November 4, 2014; Richard Milne, "Bildt Warns of British 'Balkanisation'," *Financial Times*, June 3, 2014, http://www.ft.com/cms/s/2/1a45b9bc-e258-11e3-89fd-00144feabdc0.html#axzz3J3Fx0bra, accessed November 13, 2014.

37. Surowiec, "Toward Corpo-nationalism," 140.

38. Wendy Bracewell and Alex Drace-Francis, eds., *Balkan Departures: Travel Writing from Southeastern Europe* (New York: Berghahn Press, 2009).

39. Todorova, *Imagining the Balkans*, 17.

40. Milica Bakić-Hayden, "Nesting Orientalisms: The Case of Former Yugoslavia," *Slavic Review* 54, no. 4 (1995): 917–31.

41. Vesna Goldsworthy, "Writing the Balkans," *Wasafiri* 29, no. 2 (2014): 1.

42. Nataša Kovačević, *Narrating Post/Communism: Colonial Discourse and Europe's Borderline Civilization* (London: Routledge, 2008), 16.

43. Kaneva, *Branding Post-Communist Nations*, 10.

44. Tomislav Z. Longinović, "Vampires like Us: Gothic Imaginary and 'the Serbs'," in *Balkan as Metaphor: Between Globalization and Fragmentation*, eds., Dušan I. Bjelić and Obrad Savić (Cambridge, MA: MIT Press, 2005), 47.

45. Slavoj Žižek, *Tarrying with the Negative: Kant, Hegel, and the Critique of Ideology* (Durham: Duke UP, 1993).

46. Todorova, *Imagining the Balkans*, 13.

47. Bjelić, "Blowing up the Bridge," 9.

48. Todorova, *Imagining the Balkans*, 13.

49. Svetlozar Andreev, "The Unbearable Lightness of Membership: Bulgaria and Romania after the 2007 EU Accession," *Communist and Post-Communist Studies* 42, no. 3 (2009): 375–93.

50. The publication of the novel in 2008 coincided with the EU temporarily suspending pre-accession funds and freezing the payment of nearly half a billion Euros worth of funding to Bulgaria due to allegations of fraud and misuse by government officials.

51. Michael Hardt and Antonio Negri, *Empire* (Cambridge, MA: Harvard UP, 2000).

52. It is hard to miss Veshim's parody here of the European hankerings of this dysfunctional character, who changes his legal name from the proverbially Bulgarian "Nikola Nikolov" to the inapposite "Nottingham Forest" Nikolov after his favourite team from the English Football League Championship.

53. Rather appropriately, Terziev's alias is "Terazini" after the main character in a popular 1984 Italian TV drama about the Mafia *The Octopus* (*La Piovra*).
54. The novel's elision of the difference between Britain and Europe is interesting, given the recent trend in the UK to distance itself from "Europe".
55. Mikhail Veshim, *Anglijskijat Sased*t [*The English Neighbor*] (Sofia: Ciela, 2008), 50.
56. Ibid., 71.
57. Morley and Robins, *Spaces of Identity*, 128.
58. See chapter 8 in this volume.
59. Veshim, *The English Neighbor*, 139.
60. Brett Neilson, *Free Trade in the Bermuda Triangle ... and Other Tales of Counterglobalization* (Minneapolis: University of Minnesota Press, 2004), xxix.
61. Morley and Robins, *Spaces of Identity*, 134.
62. Ibid., 187.

BIBLIOGRAPHY

Andreev, Svetlozar. "The Unbearable Lightness of Membership: Bulgaria and Romania after the 2007 EU Accession." *Communist and Post-Communist Studies* 42, no. 3 (2009): 375–93.
Bakić-Hayden, Milica. "Nesting Orientalisms: The Case of Former Yugoslavia." *Slavic Review* 54, no. 4 (1995): 917–31.
Bjelić, Dušan I. "Introduction: Blowing up the Bridge." In *Balkan as Metaphor: Between Globalization and Fragmentation*, edited by Dušan I. Bjelić and Obrad Savić, 1–22. Cambridge, MA: MIT Press, 2005.
Bracewell, Wendy and Alex Drace-Francis, eds. *Balkan Departures: Travel Writing from Southeastern Europe*. New York: Berghahn Press, 2009.
Cheaure, Elisabeth. "Infinite Mirroring: Russia and Eastern Europe as the West's 'Other'." In *Facing the East in the West: Images of Eastern Europe in British Literature, Film and Culture*, edited by Barabra Korte, Eva Ulrike Pirker, and Sissy Helff, 25-41. Amsterdam: Rodopi, 2010.
Cilauro, Santo, Tom Gleisner, and Rob Sitch. *Molvanîa: A Land Untouched by Modern Dentistry*. Jetlag travel guide. Woodstock, NY: The Overlook Press, 2004.
"De-Balkanisation," *Financial Times*, October 15, 2009. http://www.ft.com/cms/s/0/2727cdd2-b9cc-11de-a747-00144feab49a.html#axzz1eY6St7Ob, accessed January 25, 2011.
Fleming, Katherine E. "Orientalism, the Balkans, and Balkan Historiography." *The American Historical Review* 105, no. 4 (2000): 1218–33. http://www.jstor.org/stable/2651410, accessed December 19, 2008.
Frey, William. "Immigration and Demographic Balkanization." In *America's Demographic Tapestry: Baseline for the New Millennium*, edited by James W. Hughes, and Joseph J. Seneca, 78–97. New Brunswick, NJ: Rutgers UP, 1999.
Fukuyama, Francis. "The End of History?" *The National Interest* (Summer 1989): 3–18.

Goldsworthy, Vesna. "Writing the Balkans." *Wasafiri* 29, no. 2 (2014): 1–3.

The Guardian, "Greek Elections: The Replay Deepens the Divide," June 17, 2012. http://www.theguardian.com/commentisfree/2012/jun/17/greek-elections-replay-deepens-divide, accessed July 12, 2014.

Hammond, Andrew. *The Debatable Lands: British and American Representations of the Balkans*. Cardiff: University of Wales Press, 2007.

Hardt, Michael and Antonio Negri. *Empire*. Cambridge, MA: Harvard UP, 2000.

Huntington, Samuel. *The Clash of Civilizations and the Remaking of World Order*. London: The Free Press, 2002.

Ignatieff, Michael. *Blood and Belonging: Journeys into the New Nationalism*. New York: Farrar, Strauss and Giroux, 1993.

Kaneva, Nadia, ed. *Branding Post-Communist Nations: Marketizing National Identities in the "New" Europe*. London and New York: Routledge, 2012.

Kaplan, Robert. *Balkan Ghosts: A Journey through History*. New York: Vintage, 1994.

Kovačević, Nataša. *Narrating Post/Communism: Colonial Discourse and Europe's Borderline Civilization*. London: Routledge, 2008.

Longinović, Tomislav Z. "Vampires like Us: Gothic Imaginary and 'the Serbs'." In *Balkan as Metaphor: Between Globalization and Fragmentation*, edited by Dušan I. Bjelić and Obrad Savić, 39–60. Cambridge, MA: MIT Press, 2005.

Mandela, Nelson. "Our Common Victory, the Victory of Democracy and Non-racialism, Is within Our Grasp. Address to Parliament (1990)," *Macleans*, December 5, 2013. http://www.macleans.ca/politics/ottawa/nelson-mandela-our-common-victory-the-victory-of-democracy-and-non-racialism-is-within-our-grasp/, accessed November 27, 2014.

Milne, Richard. "Bildt Warns of British 'Balkanisation'," *Financial Times*, June 3, 2014. http://www.ft.com/cms/s/2/1a45b9bc-e258-11e3-89fd-00144feabdc0.html#axzz3J3Fx0bra, accessed November 13, 2014.

Migration Observatory. "Bulgarians and Romanians in the British National Press: 1 December 2012–1 December 2013." August 18, 2014. http://www.migrationobservatory.ox.ac.uk/reports/bulgarians-and-romanians-british-national-press, accessed November 15, 2014.

Morley, David and Kevin Robins. *Spaces of Identity: Global Media, Electronic Landscapes and Cultural Boundaries*. London and New York: Routledge, 1995.

Neilson, Brett. *Free Trade in the Bermuda Triangle . . . and Other Tales of Counterglobalization*. Minneapolis: University of Minnesota Press, 2004.

Neuberger, Benyamin. "The African Concept of Balkanisation." *The Journal of Modern African Studies* 14, no. 3 (1976): 523–29.

Norris, David A. *In the Wake of the Balkan Myth: Questions of Identity and Modernity*. New York: St Martin's, 1999.

Pfaff, William. "Greece's Balkan Inheritance Is Heavy," *Chicago Tribune*, May 15, 2012. http://articles.chicagotribune.com/2012-05-15/opinion/sns-201205151630--tms--wpfafftr--v-a20120515-20120515_1_balkan-peoples-century-greek-civilization, accessed November 4, 2014.

Rushdie, Salman. *Imaginary Homelands*. London and New York: Penguin, 1992.

Said, Edward W. *Orientalism*. London and New York: Penguin, 1978.

Saunders, Robert A. "Brand Interrupted: The Impact of Alternative Narrators on Nation Branding in the Former Second World." In *Branding Post-Communist Nations: Marketizing National Identities in the "New" Europe*, edited by Nadia Kaneva, 49–75. London and New York: Routledge, 2012.

Surowiec, Paweł. "Toward Corpo-nationalism?: Poland as a Brand." In *Branding Post-Communist Nations: Marketizing National Identities in the "New" Europe*, edited by Nadia Kaneva, 124–44. London and New York: Routledge, 2012.

T.J. "Scottish Independence and the Balkans: The Balkanisation of Britain?," *The Economist*, April 4, 2012. http://www.economist.com/blogs/easternapproaches/2012/04/scottish-independence-and-balkans, accessed November 4, 2014.

Todorova, Maria. *Imagining the Balkans*. Updated edition. Oxford: OUP, 2009.

Veshim, Mikhail. *Anglijskijat Sased*. [*The English Neighbor*]. Sofia: Ciela, 2008.

Wolff, Larry. *Inventing Eastern Europe: The Map of Civilization on the Mind of the Enlightenment*. Stanford, CA: Stanford UP, 1994.

Žižek, Slavoj. *Tarrying with the Negative: Kant, Hegel, and the Critique of Ideology*. Durham: Duke UP, 1993.

Chapter 7

EUrientation Anxieties

Islamic Sexualities and the Construction of Europeanness

Piro Rexhepi

In an interview in 2009, Ismail Kadare who had just received the Prince of Asturias Award, addressing his position as a dissident writer in communist Albania, argued that, "what excited suspicion [by the Albanian communist regime] was, 'why does the western bourgeoisie hold a writer from a Stalinist country in high esteem?'"[1]. Yet, the communist regime not only allowed the Albanian writer to travel to France (a very rare privilege reserved only for those close to the regime) but engaged in promoting his rise to prominence in European literary circles. For the communist regime, Kadare provided a historical fiction that, as Morgan argues, "represented Albanian identity as something native and authentic over and against Ottoman, Soviet or, later, Maoist, influences", mirroring the regime's desire to situate Albania, not only as a constitutive part of Europe, but as its guardian of the frontier between Europe and its eastern Others[2]. As Morley and Robins put it,

> This desire for clarity, this need to know precisely where Europe ends, is about the construction of a symbolic geography that will separate the insiders from the outsiders (the Others). Implicit in these words is the suggestion that the next Iron Curtain should divide Europe from, and insulate it against, the Islamic Other[3].

For the Europeans, Kadare presented an opportunity to gaze inside what was considered one of the most isolated communist regimes, providing semi-fictionalized Orientalist narratives of oppression and violence supposedly endured by Albanians under the Ottoman Empire, which he later argued was a metaphor for the communist regime. Kadare's stories, then as now, provide the European postcolonial market place with the possibility of both objectifying and commodifying internalized Orientalist cultural productions in the service of European enlargement, particularly as Kadare's narrative is one of Albania's escape from its Islamic and communist pasts into the fold of European belonging.

In *Brown Skin, White Masks* (2011), extending on the concept of "native informer" in postcolonial studies, Hamid Dabashi calls this phenomenon "comprador intellectuals", namely, native informers who through the "inversion of facts by fantasy [and] of truth by politics" engage in legitimizing colonial and neocolonial formations[4]. The intersection of gender, sexuality and Islam has been central in the construction of what El-Tayeb calls "escape narratives" by authors such as Hirsi Ali, Salman Rushdie and Azar Nafis, who in escaping from their "backward" societies find freedom and liberation in the West and/or invite the West to control and reform their societies[5].

This chapter explores the intersections of Islam and sexuality in cultural texts in Albania and Bosnia to gain an insight in how essentialized identity markers of Muslims in the Balkans are framed to either correspond to or contradict the idea of belonging to Europe. Cultural texts, particularly literature and film, have been key in inventing a European identity for Muslims in the Balkans in the face of European enlargement. They are not only Western European Orientalist fantasies of projecting Muslims in the Balkans as objects of reform and Europeanization but also a form of internalized Islamophobic narratives that in effect seek to disconnect Muslims in the Balkans from the *Ummah*. If in the 20th century, secular and socialist nation and state building projects have constituted themselves against fictitious *Islamic sexualities*[6] in the Balkans, today these sexualities are employed and renamed in the service of European enlargement.

The construction of Islamic sexualities is best explored by examining the cultural productions of the secular-modern compromise[7], particularly universalizing neoliberal as well as socialist productions of Islamic sexualities and subjectivities within broader projects of "liberation". Throughout these cultural productions, the sexualized Muslim subject in the Balkans became the screen onto which European fantasies of civilizing Muslims are projected and heteronormative sexualities are constructed. At times, these Orientalist, homophobic and Islamophobic projections have also been adopted by Muslims in the Balkans as a way of resisting both European and Balkan colonial identification, which is why their interrogation is key in understanding how Muslims in the Balkans continue to be produced as suspect others. Thus, by looking at Albanian and Bosnian representation of sexuality in postcolonial cultural texts, this chapter examines how internalized Orientalist and Islamophobic cultural representations of Islamic sexualities seek to ease European and Balkan anxieties about Islam, while being eager to persuade the European and Balkan gaze of their "Europeanness". Queer critique and postcolonial scholarship are therefore key in subjecting the European enlargement discourse in the Balkans to critical analyses that move beyond the now traditional discourse of post-socialist "return to Europe" and its critique.

Drawing from queer and postcolonial theory, I look at the representation of queer Muslims in contemporary semi-realistic historical fiction and film to explore the construction of heteronormative secular and nationalist narratives. I argue that complex queer subjectivities among Muslims in Albania and Bosnia are essentialized and reduced to Eurocentric binary sexualities to promote European belonging in these two countries. Specifically, I look at how these attempts to incorporate sexual orientations in the service of European orientations change over time to assure Bosnia's and Albania's compatibility with dominant European epistemological and ontological categories of gender and sexuality. If in the Albanian historical novel the queer Muslim is employed in the production of the heterosexual European Albanian, in Bosnian film, the queer Muslim is staged as a sexualized victim who can only find salvation by either escaping to Europe or bringing Europe home to Bosnia. Sexual orientations thus are not only articulated and renamed in relation to Europe, but they become the markers of European orientations. In this context, cultural texts trade sexualities in the European postcolonial and postmodern cultural marketplace where the division between history and fiction is neutralized, contributing to the legitimization of larger processes of European enlargement.

There are two considerations that need to be addressed here: how postcolonialism and queer theory, respectively, figure in the Balkan context. The last two decades have seen an upsurge of postcolonial studies of the Balkans. Todorova's *Imagining the Balkans* became the canonized text that sought to locate the Balkans as the "in-between" space of civilized Europe and the uncivilized other[8]. More recently, there have been attempts to align postcolonial and post-socialist analysis in the Balkans under frameworks that seek to explore the intersectional "post" in colonialism and socialism[9]. Most of these studies suggest that, unlike Orientalism in India where "Gandhi and the Hindu internalized Orientalized stereotypes to resist their colonial identification [. . .] in the Balkans [. . .] people subverted their own identities by Orientalizing one another"[10]. While these analyses are important in understanding the overall Othering of the Balkans, it is important to note that Muslims in the Balkans cannot be grouped in the "in-between" space as, unlike non-Muslims, they were projected as the Others by both Western and Eastern European imperial and colonial formations. Moreover, Muslims were subjected to Orientalist identification before, during and after socialism. The expansion of the Yugoslav Kingdom, for instance, took place at the expense of Muslim majority populated areas of Bosnia, Kosovo, Sandžak and Macedonia where Yugoslav Orientalist accounts of the inter-war period informed socialist policies on the modernization of the Muslim population. Frequently, it was intellectuals who dominated the discourse on "what is to be done with the Muslims" before and after the Second World War. The two most noted figures, Ivo Andrić and Vasa Čubrilović, advocated the expulsion or assimilation of Muslims from the Yugoslav Kingdom[11]. In Socialist Yugoslavia, they both went on to become successful public intellectuals, Andrić receiving the Nobel Prize in literature in 1961 and Čubrilović establishing the Institute for Balkan Studies at the University of Belgrade in 1970. I am not arguing here that the rest of the Balkans were not subjected to textual colonization and Balkanist and Orientalist prejudice but that parts of the Balkans with majority Muslim populations, such as Albania and Bosnia and Herzegovina, also experienced forms of imperial and colonial rule both by Western and Central European powers and by other Balkan neighbours[12]. If the imperial rule of the Austro-Hungarian Empire over Bosnia and Herzegovina and in the case of Albania through the European-backed International Control Commission both took place in the period preceding the Great War, similar colonizing projects were enacted by the Yugoslav Kingdom with the end of that war. In this context, I argue that instead of addressing the "writing-back" to Europe, Balkan postcolonial and post-socialist scholarships should explore the implications of "writing together" with Europe in Orientalizing Muslims in the Balkans. In this intersection, I examine Orientalist depictions of Islamic sexualities in the Balkans in the process of Europeanization through Queer theory, which can provide a possibility for, as Schippert argues, "undoing, or recalibrating, of binary terminology of religion and secularism"[13], and which may in turn, as Jakobsen and Pellegrini argue, "open new configurations in the political debates structured by them"[14], hopefully deflecting and deconstructing fixed binary representations of essentialized Muslim subjectivities in the Balkans.

In the context of Queer theory, I am particularly guided by Halberstam's reading of queer, postcolonial and Black feminism that seeks to examine "the negation of the subject rather than her formation, the disruption of lineage rather than its continuation, the undoing of self rather than its activation"[15]. Building on this remark, I examine what alternatives to Europe are relegated to the background, are un-read or hidden in the process of European orientations. The need to sustain Balkan Muslim orientations towards Europe is tantamount to turning away from other orientations or deviating from the set path of progress, modernity and Europeanization. In this sense, I find Ahmed's "Orientations: Toward a Queer Phenomenology" inspirational in thinking of this process in terms of sexual orientations. As she points out,

> The temporality of orientation reminds us that orientations are effects of what we tend toward, where the "toward" marks a space and time that is almost, but not quite, available in the present. In the case of sexual orientation, it is not then simply that we have it. To become straight means not only that we have to turn toward the objects given to us by heterosexual culture but also that we must turn away from objects that take us off this line[16].

Ahmed notes how "the queer object, the one out of line, on a slant, the odd and strange one, is hence encountered as slipping away, as threatening to become out of reach"[17]. Expanding on Ahmed's work, I explore how the queer Muslim in Albanian and Bosnian cultural texts is not only represented as dangerous on his own but that he also has the potential of corrupting others, particularly those who do not fully conform to the desired European orientation. In this sense, these cultural texts not only produce European orientations through sexual orientations, but also seek to "rescue" queer subjects and set them on a straight path. While Queer theory has interrogated these processes queerly, it is important to note here that Queer theory itself has become complicit with the Europeanization discourse[18].

Thus, this chapter examines how post-Ottoman and post-socialist sexual orientations have become the markers of European orientations for the Balkans by deconstructing the representation and convergence of sexuality and Islam with notions of (straight) Europeanness. In the first part, I examine representations of queer Muslims in Albanian literature. I specifically look at how European orientations in contemporary Albanian literature are at times constructed against the queer Muslim as a renegade of the Ottoman past that continues to haunt the Albanian orientation towards Europe and at times, sympathetic narratives towards homosexuality are employed to advance Albania's European progress and emancipation. In the second part, I look at the Bosnian film *Go West* (2005) where the queer Muslim is employed as a victim of his Balkan Islamic and socialist pasts that can only be saved by escaping the Balkans and going West. In other words, the straightening of the queer Muslim becomes the European orientation for the entire nation.

QUEER ISLAMIC PASTS AND EUROPEAN FUTURES IN ALBANIAN LITERATURE

Published in 1986, *The Black Year*[19] is considered one of the most accomplished novels by Ismail Kadare. Set in 1913 Albania, a year after partition from the Ottoman Empire, the novel traces the arrival of a German prince appointed by European powers to rule Albania with an accompanied International Commission for Control to guarantee his reign. In the background, a Muslim uprising seeks to overthrow the foreign Christian prince in favour of an Ottoman Muslim one. The Muslim uprising is led by one of the main characters of the novel Kuz Baba, depicted as a ruthless, uncontrolled, hypersexualized Muslim, who in fighting to preserve Islam in Albania, is actually fighting to preserve his privilege to have access to men. Thus, in the midst of war that will decide the fate and future of Albania, Kuz Baba can't be bothered with the politics of war but is instead consumed by grief and yearning for his murdered lover and a fresh found desire for the Dutch soldiers of the new

German prince, "So taken he is by thinking about boys that since he has seen the Dutch he is obsessed with fetching one as a slave"[20]. Kuz Baba's violent, vulgar, irrational and uncontrolled sexuality throughout the novel serves to construct the character of Shestan, a beautiful, rational, heterosexual, naïve soldier who along with his friends, decides to fight in favour of the German Prince and therefore for the European future of Albania. Shestan's early lack of determination matures when he reads his first newspaper in Albanian and comes across a picture of Albania depicted as "girl or a young woman laying on a hospital bed, surrounded by masked surgeons with knifes and seizers in their hands"[21]. Against a tableau of chaos and ambivalence, Shestan's deep felt sympathy towards the representation of Albania as a fragile woman under threat by masked surgeons representing both the encroachments of neighbouring states, as well as European powers to divide Albania, produces him as the ideal male citizen. Kadare projects and parallels the chaos of an infantile state with the infantile Shestan who is then structured and matured through the Oedipus complex against Kuz Baba's subject. For Shestan's sexuality to mature, Kuz Baba's un-sublimated and un-sacrificial sexuality cannot be oriented towards the advancement of the nation and as such cannot represent the future but only a failed past. Shestan's coming of age here is employed to imply and register Albania's coming of age and into hetero-order, equated here with returning to, or rediscovering Europe.

In order to establish a semblance of order in an ambivalent time and space, Kadare has to work against multiple sexual subjectivities that don't always conform to the homo-hetero binaries that he wants to introduce as a hetero-ordering device. Kuz Baba is not simply a homosexual but represents an entire homoerotic culture modelled after the *Bejtexhi*[22] tradition that escapes the homo-hetero binaries as well as the gendered male-female order. In this context, Kadare's depiction of the queerness of Bejtexhi homoerotics is not reductive, albeit, he does mock its sentimentalities. For instance, Kuz Baba claims that he was told by a certain dervish that "like women, dylbers[23] must be covered in hijabs to avoid scenes of jealous outbursts by their lovers should someone look at them – such is desire – wherever it appears, the knife is not too far"[24]. The use of the term "dylber" and Kuz Baba's style of stories and songs are derived from Bejtexhi poets who addressed poems to their male lovers in Ottoman Albanian language. The production of the homo-hetero binaries through the ridicule of the Bejtexhi tradition in Kadare's work is manifold. The Bejtexhi poets, who mainly wrote in Ottoman Albanian using the Arabic, Persian or Ottoman alphabet, addressed homoerotic themes that are not compatible with the homo-hetero regime. They adopted cross-gendered metaphors for themselves and their lovers while frequently equating their love for their *dylbers* with their love for Islam[25]. While Kadare exploits the Bejtexhi tradition to legitimize his historical fiction, he uses irony to banalize its homoerotic aesthetics. This is not accidental, as it appears at a critical juncture of orientations, both sexual and geopolitical. In *The European Identity of Albanians* for instance, Kadare explicitly states that the Bejtexhi poetry had "a hidden agenda to unman and morally weaken" the Albanian man, as "it needed no more than a few 'boys' and 'fags' of that sort for not freedom, but the very idea of freedom to disappear forever"[26]. National anxieties around queer sexualities in Albania, which Kadare frequently locates in various Islamic settings such as a Bektashi Tekke or a dervish, are not specific only to his writings. Contemporary Albanian literary works have frequently constructed the national male character against Islamic sexualities and subjectivities by valorizing his ability to overcome such temptations and re-orient himself towards Europe and hetero/homo binaries.

The contemporary cursory employment of Islamic sexualities in different modalities to locate the ideal Albanian heterosexual in relations to Europe emerges at a time when old anxieties around fractured and unfinished European orientations become subsumed in contemporary EU enlargement debates. These debates, reflected in the literary taste for "belonging to Europe" narratives, expose old and new contradictions of historical narratives in Albanian literature. For example, Ben Blushi one of the most popular authors in Albania in the 2010s, in *Otello, the Moor of Vlora*[27] (2009) employs the queer "foreign" Muslim to reinforce a totalizing narrative of heteronormative European belonging by taking the "before the Ottomans arrived" route. Set between 1300 and 1400, in pre-Ottoman Albania, *Othello, the Moor of Vlora*, recounts the fall of Vlora to the Ottomans through the personal story of Othello. Othello, an African slave, ends up in Albania having been purchased by a Venetian family whose patriarch takes him along on a trip to Vlora to visit his relatives. The family ties between a Venetian family and the ruling family of Vlora, as a re-occurring theme in the book, reinforce Albania's historical relations with Europe before the Ottoman invasion. In Vlora, coming under suspicion for murder, Othello ends up in prison where he meets Hamit, a sly Muslim queer who seduces Othello and introduces him to homoerotic love. When Othello tries to seduce a new Albanian prisoner, Andrea, he resists engaging in anything more than just touching and pretends to be sleeping while Othello admires his body. Sexuality here is attributed to the racial and religious Other. While both Othello and Hamit are presented as feeble men who fall prey to their uncontrolled desires, Andrea's heterosexuality is saved through his resolution to join the Albanian army and defend Vlora from the arriving Ottoman armies. In the text, Andrea's resistance to sexual deviant behaviours and his preservation of heterosexual integrity is equated with his sacrifice for the nation. In the end, the Ottomans defeat the Albanians. Hamit who has now joined the Ottoman forces captures Andrea and out of resentment for Othello's love towards Andrea, cuts Andrea's head

off and paints it in oils and perfumes. This corporal disfigurement and sub-
sequent feminization of Andrea's head servers to remind the reader of failed
Albanian heterosexuality in the face of Ottoman conquest. Only through the
disintegration of his body however, and its subsequent feminization, could
Hamit subdue Andrea's heterosexual masculinity. The fall of Albania to
Ottomans here registered in the disarticulation and feminization of Andrea's
body suggests that Albania's temporary misalignment from Europe during the
Ottoman rule did not and could not convert Albanians into Ottomans, as this
could have only been attained through death.

Similarly, in *To Live in an Island*[28] (2008), the character of Ali Tepelena, a
semi-realistic depiction of the Ali Pash Tepelena[29], is styled as a queer despot
who seduces young Christian men for his harem. His homoerotic sexuality is
equated with Islam as a foreign infliction in the body of the nation that cannot
be purged but only assimilated. The main character Arianit Komneni reflects
on how "Islam has been pushed onto our beds, our homes and our souls" and
that "now we can't kill this foreign beast as we will hurt ourselves [. . .] if
we want to live in peace with it, we have to tame the wildness of the beast,
feeding it with our Christian body and soul"[30]. The foundational narrative
of Albanian identity here emerges as a diluted, damaged and compromised
hybrid of wild Islam penetrating the loving Christianity or, to use Bhabba's
concept, the establishment of a "third space of enunciation"[31]. Here, Blushi,
while destabilizing the boundaries of "us" and "them", employs the Christian ethics of victimhood and sacrifice to suggest that, as Christ carries the
burden of sin in being reborn free, so the Albanian man in being reborn as
European must tame Islam and bring it under control. While Blushi operates
through pre-Ottoman Christianity to establish the Europeanness of Albanians,
he also acknowledges Islam's inauspicious infiltration of the Albanian body
providing somewhat more complexity, albeit still in the form of an Orientalist
and fictionalized history. Kadare, on the other hand, denies the existence of
an Islamic dimension of Albanian "Europeanness", particularly because he
believes that this definition of Albania's European identity was preserved as
preserved in northern Albanian Catholicism, which he conceives and utilizes
as an orienting device towards the Balkans and Europe[32].

It is important to note here that the dialectical tensions around Islam, sexuality and belonging to Europe are not framed in opposition to homosexuality
per se, but specifically Islamic "queer" sexualities. In Kadare's *Beauty Pageant for Men in the Accursed Mountains*[33] (1996), unlike Islamic sexualities,
the Catholic Albanian homosexual is ontologized through ancient Greek
mythology and rendered a victim-hero rather than a villain. The situation of
Catholic homosexuality in the registry of ancient Greek and thereby European
Albanian homosexuality serves as an ordering narrative that seeks to save the
Albania heterosexual from Islam while introducing homo-hetero binaries as a

protection from the uncategorizable abjection. Situating the narrative in northern Catholic Albania, the hero of the novel, Gaspër Cara, is portrayed as a kind, emancipated citizen from the capital who suffers his homosexuality in silence. Gaspër Cara's love for Prenk Curri, a confident highlander and suffering-in-silence desired heterosexual, is committed, stable and exclusive. In contrast to Kadare's licentious queer Muslim characters who have multiple lovers and frequently abuse them, Gaspër's love for Prenk, while homosexual and tragic, is still depicted as possible. It is also interesting to note that the construction of Gaspër Carra as a modern European homosexual is enacted through his dress "of the latest fashion" and his reading of Oscar Wilde's *The Ballad of Reading Gaol*. The civilized look and behaviour enable him to engage with the rest of the local Europeanized intelligentsia who not only understand him but sympathize with his condition. The difference in the portrayal of Islamic and northern Albanian Catholic sexualities is therefore relational to European belonging. Carra is not projected as a threat, as his European homosexuality keeps heterosexuality intact and stable. Islamic sexualities, on the other hand, are projected as destabilizing, impossible and failed. Indeed, in an interview after his reception of the Man Booker Prize International, asked what he made of Lord Baryon's account of "Greek love" among Albanians in the court of Ali Pasha Tepelena, Kadare replied that "what Byron saw had nothing to do with Ancient Greece, [. . .] It came with the Ottoman occupation and was paedophile, little boys"[34]. The desire to pathologize and discredit Ottoman Albania and by extension Islamic sexualities as failed and perverse serves as a reminder of the continued Albanian anxiety around the desired integrity of their European orientations. The introduction of the Catholic homosexual as a victim on the other hand, at a time when certain homosexual bodies are integrated into European citizenship, suggests that while Islamic sexualities cannot be fully expelled, they can be stabilized and assimilated into the homo-hetero binaries and renamed in the grammar of European sexualities. Indeed, in examining "complex entanglements of culture and politics involved in the processes of renaming" in chapter 3 in this volume, Milevska points out how renaming processes not only rely on "violence by signification" but also "shap[e] national, cultural and personal identities in the Balkans" between post-socialist Balkan societies and Europe. Europe then presents the possibility to redeem and escape past failed sexualities, renaming, straightening and administering their permission as a testament to tolerance and diversity. Going to Europe as a way of escaping the past coincides with European integration discourses built around "returning to Europe" as an escape from violent non-European pasts, particularly Islamic or socialist pasts. The temporality of these cultural productions, as Čvoro points out in chapter 8 in this volume, reiterates European enlargement geopolitics by creating "a sense of historical inevitability about the 'accession' from centralised economies, conflict, and leftovers of imperial rule (Ottoman, Austro-Hungarian and Soviet) towards deregulated markets, stability and European democracy". Indeed, in the Bosnian film *Go West,* socialist and Islamic violent pasts merge to produce Europe as not just the desired, but the only possible destination.

GO WEST

Go West (2005)[35] is the first and one of the most controversial gay-themed films made in Bosnia and Herzegovina. It tells the story of a gay couple during the conflict in 1992. Kenan, a Bosnian Muslim and his Serbian boyfriend Milan, take refuge in Milan's Serb village where Kenan must cross-dress to pass as Milan's fiancée. The film is typical of the post-war Balkan cinema where the negative stereotypes circulating in the West about the Balkans are appropriated in films at home. Films like *Before the Rain* (1994, dir. Milčo Mančevski), *Underground* (1995, dir. Emir Kusturica) and *Pretty Village, Pretty Flame* (1996, dir. Srđan Dragojević) construct ahistorical discourses that deny the socialist past. The Balkans are portrayed as stuck in time with no clear distinction of the past and the present where the familiar narrative is one of perpetual conflict and ethnic and religious hatred. Working in similar linear narratives, representing the Balkans as the "in-between" space that divides Europe from the East yet belongs to neither, in *Go West* the gay couple is removed from this space of in-betweenness and situated outside the Balkans. Unlike the rest of the characters in the film, the gay couple is urban, they smoke marijuana and one of them plays the cello; they have arrived at modernity while their families and surroundings are projected as pre-modern, brutal and insane. The "semiotic modalities" of the film (visual image, sound, action, gestures, layout etc.)[36] are rooted in the representation of the Balkans or Balkanism as "imputed ambiguity"[37]. War, destruction, scenes of wailing, superstition, curses and blessings are present throughout the film to capture the wild Balkans, while the only sane people are the gay couple who are trying to "Go West" and Milan's father, who has previously lived in the West. Thus early in the film, it becomes clear that those who have not been in touch with the West or do not emulate it are wild and barbaric and responsible for the war. All three characters observe the madness of the war around them in dismay and helplessness. The gay subjects here not only represent the West explicitly but also symbolize the West distantly observing the Yugoslav wars and denying to have anything to do with them. Yet for this narrative to work, any hint of Europeanness, including the socialist past, had to be negated in both the characters and the semiotic modalities of the film, by evoking a pre-socialist Balkans, just out of the Ottoman Empire but not fully in Europe.

To escape the conflict, the couple forges a marriage to obtain papers and move West. In the meantime however, Milan is called to serve in the Serb army. Kenan has to cross-dress daily to maintain his appearance as Milan's wife among the suspicious locals. Although the post-conflict rhetoric "we all suffered equally" is used as a levelling device throughout the film, the more obvious representation of the character here is based on traditional Orientalist representations of the Muslim man as effeminate, neurotic and prone to emotional outbursts, all the while his Serbian boyfriend practises martial arts, always reasons and bears his sufferings in silence. Kenan lacks any agency and will to the point that when Ranka, a local Serbian woman from the village, discovers his secret, he gives in to her sexual demands. Having discovered their affair on a visit home, Milan returns to the front and dies.

In a study of representations of women in post-war Japanese film, Coats notes that post-war narratives on screen can retrospectively provide a powerful means to re-imagine past conflicts in terms suitable to current national identifications[38]. From this angle, *Go West* is both a film about a past and present war in that the sympathetic identification with the gay characters is employed against both past and present. The main protagonist, Kenan Distar, notes "there is war in my country. Serbs, who are Christian Orthodox hate the Muslims. Muslims who are Muslim, don't like the Serbs . . . while the war may finish one day . . . they will all still hate homosexuals, as in the Balkans, it is easier to have a slayer in the family than a faggot". The representation of homophobia in the Balkans as timeless and innate suggests another war, a civilizational one, where gays come to represent the desire to *Go West*, whereas the unification with Europe is only possible through the Balkans *coming out* of the Islamic and socialist closet. By anchoring gay characters to the West, their victimization then functions as a hidden desire of all other Bosnians who want to be European. Yet, while Europe may claim certain gays, it is not ready for the rest of the society.

The projection of the homosexual characters as not of the Balkans but foreign to it poses the question of why gays are frequently rendered more modern than others in the peripheries? The politics of time and "who has arrived in modernity and who has not?", as Butler agues, are "all raised in the midst of very serious political contestations"[39]. Is it because, as Massad argues, sexuality is "a product of specific Euro-American histories and social formations" and therefore "not universal *or necessarily universalizable*"[40], or is it because the West has "nationalized gayness" by perpetuating a homonormative approach to subjectivity and belonging? Indeed, the Serbian film *Parada* (2011), arranged around former war enemies uniting to protect the gay pride in Belgrade, suggests that gay rights may be a particularly effective point of post-conflict inter-ethnic dialogue and solidarity in moving towards Europe. The invitation to belong in Europe through the gay parade then

centres the queer rights discourse as the terrain where anxieties over Europeanization take place, leaving the Balkans in effect homophobic.

In the last scene, Kenan is being interviewed by the French actress Jeanne
Moreau somewhere in Western Europe in 1993. "That's all" he says. "I no
longer have a house, a cello, a country, I lost my family and I lost Milan. . . . I
am only left with my music." Kenan then goes on to play an imaginary cello
while on the screen we see Bosnian graves. Back in the studio Moreau says,
"I am sorry but I don't know what to say". Kenan replies by saying "you
should say I should play louder". The affect and identification of viewers
with Kenan is meant to induce a problem-solution imperative with the viewer,
where the solution for the Balkan ambiguity is Europe. There are no other
imaginable alternatives for the post-socialist, post-conflict and post-traumatic
disorder of the Balkans but Europe. The credits roll with the song *Go West* by
the famous Bosnian composer Enes Bure Zlatar: "I am powerless. . . . I'll go
with sunset . . . Go West. I'll go with sunset, Go West".

CONCLUSION

The intersection of sexuality and Islam, discussed in this chapter as orientation points in the construction of European identity for the Muslims in
the Balkans, is guided by a hegemonic desire to "clean" themselves from
their Islamic pasts in favour of histories that support totalizing narratives of
Europeanness. El-Tayeb for instances notes how "those perceived as non-
European constantly have to prove that their presence is legitimate, for there
is no space within Europe that they can claim as their own, in which their
status of belonging is undisputed"[41]. In this context, the confluence of sexual
orientation and European orientation in Albanian and Bosnian literature and
film has been complex, contradictory and corrective. By corrective, I mean
the desire to write a totalizing history in such a manner that the destabilizing subjectivities and lived experiences that fail to conform to the European
oriented politics of local elites are at times rendered invisible or attacked as
Oriental renegades of Ottomanism and Islam.

As questions around Muslim integration inside the European Union are
framed around *coexistence*, in Bosnia and Kosovo they have been framed in
terms of *orientations* towards Europe; both concepts suggesting incompat-
ibility, distance, failure and perhaps impossibility. While the idea of coexistence suggests that Muslims are, as Asad argues, "external to the essence of
Europe" so that "'coexistence' can be envisaged between 'us' and 'them'"[42],
"orientation" towards the European Union raises the question of alternative
orientations. Reinforcing the idea of a European orientation suggests that
there is an alternative, a possibility, a desire among these populations against
which European orientation is enforced. In other words, against which other

futures are the Muslims in the Balkans being directed towards the EUropean future? As European enlargement presents itself as an unmarked category, as the self-evident and only possible orientation for the Balkans, the queer Muslim is employed to stabilize Balkan anxieties about belonging in Europe and discipline its disoriented bodies. Thus, if in the Bosnian film *Go West*, the queer Muslim can only be liberated by escaping to Europe, which produces Europe as a safe space free of homophobia and the centre of progress, in recent Albanian literature, the queer Muslim is employed in the production of the "European" Albanian heteronormative homosexual or heterosexual. I therefore argue that these fictional accounts of Islamic sexualities are not only traded in the postcolonial and postmodern market place, always in need for new Others that can be co-opted and incorporated, they also allegorize the anxieties of the Islamic self as an unfinished queer self that fails to follow European orientations.

NOTES

1. Alison Flood, "'I Am Not a Political Writer' Says Ismail Kadare," *Guardian*, March 29, 2009.
2. Peter Morgan, "Greek Civilization as a Theme of Dissidence in the Works of Ismail Kadare," *Modern Greek Studies (Australia and New Zealand)* 15 (2011): 16–23.
3. David Morley and Kevin Robins, *Spaces and Identity: Global Media, Electronic Landscapes and Cultural Boundaries* (London: Routledge, 1995), 190.
4. Hamid Dabashi, *Brown Skin, White Masks.* (London: Pluto Press, 2011), 6.
5. For more on this subject, see: Fatima El-tayeb, *European Others: Queering Ethnicity in Postnational Europe* (Minneapolis: University of Minnesota Press, 2011) and Mayanthi L. Fernando, *The Republic Unsettled: Muslim French and the Contradictions of Secularism* (Durham, NC: Duke University Press, 2014).
6. While the term "Islamic sexualities" is used here to illustrate the specific construction of Orientalist Muslim male sexuality, this is by no means an endorsement of the frequently used, generalized term "Islamic sexualities". For more on this subject, see Félix Boggio Éwanjé-Épée and Stella Magliani-Belkacem, "The Empire of Sexuality: An Interview with Joseph Massad," *Jadaliyya*, March 5, 2013, available at http://www.jadaliyya.com/pages/index/10461/the-empire-of-sexuality_an-interview-with-joseph-m, accessed June 20, 2015; and Joseph A. Massad, *Islam in Liberalism* (Chicago: University of Chicago Press, 2015).
7. What I want to complicate here is the understanding that secularism is a universal and neutral norm, and not a by-product of Christian teleology of rights, governance and temporality and its compromise with modernity and secularism.
8. Mariija Nikolaeva Todorova, *Imagining the Balkans* (New York: Oxford University Press, 1997). See also Milica Bakić-Hayden, "Nesting Orientalisms: The Case of Former Yugoslavia," *Slavic Review* 54, no. 4 (1995); Larry Wolff, *Inventing Eastern Europe: The Map of Civilization on the Mind of the Enlightenment* (Stanford,

CA: Stanford University Press, 1994); and Vesna Goldsworthy, *Inventing Ruritania: The Imperialism of the Imagination* (New Haven, CT: Yale University Press, 1998).

9. See, for instance, Dušan I. Bjelić and Obrad Savić, *Balkan as Metaphor: between Globalization and Fragmentation* (Cambridge, MA: MIT Press, 2002); Nataša Kovačević, *Narrating Post/communism: Colonial Discourse and Europe's Borderline Civilization* (London: Routledge, 2008); and Vedrana Velickovic, "Belated Alliances? Tracing the Intersections between Postcolonialism and Postcommunism," *Journal of Postcolonial Writing* 48, no. 2 (2012): 164–75.

10. Bjelić and Savić, *Balkan as Metaphor*, 4.

11. See, for instance, Vaso Čubrilović, "Iseljavanje arnauta," in Robert Elsie, *Gathering Clouds: The Roots of Ethnic Cleansing in Kosovo and Macedonia* (Peja, Kosovo: Dukagjini Balkan Books, 2002), 97–130; and Bogdan Krizman, "Elaborat dra ive andrica o albaniji iz 1939, godine," *Časopis za suvremenu povijest* 9, no. 2 (1977): 77–89.

12. For more on this issue, see: "Preliminary Provisions for Agrarian Reform" (February 25, 1919); "The Decree on the Colonization of the Southern Regions" (September 24, 1920); "The Law on the Colonization of Southern Regions" (June 11, 1931); "The Law on Regulation of Agrarian Relations in the Former Regions of Southern Serbia and Montenegro" (December 1931); and "The Law on Settlement Southern Regions" (December 15, 1921). See, for instance, Vladan Jovanović, *Jugoslovenska država i Južna Srbija, 1918–1929: Makedonija, Sandžak, Kosovo i Metohija u Kraljevini SHS* (Beograd: INIS, 2002).

13. Claudia Schippert, "Implications of Queer Theory for the Study of Religion: Entering the Third Decade," *Religion and Gender* 1, no. 1 (2011): 66–84.

14. Janet R. Jakobsen and Ann Pellegrini, "Introduction," in *Secularisms* (Durham, NC: Duke University Press, 2008), 10.

15. Judith Halberstam, *The Queer Art of Failure* (Durham, NC: Duke University Press, 2011), 125–26.

16. Sara Ahmed, "Orientations: Toward a Queer Phenomenology," *GLQ: A Journal of Lesbian and Gay Studies* 12, no. 4 (2006): 554.

17. Ibid., 566.

18. See, for instance, Sushila Mesquita, Maria Katharina Wiedlack, and Katrin Lasthofer, *Import—Export—Transport: Queer Theory, Queer Critique and Activism in Motion* (Wien: Zaglossus, 2012).

19. Ismail Kadare, *Viti i mbrapshtë: Roman* (Tiranë: Onufri, 2009), 469.

20. Ibid.

21. Ibid., 476.

22. For more on the Bejtexhi Literature, see Robert Elsie, *History of Albanian Literature* (New York: Columbia University Press, 1995).

23. In colloquial Albanian, *dylber* refers to an attractive male who uses his beauty to seduce other men. See, for instance, Gjergj Filipaj, "Masculinity Representation in Kosovo Television Media" (Prishtina: Qendra Kosovare për Studime Gjinore [Kosovar Center for Gender Studies], 2009), 44.

24. Kadare, *Viti i mbrapshtë*, 436.

25. See, for instance, one of the most noted Albanian Bejtexhi poets, Nazim (Frakulla) Berati, who in the late 18th century, writes to his *dylber*: "I am Ferhad, you

are Shirin, You're a falcon, I'm a rock dove, I am Muslim, you are Islam, I'm the faithful, you are imam" (Muhamet Kycuku dhe Nezim Frakulla. *Erveheja dhe vjersha të tjera*, Albanian National Library, inventory Nr.000000486/drs.1.f.3, 1824, 127). For more on Nezim Berati, see Genciana Abazi-Egro, *Divani shqip* (Tiranë: Botimet Toena), 2009.

26. Ismail Kadare, *European Identity of Albanians* (*Identiteti evropian i shqiptarëve një "sprovë"*) (Tiranë: Onufri, 2006).

27. Ben Blushi, *Otello arapi i vlorës* (Tiranë: Toena, 2009).

28. Ben Blushi, *Të jetosh ne ishull* (Tiranë: Toena, 2008).

29. For more on Ali Pasha of Tepelena or Ali Pasha of Yannina (1740–1822), see K. E. Fleming, *The Muslim Bonaparte: Diplomacy and Orientalism in Ali Pasha's Greece* (Princeton, NJ: Princeton University Press, 1999).

30. Blushi, *Të jetosh në ishull*, 403.

31. See, for instance, Homi K. Bhabha, *The Location of Culture* (London: Routledge, 1994), 37.

32. In Kadare's works of both literature and literary criticism, the Catholic Albanian North represents a space not fully contaminated by the Ottoman Empire and fanatically engaged in preserving "Albanianess" in the ancient Greek tradition, and therefore proto-European. For more on Kadare's use of Greek mythology, see Morgan, "Greek Civilization," 16–23. See also Kadare, *European Identity of Albanians*.

33. Ismail Kadare, "Beauty Pageant for Men in the Accursed Mountains [Konkurs bukurie për burrat në bjeshkët e namuna]," in Ismail Kadare, *The Theft of the Royal Sleep* (*Vjedhja e gjumit mbretëror*) (Elbasan: Onufri), 117–55.

34. Duncan Fallowell, "Will the Real Mr Kadare Please Stand Up?" *Telegraph*, April 23, 2006.

35. Imamović, Ahmed, and Enver Pusca, *Go West*, directed by Ahmed Imamović (Charlottesville, VA: Water Bearer Films, 2008), DVD.

36. David Lazar, *The Body of Brooklyn* (Iowa City: University of Iowa Press, 2005), 12.

37. Todorova, *Imagining the Balkans*, 17.

38. Jennifer Coates, "Victims and Bystanders: Women in the Japanese War-Retro Film," *Media, War & Conflict* 6, no. 3 (2013): 234.

39. Judith Butler, *Gender Trouble* (New York: Routledge, 1990), 1.

40. See, for instance, Éwanjé-Épée and Magliani-Belkacem, "The Empire of Sexuality".

41. El-tayeb, *European Others*.

42. Talal Asad, *Formations of the Secular: Christianity, Islam, Modernity* (Stanford, CA: Stanford University Press, 2003), 165.

BIBLIOGRAPHY

Abazi-Egro, Genciana. *Divani shqip*. Tiranë: Botimet Toena, 2009.

Ahmed, Sara. "Orientations: Toward a Queer Phenomenology." *GLQ: A Journal of Lesbian and Gay Studies* 12, no. 4 (2006): 543–74.

Asad, Talal. *Formations of the Secular: Christianity, Islam, Modernity*. Stanford, CA: Stanford University Press, 2003.

Bakic-Hayden, Milica. "Nesting Orientalisms: The Case of Former Yugoslavia." *Slavic Review* 54, no. 4 (1995): 917–31.

Bhabha, Homi K. *The Location of Culture*. London: Routledge, 1994.

Bjelić, Dušan I., and Obrad Savić. *Balkan as Metaphor: Between Globalization and Fragmentation*. Cambridge, MA: MIT Press, 2002.

Blushi, Ben. *Otello arapi i vlorës*. Tiranë: Toena, 2009.

———. *Të jetosh ne ishull*. Tiranë: Toena, 2008.

Butler, Judith. *Gender Trouble*. New York: Routledge, 1990.

Coates, Jennifer. "Victims and Bystanders: Women in the Japanese War-Retro Film." *Media, War & Conflict* 6, no. 3 (2013): 233–48.

Čubrilović, Vaso. "Iseljavanje arnauta." In *Gathering Clouds: The Roots of Ethnic Cleansing in Kosovo and Macedonia*, edited by, Robert Elsie. 97–130. Peja, Kosovo: Dukagjini Balkan Books, 2002.

Dabashi, Hamid. *Brown Skin, White Masks*. London: Pluto Press, 2011, 6.

Elsie, Robert. *History of Albanian Literature*. New York: Columbia University Press, 1995.

El-Tayeb, Fatima. *European Others: Queering Ethnicity in Postnational Europe*. Minneapolis: University of Minnesota Press, 2011.

Éwanjé-Épée, Félix Boggio, and Stella Magliani-Belkacem. "The Empire of Sexuality: An Interview with Joseph Massad." *Jadaliyya*, March 5, 2013. http://www.jadaliyya.com/pages/index/10461/the-empire-of-sexuality_an-interview-with-joseph-m, accessed June 20, 2015

Fernando, Mayanthi L. *The Republic Unsettled: Muslim French and the Contradictions of Secularism*. Durham, NC: Duke University Press, 2014.

Filipaj, Gjergj. "Masculinity Representation in Kosovo Television Media." Prishtina: Qendra Kosovare për Studime Gjinore [Kosovar Center for Gender Studies], 2009.

Fleming, K. E. *The Muslim Bonaparte: Diplomacy and Orientalism in Ali Pasha's Greece*. Princeton, NJ: Princeton University Press, 1999.

Imamović, Ahmed, and Enver Pusca. *Go West*. DVD. Directed by Ahmed Imamović Charlottesville, VA: Water Bearer Films, 2008.

Goldsworthy, Vesna. *Inventing Ruritania: The Imperialism of the Imagination*. New Haven, CT: Yale University Press, 1998.

Halberstam, Judith. *The Queer Art of Failure*. Durham, NC: Duke University Press, 2011.

Jakobsen, Janet R., and Ann Pellegrini. "Introduction," in *Secularisms*, 1–35. Durham, NC: Duke University Press, 2008.

Jovanović, Vladan. *Jugoslovenska država i Južna Srbija, 1918–1929: Makedonija, Sandžak, Kosovo i Metohija u Kraljevini SHS*. Beograd: INIS, 2002.

Kadare, Ismail. "Beauty Pageant for Men in the Accursed Mountains [Konkurs bukurie për burrat në bjeshkët e namuna]." In *The Theft of the Royal Sleep* [*Vjedhja e gjumit mbretëror*], 117–55. Elbasan: Onufri, 1999.

———. *European Identity of Albanians* [*Identiteti evropian i shqiptarëve një "sprovë"*]. Tiranë: Onufri, 2006.

———. *Viti i mbrapshtë: Roman*. Tiranë: Onufri, 2009.

Kingdom of Serbs, Croats and Slovenes, "Preliminary Provisions for Agrarian Reform," February 25, 1919; "The Decree on the Colonization of the Southern Regions," September 24, 1920; "The Law on the Colonization of Southern Regions," June 11, 1931; "The Law on Regulation of Agrarian Relations in the Former Regions of Southern Serbia and Montenegro," December 1931; and "The Law on Settlement Southern Regions," December 15, 1921.

Kovačević, Nataša. *Narrating Post/communism: Colonial Discourse and Europe's Borderline Civilization.* London: Routledge, 2008.

Krizman, Bogdan. "Elaborat dra ive andrica o albaniji iz 1939, godine." *Časopis za suvremenu povijest* 9, no. 2 (1977): 77–89.

Lazar, David. *The Body of Brooklyn.* Iowa City: University of Iowa Press, 2005.

Massad, Joseph A. *Islam in Liberalism.* Chicago: University of Chicago Press, 2015.

Mesquita, Sushila, and Maria Katharina Wiedlack, and Katrin Lasthofer. *Import—Export—Transport: Queer Theory, Queer Critique and Activism in Motion.* Wien: Zaglossus, 2012.

Morgan, Peter. "Greek Civilization as a Theme of Dissidence in the Works of Ismail Kadare." *Modern Greek Studies (Australia and New Zealand),* 15 (2011): 16–23.

Morley, David, and Kevin Robins. *Spaces and Identity: Global Media, Electronic Landscapes and Cultural Boundaries.* London: Routledge, 1995.

Muhamet Kycuku dhe Nezim Frakulla. *Erveheja dhe vjersha të tjera.* Albanian National Library, inventory Nr.000000486/drs.1.f.3, 1824, 127.

Schippert, Claudia. "Implications of Queer Theory for the Study of Religion: Entering the Third Decade." *Religion and Gender* 1, no. 1 (2011): 66–84.

Todorova, Maria Nikolaeva. *Imagining the Balkans.* New York: Oxford University Press, 1997.

Velickovic, Vedrana. "Belated Alliances? Tracing the Intersections between Postcolonialism and Postcommunism." *Journal of Postcolonial Writing* 48, no. 2 (2012): 164–75.

Wolff, Larry. *Inventing Eastern Europe: The Map of Civilization on the Mind of the Enlightenment.* Stanford, CA: Stanford University Press, 1994.

Part V

ACCESSING

Chapter 8

Transitional Aesthetics

Apprehending Time between the Balkans and Europe in Contemporary Art Practices

Uroš Čvoro

This chapter examines how select artists from former Yugoslavia use temporality as a medium to apprehend certain political, social and cultural paradoxes of their experience of living between the 'Balkans' and 'Europe'. In the countries of former Yugoslavia, the last two decades have been defined by political and economic crises that have fused into a permanent condition. The explosion of the war in the 1990s (defined differently in different successor states, e.g. 'homeland war' in Croatia), marked the beginning of that period, and twenty years later the region still remains caught in the process of 'constant and unfinished transition' towards (alleged) European values of market economy and functional democracy, and away from the perceived 'Balkan barbarism'[1]. Artists Katarina Zdjelar and Tanja Ostojić, whose work I discuss below, respectively articulate cultural phenomena that are neither completely 'European' nor completely 'Balkan'. Using Walter Benjamin's concept of historical time, I argue that Zdjelar's and Ostojić's works interrogate a permanent state of temporal 'in-betweenness' that critically mirrors the permanent state of transitional uncertainty in the region: a state of being in-between alleged European (post)modernity and Balkan (pre)modernity[2]. In particular, I consider how transitional aesthetics in Zdjelar and Ostojić's practice – defined by their images of 'temporal clashes' – provides us a means for thinking through translation and migration. While there are other examples of transitional aesthetics in artistic practices in the region, I suggest that the way in which these artists engage with migration and language as key modes of the Balkans' transition to Europe provides an exemplary case study for considering the encounter between the two regions. While Zdjelar's work suggests translation to be an unfinished process of synchronizing temporalities (one temporality trying to 'catch up' with the other), Ostojić articulates migration not just as an experience of multiple and different temporalities, but as grounded in series of events that blur the distinction between artistic practice, civil status and political agency.

By way of a preamble, I find a useful articulation of the relevance of temporality for how we understand issues of trans-European migration and translation in Vladimir Nikolić's work *Death Anniversary* (2004) (figure 8.1), which stages an encounter between two forms of experience and aesthetics of time. For *Death Anniversary*, Nikolić employed a professional weeper and visited the gravesite of Marcel Duchamp in Rouen on the 36th anniversary of his death. The work features footage of Nikolić sombrely standing over the tombstone, while the weeper wails a mournful dirge about Duchamp's legacy. According to Nikolić, his intention was to take 'a true Balkan artist' to 'the wrong place'; to stage an encounter between the irreducible cultural difference of the shepherdess from Montenegro performing an obsolete social ritual and what Nikolić describes as 'the ultimate point of art universality', symbolized in the Godfather of European modernism[3]. *Death Anniversary* is ostensibly about European perception of art 'from the Balkans', and uses an idiosyncratic cultural form as a strategy to make visible the processes of identity branding engaged by an artist to gain visibility on the global art circuit.

Figure 8.1 Vladimir Nikolic, Death Anniversary, 2004, Video installation, 4'00". *Source*: Courtesy of the artist.

Nikolić performs the mourning ritual for Duchamp by staging an encounter between 'Europe' and 'Balkan', which have for several decades served as key framing devices for art from former Yugoslavia[4]. Yet *Death Anniversary* also complicates this encounter by reassembling the elements that constitute its historical, cultural and temporal parameters.

Death Anniversary positions the figure of the weeper as the 'Balkans readymade': an archaic cultural form symbolizing the historically frozen Balkans, yet one with a distinctly pragmatic element. In hiring a weeper, Nikolić outsources the affective labour of mourning for Duchamp (and for history), allowing him to remain preoccupied with the 'proper' art business of presenting cultural capital in order to gain recognition on an international stage. Nikolić thus treats the cultural specificity of his work not just as a way of making explicit the complex relationship between art history and constructions of identity, but also as a form of cultural remembrance. The performance of weeping is not only crucial for the sense in which *Death Anniversary* suggests repetition of history through ritual (commemorating death), but also to the way it repeats a particular sense of history through weeping as a medium: the weeper operates not just as a medium for repeating history, but is also a medium for articulating a culturally specific feeling of time. The flow of history is suspended in the performance, reflecting the external perceptions of the historically frozen Balkans. *Death Anniversary* thus creates a symbolic universe that 'Balkanises' Duchamp by framing him – and his legacy – through the cultural lens of the 'dark side' of civilization, still 'plagued' by the residue of history. Nikolić articulates a sense of temporality that is fixed 'in-between' Europe and the Balkans. This temporality is symptomatic of a much broader and as yet uncharacterized phenomenon in contemporary art practices emerging from former Yugoslavia, which I describe as 'transitional aesthetics'.

TRANSITIONAL AESTHETICS

The works I will discuss here raise the issue of the post-1989 phenomenon of transition as being, paradoxically, one of a state rather than a temporary phase. In one sense, the work by Zdjelar and Ostojić can be understood as attempts to capture an experience of time and temporality that represents their political reality. As artists from the countries of former Yugoslavia, they are interested in the way that post-socialist transition is experienced and represented in the region. The term 'transition' has been one of the key framing devices for the economic and political changes in former Yugoslavia in the last two decades. In May 1999, the international community set 'transition' as one of the explicit aims for the region's post-communist and post-conflict European integration process, known as Stabilization and Association

Process[5]. These macro policies created a sense of historical inevitability about the 'accession' from centralized economies, conflict and leftovers of imperial rule (Ottoman, Austro-Hungarian and Soviet) towards deregulated markets, stability and European democracy. In this designation of the term transition I draw on the work of scholars that articulate transitional economies not as 'bridges' between socialism and capitalism, but rather as permanent states of historical and temporal 'in-between' with their own dynamics and with the destination looking nothing like the contemporary Euro-American world[6]. These accounts position the temporal schema of transition as 'an expectation' located after the failure of modernity, but in the face of an uncertain present and future. Transition thus does not really operate as an event with clear temporal boundaries, defined by a starting and end point and framed by past and future, but rather as 'between time' with its own characteristics[7].

In this respect, I am interested in the ways in which Zdjelar and Ostojić establish transition as a displaced 'space of identity' defined by a temporality. While much has been said about the historical, symbolic and geopolitical contours of Balkans-EU relations, here I am interested in the temporal settings of this relation. This sense of 'not-quite-there' is also key to articulating my personal position in thinking though the temporal dimensions of history and collective identity in the Balkans. Since leaving my hometown Mostar in 1992, I lived in Croatia, Slovenia and Serbia, before finally moving to Australia. During every step of this journey, I occupied the position of 'not-quite-there' outsider who is continuously required to narrate their personal history of displacement: in Mostar, we were 'unpatriotic' Serbs who stayed in the city besieged by Serbian forces; in Croatia, we were Serbs; in Slovenia, we were Bosnian Southerners; and in Serbia, I was 'accused' of being a Muslim. In Australia, I became a refugee with a weird name and a foreign accent. This experience of a peripheral condition, occupied too by increasing numbers of displaced peoples, particularly those currently arriving into Europe, has informed my critical engagement with collective identity formations.

While primarily concerned with transition in this regard, the work of Ostojić and Zdjelar is also related to broader discussions of the relation of time to representations of cultural memory[8], ontological understanding of time in art[9] and critical postcolonial projects[10]. In exploring the ways in which transition can be articulated through art and images, Ostojić and Zdjelar's work should also be positioned in relation to recent considerations of time in art designated under the rubric of 'contemporary'[11]. However, here I am primarily interested in the way in which specific images or objects are used in art in order to show how different experiences of time fail to synchronize in the present. To develop this point, I turn to Walter Benjamin's formulation of the relation between images and time.

Benjamin's perspective on historical time operates through the visual logic of collage. His central temporal image – the dialectical image – is produced by juxtaposing historical objects that originate from different times. Elsewhere I discussed the potential of the dialectical image to serve as a critical framework for understanding the present[12], and here I want to emphasize the double temporality that underpins Benjamin's understanding of history: one that sees history as the linear progression, and the other that is the revolutionary freezing of history. Benjamin's rethinking of temporality emerges out of dialectical suspension of history between these two temporalities, and functions as the key principle of transitional aesthetics.

Here we can ask what does it mean to suggest that Benjamin's temporal montage is the key principle of transitional aesthetics? In one sense, it refers to the way in which Nikolić, Zdjelar and Ostojić create works that recall different historical times as a way to understand the present. In the context of the Balkans, this gesture is charged with emotional and political stakes, because during the collapse of Yugoslavia in the 1980s and early 1990s political leaders often used historical montages to inflame nationalism by conflating the past and future into the present[13]. Here we only need to recall the infamous 1989 Kosovo speech by Slobodan Milošević, which initiated the rise of Serb nationalism by conflating the Serb martyr mythology of the battle of Kosovo in 1389, nationalist grievances from 1989, and the future destiny of the so-called 'heavenly nation'. By contrast, in the works discussed here, historical montage is used not to construct a historical (or nationalist) teleology, but precisely to subvert it. The temporal montages created by Zdjelar and Ostojić articulate the way in which clashes between different experiences of time problematize the present.

Transitional aesthetics in Zdjelar and Ostojić's practices are about actively inhabiting the transitional time between Balkans and Europe. Both works capture the process of moving towards something (learning English language or getting a visa for the EU) where that something is the condition of desired inclusion. Both works are attempts to catch up with time of the centre: to be able to speak English and to be able to move freely across borders. Yet, in Zdjelar's work, this is also a montage between socialist temporality (the redundant labour of unemployed workers), and the temporality of global capital (iPod as a device that compresses music into a digital flow of thousands of files). In Ostojić's *Looking for a Husband with EU Passport* (2000–2005), the interplay between Balkan and European time-settings is revealed by performing the stages of the bureaucratic procedure of migration: filling out the paperwork, standing in line, marrying and crossing the border.

SHOUM

Katarina Zdjelar's video work *Shoum* (2009) captures the process and struggle through which linguistic expression is incorporated from an exterior source.

The work shows two middle-aged men from Belgrade transcribing the lyrics of the eighties hit song *Shout* (1985) by the English new wave band Tears for Fears (figure 8.2). As neither of the men understands English, *Shoum* shows their attempts to write down the lyrics while listening to the song on an iPod. The men translate the lyrics into phonetic English (the title of the work is taken from their pronunciation of the word 'shout'), treating the language as a code to be deciphered and taking turns in guessing the possible pronunciation of English language. The work ends with a black screen and the voice of one of the men singing his version of the lyrics.

Shoum recalls the strategies used by artist Candice Breitz in her video work *Karaoke* (2000), which features migrants struggling with English lyrics of famous pop songs. In her analysis of Breitz's work, Jill Bennett calls this struggle a 'bad performance', suggesting that people in the video resemble actors struggling with a script[14]. Like Breitz, Zdjelar makes the on-screen presence of the two protagonists in *Shoum* palpable in the struggle to read a script. The key difference however is that in *Shoum* the contemporary portable device for playing music (iPod) is contrasted with transcribing as a

Figure 8.2   Katarina Zdjelar, Shoum, 2009, still from video DVD, 7′00″, loop. *Source:* Courtesy of the artist and SpazioA, Pistoia.

traditional ('primitive') mode of capturing the script. Their labour of capturing language in this way slows down the experience of the song into series of stops and starts. As the video progresses, they show signs of frustration with the process. At one point, one of the men exasperatedly utters 'Fucking English!' in the face of his inability to pronounce the words or perform the language. As Zdjelar explains, *Shoum* is about the way that language (of the centre) is understood at the (isolated) periphery:

> Cut off from the lingua franca of a globalized world, with perseverance these two men create something of their own that lies between the foreign and the familiar[15].

In this sense, *Shoum* stages a process of the periphery attempting to catch up by learning the language of the West and the code of a popular song. This is highlighted by the juxtaposition of the then latest technology (iPod) with 'retro' popular culture (the song *Shout* dates from the 1980s). English language mediates between the two layers of temporality, yet the inability of the two men to understand English means they are also completely oblivious to the meaning of the cultural-temporal codes. This motif of language in *Shoum* references the discourse of migration where language proficiency is one of the key requirements for 'the right' orientation from the Balkans to the West as a space of desirable imagery and music[16]. This relation to time manifests itself in *Shoum* through the cultural 'otherness' of the men, demonstrated through their relative unfamiliarity with English as the global language, and their simultaneous attraction to the cultural and temporal codes of 'Western' popular culture. The two men never raise the question of the meaning of the words, or their translation into Serbian, remaining focused on learning the script. Zdjelar calls this 'para-poetics', describing the struggle with learning a new language that results in violating the linguistic rules of expression[17].

Zdjelar captures temporality in the process of translation. Or rather, she captures the clash between different temporalities in the process of incomplete and incorrect translation from the fast-moving (absent) centre of contemporary capital to the economically stumbling post-socialist periphery. In this sense, post-socialist translation is manifested in *Shoum* as 'a process of a never-finished synchronization among multiple temporalities'[18], which results in series of tensions between different understandings, experiences and representations of time. This point is developed by Zdjelar, but originates in the performance that inspired her work.

Shoum was inspired by a performance from 2008 *Bulgarian Idol* in which candidate Valentina Hassan 'misunderstood' English while learning to sing Mariah Carey's pop-hit *Without You* (1993). With no knowledge of English, Hassan learned the lyrics mimetically by repeatedly listening to the song. As result, her phonetic pronunciation dislocated the linguistic signifiers of English, rendering it sound poetry. The chorus line 'I can't live if living is without you, I can't live anymore' became 'Ken lee tu libu dibu douchoo, ken lee meju more', turning the performance into a humorous and playful rearrangement of the English language. Since it first aired on television, the footage of Hassan's audition went viral online, and her consequent Internet celebrity status brought her back for a second performance of 'Ken Lee' on a Bulgarian talk show.

Hassan's popularity ostensibly stems from the comedic effect of the audition, her pronunciation of English and limited vocal skills, and in particular the contrast between her earnestness and obliviousness. When asked by one of the panel judges 'What language was that?', she replies with an assured 'English'. Hassan struggles with language in the same way that the protagonists of *Shoum* do. Both capture the process of incorporating language from an exterior space, and their mental and bodily struggle to take command of that language as a tool for identification. The enjoyment (or discomfort) of watching this struggle acts as a powerful reminder of the cruel voyeurism inherent to contemporary popular culture that largely mirrors larger geopolitical relations. Yet crucially, both Hassan's performance and *Shoum* also highlight the way in which this process connects to a specific history.

Hassan's performance and *Shoum* evoke the long-standing association of post-socialism in Eastern European societies with an almost slavish embrace of Western popular culture[19]. Since the early 1980s, the immense popularity of Western culture in post-socialist societies operates as the sphere that replaces the imposed ideology of socialism, offering instead the rhetoric of individualism and freedom. In this context, the influx of popular culture finds its equivalent in the influx of economic deregulation and privatization, raising questions about the way in which transition and accession to EU translates into local contexts. In this sense, the para-poetics of the English language in *Shoum* becomes a reflection of broader political misunderstandings in recent years. Telling examples here are the two main responses to the post-2008 implosion of the Greek economy. On the one side was the German version that blamed 'Greek laziness', while on the other was the Greek version of 'German financial neo-imperialism'. Regardless of which version we agree with, in an important sense they represent the inability of each side to translate the demands of the other side, or the inability of both sides to fully grasp and incorporate the language of global capital.

Yet Zdjelar's positioning of the two men as the interpreters of English raises another question in terms of our understanding of their socio-economic and cultural identity. Even though the men are never fully visible – aside from occasional glimpses – their voices and hands play a central part in the work. The rough texture of their hands is crucial here because it points to a class identity: they are hands of the working class worn by years of physical labour.

Their voice is even more clearly a marker of a socio-economic identity: the off-key singing that concludes the work. The 'bad performance' is the short circuit between the historical time of *Shoum* and the 'real' time of the present. The discomfort felt at the sound of the bad performance is the recognition that these men are from a generation being left behind in time. In this sense, *Shoum* is also about the voice of the Yugoslav working class, and Ken Lee is the voice of their children as the new underclass. Here the meaning of *Shoum* emerges in the interplay between local conceptions of taste and cultural identity translated into a series of oppositions that map onto transition: cosmopolitan–primitive, urban–rural, Europe–Balkans, superior–inferior.

This interplay between notions of cultural taste maps on to the rift between different types of music as key axes of sociocultural identity, encapsulated in the question, 'What music do you listen to?' As Ljerka Vidic Rasmussen argues following Pierre Bourdieu, in the post-Yugoslav space, enjoying a particular song 'is not a culturally inconsequential choice; it is an indication of musical preference that is tied to cultural affinity and one's own sociocultural identity'[20]. In this respect, during the 1980s, when the song *Shout* was released, one of key cultural lines of demarcation in Yugoslavia was carved out between the urban, cosmopolitan rock and new wave audience and the folk music audience. This division marked the sociocultural identity between the folk audience as generally from lower or working class families with limited education, and the rock/punk/new wave audience as the culturally sophisticated middle class. This sociocultural differentiation between the working class and the cultural intelligentsia in Yugoslavia is expressed in *Shoum* through the men's lack of familiarity with both the song and with the English language. Their inability to move beyond phonetic mimicry of the lyrics is a marker of a class identity, of the inability to participate in the global language of popular culture. Yet, it is in this very act that they undermine the legitimacy of that language to function as the lingua franca.

Zdjelar identifies the work of Yugoslav artist Mladen Stilinovic *An artist who cannot speak English is no artist* (1994–1996) as a key reference point for her understanding of the power dynamics implicit in language. Stilinovic's work operates in the tradition of 1970s conceptual art, using a slogan on a flag to capture a politically loaded sentiment. The directness of his work captures the essence of Zdjelar's work: cultural difference as the manifestation of institutional exclusion of former Eastern Bloc artists from the Western art business and art market. Like Stilinovic, Zdjelar positions the knowledge of the English language as a precondition for an individual's functioning in the new international art economy: being 'of one's time'. Both highlight the process of incorporating English language from an exterior source, and the way in which this process highlights the relevance of language of an unreachable temporal and spatial horizon of the West.

LOOKING FOR A HUSBAND WITH EU PASSPORT

Tanja Ostojić's *Looking for a Husband with EU Passport* (2000–2005) incorporates photography, video, installation, performance and online interaction into a powerful critique of the exploitative gender and racial politics implicit in EU migration laws. Since the establishment of the Schengen Area in 1995, Continental Europe has been split into two zones, the internal member state zone that permits mobility and another that restricts movement. As Ostojić explains, her work explicitly addresses the inequalities created by this arrangement:

> In order to claim my own rights, which I have been deprived of by current EU laws, I explicitly applied the strategy of tricking the law . . . to gain the right to move freely and live and work in diverse locations[21].

By marrying 'for papers' in *Looking for a Husband with EU Passport*, Ostojić intentionally transgresses the rules of migration and exploits the legal institution of marriage in order to gain economic independence and geographic mobility. In this sense, Ostojić's work is part of a broader artistic response to Europe's exclusionary migration policies, which uses 'ethnographic procedures and documentary tactics to expose the living conditions' and 'economic and political structures that produce those conditions'[22].

Ostojić's work proceeds by staging a series of events that cohere into a narrative as they are understood though the bureaucratic process of migration. Her work follows a temporal logic 'according to which the basis of identity and meaning shift from territorial shapes to temporal situations'[23]. *Looking for a Husband with EU Passport* uses the process of migration as the material to create series of events that remain 'in-between' the Balkans and Europe[24]. Ostojić creates a temporal montage out of migration, by layering its multiple temporalities into an (artistic) event of the performance.

This layering of multiple temporalities is already apparent in a personal advertisement released online and in art magazines by Ostojić in 2000 announcing her search for a husband, featuring a confrontational photograph of her naked, head and body shaved. The photograph is staged as an event that follows conventions of a 24-hour news cycle media narrative. It has a captivating story of an individual openly using the legal institution of marriage to transgress the rules of migration and gain economic independence and geographic mobility. Ostojić isolates her body in the photograph, where it becomes the social body, the ground from which a series of larger relationships are established (gender and the media complex, gender and migration, sex trade in migration)[25]. It operates as a dialectical image by bringing together seemingly oppositional meanings: seduction and violence; love and pragmatism; advertising and concentration camp; desperation and empowerment. It also operates as what Mieke Bal calls a 'sticky image', by layering two temporalities of historical time and real time[26]. Ostojić compresses intentionally oppositional meanings into the image, forcing us to think through the connections and slowing down our experience of time in the image. This image is then expanded into a larger story – and a larger series of events – involving documented correspondence with potential suitors, meeting the suitable candidate Klemens G. in Belgrade in 2001 in a public event that was also broadcast online, and marrying in front of two witnesses (who wrote an article about the wedding for an exhibition catalogue). Ostojić expands the contradictions contained in the image as a framework within which to deploy herself within the legal (and art) system. After receiving a visa, she moved to Dusseldorf where she lived for three years, and in 2005 Ostojić divorced and organized a 'Divorce Party' in a Berlin gallery.

Ostojić uses laws and legal institutions as the material of her work in order to repurpose the way in which they operate. The work acts as a series of events where everyday life intersects with administrative procedures[27]. Ostojić creates a temporal dialectic between events and their narration through bureaucracy and documentation. *Looking for a Husband with EU Passport* is part of Ostojić's *Crossing Borders Series* that features earlier works about getting into the EU. In *Illegal Border Crossing* (2000) Ostojić illegally entered Austria from Slovenia, which was not in the Schengen Area at that time. A few months later in *Waiting for a Visa* (2000), Ostojić unsuccessfully tried to apply for Austrian visa by queuing for six hours in front of the Austrian consulate in Belgrade. *Looking for a Husband* was the third 'action' in the series. Ostojić's success in getting into the EU and her continuing struggles with gaining permanent residence for herself and her family mean that in some ways the work is ongoing.

In this sense, the work functions less as a performance than a staged event with no clear temporal boundaries. Such temporalization, which singles out certain moments, produces an alternative chronology. Ostojić does not so much stage events as much as 'shows' them through the constellation of oppositional elements built into the twin processes of migration: the EU and fortress 'Europa', mobility and stasis, humanitarianism and exploitation. Thus, every step of the process is complicated and problematized by its reverse; these events are not staged, but rather simply 'collide' with her daily life. It is difficult to distinguish between the two: she registers events not only as they actually happen, but also as they realign with her life.

Looking for a Husband with EU Passport is relevant in the context of this book as a shift in the understanding of the institutional nexus that regulates everyday life in the Balkans. Starting from a position of cynical distance towards institutions, Ostojić shifts into a new model of artistic practice:

improvisational pragmatism. In *Illegal Border Crossing*, the meaning of the work is framed by the pragmatic, yet dangerous, solution to her geographic immobility. In illegally crossing the border, Ostojić, like so many migrants, successfully crosses the border, but foregoes all legal rights in doing so. *Waiting for a Visa* documents Ostojić's participation in an exercise of following protocol. Her act of queuing was predestined to fail precisely because she was a private citizen with no symbolic, political or cultural capital. The work was intended to show the cynicism and failure of the process: the impossibility of gaining access to the Austrian consulate without the right connections. The situation of *Waiting for a Visa* was framed by Ostojić's institutional invisibility and geographic immobility of standing in one spot for hours, recalling the trope of spatial and temporal immobility of the Balkans in relation to the EU.

In *Looking for a Husband with EU Passport* Ostojić becomes an entrepreneur of the self who strategically manipulates her identity to collapse her human capital into artistic and cultural capital. Her subjectivity shifts from being an outsider unsuccessfully waiting for a visa, 'bare life' illegally crossing the border, to becoming an artist that actively inhabits and manipulates the administrative process. Ostojić gets the visa by soliciting an artist husband and stating that she and Klemens G. met on an arts project. This is crucial because in doing so, Ostojić massages the information to suit the requirements of the visa application. She crosses the border by turning her art labour into variable capital. As Peter Osbourne argues,

> Art is a kind of passport. In the new transnational spaces, it figures a market utopia of free movement, while in actuality it embodies the contradiction of the mediation of this movement by capital[28].

In this sense, Ostojić's work is about the way in which the international positioning of the artist dictated by the politics of identity is already inscribed into the contemporary art system. This raises the question of participation of artists from the periphery 'catching up' and participating in international art events. In the decade since the start of transition, the question of artists designated with the prefix 'from' on the international scene has been crucial in understanding practices from former Yugoslavia. Serbian art historian Miško Šuvaković uses the term 'Soros realism' to describe the emergence of a style of artworks and exhibitions such as *Manifesta*, which created a specific type of a work of art that was 'political' within the acceptable boundaries of the EU model of pluralism and multiculturalism. According to Šuvaković, the activities of the Soros network and exhibitions such as *Manifesta* created an international 'second division' of art that acts as the feeder body of young talent for the international art circuit without endangering the art system[29]. In this respect, Ostojić's work aligns with other younger artists from former

Yugoslavia that deals with the politics of being labelled as an artist 'from the Balkans'. Here I should mention works such as *Attack* painting series by Mladen Miljanović, which uses the language of military maps to plan how to get accepted into prestigious exhibitions in European art centres. Also, Šejla Kamerić's work *EU/OTHERS* for *Manifesta 3* in Slovenia installed on the Tromostovlje bridge in the centre of Ljubljana, used border-crossing signs to differentiate EU passport holders from 'others'. *EU/OTHERS* articulates the dynamic of keeping borders between Europe and Balkans by positioning Slovenia as the 'last outpost of Europe' at that point. What the work of these artists attempts is to make visible the Balkans-EU relation in the physical and symbolic spaces where they intersect, their usual invisibility and regulatory power.

ONGOING TRANSITION

The experience of transition is in large part an attempt to address the promise of the future while attempting to deal with the past that is constantly being called upon to show what is being left behind. In this respect, Zdjelar and Ostojić may be regarded as engendering a language of 'in-between' time, by making visible fragments of the past that problematize this act of leaving the past behind. By making visible the temporality (and historicity) of relevant events and media images, they capture some of the political reality that surrounds them, and the ways in which this political reality manifests itself in social relations. Two and a half decades after the start of transition of former Yugoslav countries from socialism into capitalism, most of the successor states find themselves in similar political and economic positions. While the member states Slovenia (2004) and Croatia (2013) have been included but relegated to the economic and political periphery of the EU, non-member states Bosnia and Herzegovina, Montenegro, Serbia and Macedonia remain caught in the perpetual cycle of 'in-betweenness'. Artistic strategies articulated here as transitional aesthetics apprehend this situation by highlighting the intrinsic relationship between the political pragmatics driving the neoliberal austerity measures enforced by the EU, and nationalism as the driver of the resistance to them. As Tanja Petrović argues in her account of post-1999 public discourses (following the establishment of the Stabilization and Association Process in the Balkans), rather than offering an alternative to nationalist discourses from the 1990s, the EU enlargement processes support and legitimize them: by re-emphasizing the need for clear territorial demarcation, by seeking to establish a clear ethnic majority (and manageable minorities) and by re-writing the past (erasing the socialist heritage)[30]. Zdjelar and Ostojić in different ways articulate positions that reject both Europe and the Balkans as equally inadequate symbolic destinations: Western Europe and its neoliberal market is offered as a way to 'improve' the 'primitive' and 'lazy' Balkans, whereas the impassioned 'Balkanism' and its 'politically correct' version of nationalism emerge as the only remaining antidote to rampant globalization. The perceived absence of functional alternatives is understood by these artists as manifesting that transition is a crisis with no conceivable end point and permanent delay of resolution.

Zdjelar and Ostojić each attempt in different ways to address this assumed absence of alternatives by encouraging the experience of their work as 'in-between'. This critical strategy of capturing an 'in-between' temporality, of being neither-present-nor-past, exhibits a powerful homology to strategies that people in the Balkans have been using to come to terms with the lived realities of transition. Both artists attend to the ways in which transition is experienced and negotiated at the level of the everyday (the accessibility of 'Western' popular culture; opening and closing of borders). Rather than offering us images of broken narratives of fragmented temporalities, Zdjelar and Ostojić mediate transition in terms of everyday perception and strategies. As such, the meaning of their works, although very clearly located in the present socio-political predicament of the Balkans, is not entirely premised on their geographical and historical condition. In this sense, further studies can consider more broadly the ways in which transitional aesthetics can help us to articulate how art operates in other regions of Europe affected by prolonged instability. The Balkans are one key site of ongoing transition, but they are certainly not the only one in Europe. In the post-1989 Balkans, characterized by unstable economies, recurring corruption, rampant social inequalities, revived nationalism, historical revisionism and attempted normalization of fascism, artistic articulation of the present as unfinished synchronization among multiple temporalities means refusing transition to the EU as the only option. It means daring to imagine that Balkan history can lead to something better.

NOTES

1. Rastko Močnik, "Social Change in the Balkans," *Eurozine*, 2003, http://www.eurozine.com/articles/2003–03-20-mocnik-en.html, accessed January 12, 2016. For wider political and social considerations of the post-1989 transition in the Balkans, see also Igor Štiks and Srećko Horvat, *Welcome to the Desert of Post-Socialism* (London: Verso, 2015).

2. See also chapter 11 in this volume.

3. Vladimir Nikolić, "Death Anniversary", 2007, http://www.vladimir-nikolic.com/foto/about%20death%20anniversary.pdf, accessed January 12, 2016.

4. For examples, see international exhibitions such as 'Future's in the Balkans' (2003), 'In the Gorges of the Balkans' (2003), and 'In Search of Balkania' (2002).

5. Leonard J. Cohen and John R. Lampe, *Embracing Democracy in the Western Balkans: From Postconflict Struggles toward European Integration* (Baltimore: The Johns Hopkins University Press, 2011), 81.

6. Katherine Verdery, *What Was Socialism and What Comes Next* (Princeton: Princeton University Press, 1996); Susan Buck-Morss, "The Post-Soviet Condition," in *East Art Map*, ed., Irwin (London: Afterall, 2006), 494–99.

7. Jill Bennett, *Practical Aesthetics* (London: I.B. Tauris, 2012), 78.

8. Andreas Huyssen, *Present Pasts* (Stanford: Stanford University Press, 2000).

9. Peter Osbourne, *Anywhere or Not at All* (London: Verso, 2013).

10. Okwui Ewenzor, "The Postcolonial Constellation: Contemporary Art in a State of Permanent Transition," *Research in African Literatures* 34, no. 4 (2003): 57–82.

11. Terry Smith, *What Is Contemporary Art?* (Chicago: Chicago University Press, 2009).

12. Uroš Čvoro, "Dialectical Image Today," *Continuum* 22, no. 1 (2008): 89–98.

13. Ilana Bet-El, "Unimagined Communities: The Power of Memory and the Conflict in the Former Yugoslavia," in *Memory and Power in Post-war Europe: Studies in the Presence of the Past*, ed., Jan-Werner Müller (Cambridge: Cambridge University Press, 2002), 206–22, 210.

14. Bennett, *Practical Aesthetics*, 115.

15. Katarina Zdjelar, "Shoum," http://katarinazdjelar.net/shoum, accessed January 12, 2016.

16. My thanks to Zlatan Krajina for pointing this out.

17. Katarina Zdjelar, *But If You Take My Voice, What Will Be Left to Me?* (The Serbian Pavillion at the 53rd Biennale di Venezia, 2009), 76.

18. Anita Starosta, "Perverse Tongues, Post-Socialist Translations," *Boundary 2*, no. (2014): 203–27, 205.

19. On the use of 'kitsch' as a marker of self-perceived cultural and social inferiority, see chapter 4 in this volume.

20. Ljerka Vidic Rasmussen, "From Source to Commodity: Newly-Composed Folk Music of Yugoslavia," *Popular Music* 14, no. 2 (1995): 241–56, 251.

21. Tanja Ostojić, "Crossing Borders: Development of Different Artistic Strategies," in *Integration Impossible? The Politics of Migration in the Artwork of Tanja Ostojić* (Berlin: Argosbooks, 2009), 161–71, 163.

22. T.J. Demos, *The Migrant Image* (North Carolina: Duke University Press, 2013), 15.

23. Lane Relyea, *Your Everyday Art World* (London: Verso, 2013), 33.

24. For a discussion of the strategic use of 'in between' in Ostojić's practice, see Suzana Milevska, "Balkan Subjectivity as Neither," *Third Text* 21, no. 2 (2007): 181–88. See also chapter 3 in this volume.

25. On the connection between Islam and sexuality in discussions of 'European identity,' see chapter 7 in this volume.

26. Mieke Bal, "Sticky Images: The Foreshortening of Time in an Art of Duration," in *Time and Image*, ed. Carolyn Bailey Gill (Manchester: Manchester University Press, 2000), 79–99, 80.

27. On the intersection between migration, mobility and everyday life, see chapter 10 in this volume.

28. Osbourne, *Anywhere or Not at All*, 27.
29. Miško Šuvaković, "The Ideology of Exhibition: On the Ideologies of Manifesta," (Ljubljana: *Platorma SCCA*, 2002).
30. Tanja Petrović, *Yuropa: Jugoslovensko nasledje i politike buducnosti u Postjugoslovenskim Drustvima* (Beograd: Fabrika Knjiga, 2012), 189.

BIBLIOGRAPHY

Bal, Mieke "Sticky Images: The Foreshortening of Time in an Art of Duration." In *Time and Image*, edited by Carolyn Bailey Gill, 79–99. Manchester: Manchester University Press, 2000.

Bennett, Jill. *Practical Aesthetics*. London: I.B. Tauris, 2012.

Bet El, Ilana "Unimagined communities: the power of memory and the conflict in the former Yugoslavia." in *Memory and Power in Post-War Europe: Studies in the Presence of the Past*, edited by Jan-Werner Müller, 206–22. Cambridge: Cambridge University Press, 2002.

Buck-Morss, Susan. "The Post-Soviet Condition." In *East Art Map*, edited by Irwin, 494–99. London: Afterall, 2006.

Cohen, Leonard J. and Lampe, John R. *Embracing Democracy in the Western Balkans: From Postconflict Struggles toward European Integration*. Baltimore: The Johns Hopkins University Press, 2011.

Čvoro, Uroš. "Dialectical Image Today," *Continuum* 22, no. 1 (2008): 89–98.

Demos, T.J. *The Migrant Image*. North Carolina: Duke University Press, 2013.

Enwezor, Okwui. "The Postcolonial Constellation: Contemporary Art in a State of Permanent Transition." *Research in African Literatures* 34, no. 4 (2003): 57–82.

Huyssen, Andreas. *Present Pasts*. Stanford: Stanford University Press, 2000.

Milevska, Suzana. "Balkan Subjectivity as Neither." *Third Text* 21, no. 2 (2007): 181–88.

Močnik, Rastko. "Social Change in the Balkans." *Eurozine*, 2003. http://www.eurozine.com/articles/2003–03-20-mocnik-en.html, accessed January 12, 2016.

Nikolić, Vladimir. "Death Anniversary." 2007. http://www.vladimir-nikolic.com/foto/about%20death%20anniversary.pdf, accessed January 12, 2016.

Osbourne, Peter. *Anywhere or not at All*. London: Verso, 2013.

Ostojić, Tanja. "Crossing Borders: Development of Different Artistic Strategies." In *Integration Impossible? The Politics of Migration in the Artwork of Tanja Ostojić*, 161–71. Berlin: Argosbooks, 2009.

Petrović, Tanja. *Yuropa: Jugoslovensko nasledje I politike buducnosti u Postjugoslovenskim Drustvima*. Beograd: Fabrika Knjiga, 2012.

Relyea, Lane. *Your Everyday Art World*. London: Verso, 2013.

Starosta, Anita. "Perverse Tongues, Post-Socialist Translations," *Boundary 2* 41, no. 1 (2014): 203–27.

Smith, Terry. *What Is Contemporary Art?* Chicago: Chicago University Press, 2009.

Štiks, Igor and Horvat, Srećko. *Welcome to the Desert of Post-Socialism*. London: Verso, 2015.

Šuvaković, Miško. "The Ideology of Exhibition: On the Ideologies of Manifesta." Ljubljana: *Platorma SCCA*, 2002.

Verdery, Catherine. *What Was Socialism and What Comes Next.* Princeton: Princeton University Press, 1996.

Vidić Rasmussen, Ljerka. "From Source to Commodity: Newly-Composed Folk Music of Yugoslavia." *Popular Music* 14, no. 2 (1995): 241–56.

Zdjelar, Katarina. *But If You Take My Voice, What Will Be Left To Me?* The Serbian Pavillion at the 53rd Biennale di Venezia, 2009.

Zdjelar, Katarina. "Shoum." 2009. http://katarinazdjelar.net/shoum

Chapter 9

How We Survived Europe (and Never Laughed)

The Role of Liberal-Humanitarian Utopia in Croatia's Accession to the EU

Orlanda Obad

Croatia joining the European Union (EU) symbolically signalled the end of the country's long period of transition. Though arguably still incomplete[1], this long journey from socialism (starting with the dissolution of Yugoslavia in 1991) to the supposedly acceptable performances of capitalism and liberal democracy (the adoption of which formed the EU's basic criterion for granting the permission of "entry") lasted more than two decades. The sole process of joining the EU – if counted from the country's signing of the Stabilization and Association Agreement in 2001 to the accession in 2013 – took more than a decade. During those years of supervised adjustment to EU rules and regulations, the initial public excitement about the "idea" of EU (the club of the "advanced" societies) was replaced by indifference and even annoyance[2]. In some instances, the process confronted Croatian society with issues that were contested and polarizing, such as the processing of war crimes or privatization of shipyards.

Nevertheless, early on in the process, in the early 1990s, major political parties had reached a wide consensus in support of the EU, and opposing the accession was, all until the very end of the process, relegated to marginal voices on both ends of the political spectrum[3]. The formal "negotiation" process on the more specific terms of accession (such as agricultural quotas), which precedes any EU entry, was kept rather closed to the Croatian public, and some commentators asserted that the lack of access to information regarding the course of negotiations contributed to the "alienation of Croatian citizens from the EU, its goals, values and processes"[4]. Indeed, for the most part of the process, EU accession was discussed on a very broad level of nationwide commitment and choosing the right side, rather than an intelligible political process of deliberation on an ongoing transformation

("Europeanization") of the country with palpable legal, economic and political consequences. Moreover, predicting the date of accession remained a prominent fixture of the media coverage throughout the process[5].

This lack of Croatian citizens' interest was reflected in the low (and, lowest in the EU) voters' turnout in the referendum on the EU accession held in January 2012. As Dejan Jović asserts, public debates held in the period preceding the referendum on the EU accession were framed in a manner that incited the euro-sceptical voters to become *euro-indifferent*[6], that is, uninterested in the issues related to the EU and the country's accession. The resulting possibility of an unsuccessful referendum was circumvented (rather than confronted) by such last-minute manoeuvres as the loosening of the constitutional requirement of minimal voter turnout (needed for the referendum to be valid)[7].

But in order to understand the axis around which most of the arguments related to the EU revolved throughout this process – and often from differing and opposed political perspectives – I believe one first has to switch the discursive register and enter the realm of "Europe" understood as "an imaginary figure that remains deeply embedded in *clichéd and shorthand forms* in some everyday habits of thought"[8]. Then it is important to listen to the seemingly unrelated, non-elite and non-political, less carefully articulated and therefore less discernible, messy everyday accounts in Croatian buses, small talk on radio stations and anonymous comments posted below news articles on the internet. These conversations involved accounts of "how things are done in the advanced Western European countries"; of what never would have happened "if this were a *real* country and a *serious* government"; of the illogical or absurd incidents – such as inefficient bureaucracy and corruption – that could happen "only here and nowhere else", of the negatively "Balkan", "socialist", "rural" and "backward" culture and mentality which prevented the positive "development" of the country.

These *deliberately naïve* and utopian narratives of progress and Europeanness were most often used by the so-called common people in order to express frustration with the flaws of the state on various levels but also with its lack of commitment to deliberation, transparency and rule of law. Such narratives were not necessarily opposed to euro-scepticism, for it was, of course, possible to be sceptical towards the EU and still claim the positive notions of Europeanness. Or, rather, project the negative notions towards the neighbouring, mostly South-eastern European countries and also towards various segments of the country's population, such as representatives of "lower classes", peasants or various minorities. These projections were about an underlying, cultural sense of lacking, which may best be articulated through a paraphrase of a popular Croatian writer and columnist: an unspoken and yet powerful assumption that "Europe" is simply "*better than we are people*"[9]. If this incessant sense of lacking is placed at the centre of analysis, as Alexander Kiossev did in his "Notes on the Self-colonising Cultures"[10], one encounters traces of historical discursive structures echoed in the contemporary political space. According to Kiossev, there are certain forms of rationalization through which "peripheral" cultures approach their traumatic and long-standing inferiority complex and second-rate status[11]. One such form of rationalization is, as Kiossev asserts, *Westernization or Europeanization*, which confronts this supposed cultural lack eagerly and energetically, as an "'athletic' competition" in which "'civilizational' drop-back could be compensated for by 'enlightened' sprinting"[12]. *Nativism*, on the other hand, is its opposite: it responds to the same trauma with an introverted tactic of digging deep to uncover the yet-unspoiled, "'authentic substance' of the nation", which "struggles against any new corrupting influences", and which also threatens to inspire "the most vehement nationalistic ideologies and dangerous sacralizations of the 'native'"[13]. It, thus, seems possible to acknowledge Eurocentric narratives of progress and attempt to diminish the perceived civilizational delay, and to invalidate the humiliating Western gaze or declare its values distorted and false. It is even possible to reverse the inherent binary oppositions (West-East/civility-barbarity) by celebrating and cherishing what this opposition implies as uncivilized or boorish[14]. Though the tactics may vary, they all work around the basic structure of inequality between European regions, rather than dismantling its foundations.

In this chapter[15], I examine various discursive mechanisms related to *gradations of Europeanness*[16] that operated throughout the process of Croatian accession to the EU. I believe these mechanisms function across at least two mutually intertwined axes. The first one is horizontal in its direction and cartographic in its tendency to deploy the "view from the above". This mechanism ascribes civility and Europeanness to a varying degree across various parts of the continent, and although its direction is not straightforward and immutable, and is related to a number of variable determinants, it may be roughly described as descending from the (North)West towards peripheries and semi-peripheries, one of the most pronounced being placed in the (South) Eastern part of the continent – the Balkans.

The formation of this discursive axis has thus far been well-researched and documented across various historical periods and also in relation to different parts of Europe[17]. This body of research serves well to explain the discursive logics as to why a country such as Croatia, for example, would be considered by some to be "less European" than France or Sweden, but still more so than Bulgaria or Albania. However, there is another important axis, which often remains less examined *within* critical approaches to continental symbolic geographies. Namely, some of the same *differences* that are turned into *inequalities* on the horizontal axis[18] are used in vertical direction, within societies, as well. This axis uses notions related to Europeanness in order to (re)produce hierarchies and exercise exclusions/ expulsions of various segments of the population. In this chapter, I draw upon my long-term research into Croatian's perceptions of the EU in an attempt to trace the intertwining of these two axes, with a particular focus on vertical, class-related divisions.

I focus my analysis on three separate sets of interviews I conducted throughout this research. First, the interviews with the so-called Croatian negotiators with the EU, which were conducted in the middle of the nego-tiating process, at the end of 2007 and in the first half of 2008. Second, the interviews with the so-called agricultural entrepreneurs, who were successful in applying to the EU pre-accession funds for agriculture, conducted in the first half of 2010. And finally, my most recent and ongoing research with EU officials from Croatia, who have been permanently employed in various EU institutions since the country's joining the EU in 2013.

THE BALKANS, EUROPE
AND THE LIBERAL-HUMANITARIAN EUTOPIA

Among the various attempts to analyse and name discourses that grade Europeanness, a particularly apt and theoretically grounded is Attila Melegh's notion of civilizational slope or East-West slope, in which, as the author asserts, political processes such as EU enlargement are embedded. Civilizational slope arranges symbolic geography of the continent "as a descending slope of regional cultures" on which various notions associated with "civilization" gradually diminish "toward the 'East'" and the South[19].

The discursive formation of civilizational slope is not permanent or immutable. As Attila Melegh asserted, after the Second World War and until the late 1970s, European countries, both in the East and in the West, were submerged in the "discourse of rival modernities" which focused on "hard facts" and "reality": statistical data, literacy rates, industrialization, economic production and competition between the two blocs[20]. By the 1980s an impor-tant discursive shift was noted: along with the decline of the socialist system, various Eastern European dissidents began to point to its growing discursive hollowness, while in some countries political discussions of reforms were gradually replaced by debates on how to adjust the state system to the "West", understood as the prime normative role model[21]. This discursive formation, which Melegh names civilizational slope or East-West slope, (re)introduced the notion of gradually diminishing, fading Europeanness[22]. The important role of *transitional zone* between "proper" West and East was relegated to

Central Europe, a highly poeticized region whose borders were prone to incessant shifting and reshaping.

The workings of the civilizational slope continued in the countries of Central and Eastern Europe after the fall of the Berlin wall in 1989 and throughout the decades of post-socialist "transition". Its mechanisms were still discernible in various forms of EU-related narratives in Croatia during the accession, in which the country's alleged Central European identity, together with its Habsburg legacy, was widely held as useful in contrasting the disputed Balkan identity. To demonstrate the strategic status of this linkage, I quote from a typical response I retrieved in an interview I conducted with a negotiator with the EU[23], in which the symbolic significance of EU accession for Croatia was discussed:

> We always try to emphasize that we are part of Central Europe, that we are part of that Western culture and civilization, that we are significant and important – which we are – and it [the EU entry] will be the icing on the cake, I would say. . . . We deserve to be in the Union because we are like that already, and we will be, in a few years, even better.

The greater part of my interviews with negotiators in turn revolved around rather technical details of the process. Some of my interviewees, for example, expressed satisfaction with their cooperation with relevant Croatian state institutions. Others admitted to facing significant problems in convincing various representatives in Croatian institutions involved in the process to take their role and function seriously, and to respond to the negotiators' requests in a timely and cooperative manner. Some of my interviewees described their meetings in Brussels as a rather uninteresting bureaucratic set-up, which consisted in a series of predetermined and expected steps. Others recounted more vivid stories, in which, for example, nationalities of representatives of the European Commission mattered, and in which there was occasional possibility for disruption of the expected code of conduct. One negotiator, for example, recounted how he demonstratively asked to leave the meeting, because he felt unnerved by a response from an EC representative from a "new" member state that he felt was off the topic and patronizing. Representatives of the European Commission coming from newer member states, said another interviewee, did not like to be reminded that their country was in the same position as Croatia only a couple of years earlier.

Interviewees' answers were more homogenous when asked to determine which circle of countries Croatia belonged to or which its regional affiliation was. As is discernible from the quote above, negotiators most often referred to Central Europe, which was conceived as a possible shortcut to Western culture and civilization[24]. In this same *view from above* the EU was linked to an abstract, idealized goal which is to be reached through gradual perfection on the part of the accession state. In the meantime, and until this process was completed and the "ongoing transition" allegedly ended[25], the country's Central European cultural identity seemed to be employed as a guarantee that "Europeanization" is, indeed, feasible.

In order to attain a better understanding of the inner logic of the civilizational slope, and especially its utopian traits, I find it useful to follow Melegh's call for revisiting the classical work of Karl Mannheim on ideology and utopia, originally published in 1929.

"A state of mind is utopian", wrote Mannheim, "when it is incongruous with the state of reality within which it occurs"[26]. Utopian orientations, once they are actualized, "tend to shatter, either partially or wholly, the order of things prevailing at the time"[27]. Utopia is, therefore, not necessarily something unreal or impossible to actualize, as it is often described, because it has the potential to inform and thus change the existing state of affairs. Among the four types of *utopian mentality* which Mannheim defines[28], and which ranges "in an order of increasing historicity and determinateness"[29], the most pertinent to this analysis is the second one: liberal-humanitarian mentality, whose chief proponent is the middle class, and whose utopia is – an idea.

The liberal-humanitarian utopia[30] rests upon "a formal goal projected into the infinite future whose function it is to act as a mere regulative device in mundane affairs"[31]. This type of utopian mentality, thus, becomes "increasingly bound up with the process of becoming"[32]. The actual idea, which is projected into the future, becomes a norm in the present, and when it is applied to mundane proceedings, it "effects gradual improvement"[33]. Melegh claims that liberal-humanitarian utopia "almost perfectly describes the dominant discourse on Eastern and Central Europe"[34], albeit without the racial and cultural implications inherent in the concept of civilizational slope.

The liberal-humanitarian utopia is crucial in the interpretation of dominant discourses in which EU accession in Croatia was embedded. The notion of the EU as a *goal projected into the future*, which is to be achieved through gradual improvement and consistent betterment was pervasive in the pre-accession period in Croatia. To understand the ways in which the liberal-humanitarian utopia works on a horizontal level, by informing the Balkanist "gradation of nations" (where those to the East are deemed less European[35]), seems like a rather straightforward task given the analogous logics of ongoing "improvement". The challenge is to try to understand the utopia's vertical workings, whereby the values it promotes become class-related, since they may not be shared throughout all spheres of society.

In my research, this was most apparent in the interviews I conducted with the group of interviewees I referred to as agricultural entrepreneurs, all of whom were awarded EU pre-accession funds for agriculture[36]. In these interviews, issues related to symbolic and political power asymmetry were not an alluring subject of conversation. It was as if discussions of national, regional or continental symbolic geographies – the cartographic view from the above – required a certain "aesthetic disposition", which, in Pierre Bourdieu's terms, entails "a generalized capacity to neutralize ordinary urgencies and to bracket off practical ends, a durable inclination and aptitude for practice without a practical function", which "can only be constituted within an experience of the world freed from urgency and through the practice of activities which are an end in themselves, such as scholastic exercises or the contemplation of works of art"[37]. After all, the research of symbolic geography often focuses on narratives produced by well-educated and even privileged representatives of society, from aristocratic travellers of the 18th century to contemporary intellectuals and politicians.

Agricultural entrepreneurs employed references to Central Europe or the Balkans only sporadically and in passing, as an addition to other, allegedly more important topics of conversation. Matters of Eurocentric symbolic geographies and hierarchies were approached in a disengaged, colloquial manner, not as a matter of potentially serious discussion. In the later interpretation of interviews, I thus focused on the *here and now* of their immediate business practices, the purposeful actions through which they navigated the strenuous entrepreneurial routine, as well as their class dispositions which were entangled within urban/rural and socialist/capitalist dichotomies. One such disposition was mirrored in the range of ways they perceived, defined and named themselves.

At the time, I found it surprising that only one of my interviewees was unhesitant in calling himself a peasant, while the majority of interviewees agreed that, because of the amount of time they spent on administrative tasks and differing tactics of *making do*, the term "agricultural entrepreneurs" described more appropriately what they did. Also, few of my interviewees identified themselves predominantly or even solely with the entrepreneurial side of the syntagma[38].

The tension between the peasant and the entrepreneur emerged in their differing positioning on the slope, even if the group as a whole was less prone to reflecting on Eurocentric symbolic geography. In some of the accounts, and especially among those who were less explicitly identified with the entrepreneurial side of the spectrum, there still was evidence of solidarity with peasants across Croatia, but also the whole Balkan region and the European continent, by asserting that they were, in some respects, subject to similar problems and difficulties, from the unpredictable weather to the detrimental effects of the globalization of food market. However, my respondents' refusal to entertain their minds with, as Bourdieu has it, *practices without a practical function,* such as issues of Balkanist prejudice, as well as their relatedness to the "peasant class" made these interviewees' accounts less susceptible to the gradating logic of liberal-humanitarian utopia. Therefore, for example, neighbouring Bosnia and Herzegovina was referred to not only as a less developed, ultra-Balkan space, but also as a state in which certain policies related to agriculture could be even more advantageous to peasants, even if the country is not likely to become an EU member soon[39].

On the other hand, those who were more inclined or closer to the entrepreneurial end of the spectrum at times identified themselves in opposition to the so-called common peasants who were described as traditional, small, self-sustainable producers who owned but "a couple of pigs at home, and a couple of small cows" and who refused to adapt to the necessary EU changes to their own disadvantage. The entrepreneurs, as a rule, took pride in their overcoming of obstacles posed by the state and its sluggish bureaucracy as well as the various occurrences of corruption, while stressing their risk-taking, diligence and perseverance as key components of success.

In the following example, one may discern echoes of such ideals promoted by the liberal-humanitarian utopia. The goal is projected into the future, and is thought to be achievable through a series of successive progresses, while the present state of affairs calls for a vigilant and unrelenting subject.

> Since the first day, which means since '92, when I entered these, I would say, entrepreneurial waters and business, there was no fair . . . or round table, or any education related to this business in which I have not participated unless I was ill or unavailable for some reason. Which means: the main thing one needs to have is knowledge, I need to know now what is ahead of me in two-three years, I cannot wait and be surprised and say: here, I missed something, and so on. So, one has to be informed, one has to have direction and goals in his life and when one does, there is no mistake.

In the accounts of entrepreneurs, the competitiveness, expansion and the desire to move forward and upward[40] was less related to the horizontal and more closely to the vertical axis, referring to issues of class.

CLASS(ES) MATTER

An explicit and meticulous theoretical examination of the intertwining of class-related, vertical societal divisions and horizontal "civilizational" gradations within Europe is found in Ezequiel Adamovsky's work on Euro-Orientalism, a "discursive formation by means of which the West symbolically organizes and regulates its relationships with the area of the world called Eastern Europe" [41]. The author examines the creation of the discourse on Eastern Europe in 19th-century France, then traces its institutional expansion and strengthening in the 20th century, to conclude with several remarks on its current political effects.

Unlike many scholars who examined similar discursive formations, such as Balkanism, Adamovsky assigns explicit importance to the "distinctive class component" within Euro-Orientalism[42]. And such a perspective contributes to his assertion that "[t]he West is not the agent and source of Euro-Orientalism", but also, and perhaps more importantly, that all Eastern Europeans are not "equally victims of that discourse":

> [T]he agents of Euro-Orientalism are the individuals and institutions shaped by the bourgeois order, regardless of their ethnic origin or geographical location. Euro-Orientalism is one of the main discursive formations by means of which the area of the world that we were taught to call Eastern Europe was (and still is being) incorporated into the global capitalist system. Euro-Orientalism is the discourse that symbolically organizes and regulates the relationship between, on the one hand, those institutions and people (regardless of their ethnic background or national location) whose role is to help expand capitalist social forms in 'Eastern Europe', and, on the other, the 'natives' and autochthonous institutions of that area of the world. In other words, Euro-Orientalism is a form of class ideology[43].

Adamovsky refrains from questioning whether the scholars who critically researched Balkanism and Orientalism, as discursive formations akin to Euro-Orientalism, perhaps understated or disregarded "hints of class ideology" in their works[44]. Some of the research, such as Andrea Matošević and Tea Škokić's[45], is alert to the importance of vertical societal divisions in the production of (contemporary) Balkanisms, and in particular those arising from the urban/rural dichotomy. For the time being, however, we shall put aside suspicion that Balkanism is not solely or even predominantly based on "ethnic background or national location"[46], and examine the mechanics of inclusion and exclusion employed in Euro-Orientalism.

In line with the "liberal-bourgeois ideology and narrative of civilization" inherent in it, Euro-Orientalism values one's capability to exert "manners and customs of the (Western) upper middle class", to appropriate "'rational' and politically acceptable behaviour", and to attain "a high degree of economic and cultural progress"[47]. It should come as no surprise, then, that in 19th-century France "the workers were constantly compared to the barbarians past and present . . . while the Russian nobility was usually accepted as fully European"[48]. While Euro-Orientalism today still participates in various gradations of Europeanness across the continent, we should keep in mind that its "derogatory effect . . . also regulates the relations between the elites and the people and between people who perceive themselves as Western or modern in different degrees"[49]. The same binary oppositions – civilized/uncivilized, progressive/backward, rational/irrational – which are used to distinguish between more and less European nations are applied within societies, as well.

The research critical geographer Merje Kuus conducted with EU officials in the Brussels' European Quarter, indeed, reveals few explicitly Orientalist notions related to Eastern Europeans who were employed with EU institutions after the enlargements in 2004 and 2007[50]. The mechanism that this researcher once termed "gradation of Europeanness"[51] is still operating, albeit through more elusive means which may have to do with geography as much as with certain class dispositions. Kuus, for example, mentions that the distinctive style, which is described as desirable among EU officials, has to do with becoming "urban"[52]. Urban, that is, in the sense of a great Western metropolis, such as London or Paris, but not Bucharest, Zagreb or Skopje. Even if within EU institutions a single, homogenous image of an ideal EU official is not necessarily fostered, adepts will be able to recognize various class dispositions or distinguish between several distinctly national (and regional) styles. But these are Western European – French, Italian or Scandinavian – while markers of eastern/central Europeanness, once again, are more easily determined through the lack thereof. Also, "casual self-confidence in movement, posture, and approach, with clothing and accessories only in a supporting role – a certain urbanity of continental *noblesse de robe* – still marks a person who is *un*likely to come from central Europe"[53].

> It is not a certain look, it is a certain ease. That ease is not monolithic, just as Western Europe is not homogenous. It comes in a finer mesh of economic and cultural capital. For it is not enough to dress a certain way; one also has to look natural in it: to stand and walk and interact with a style that matches the clothes. One has to have the certainty of taste that comes from knowing one's strong position in the field of power[54].

Precisely because manners of conduct and personal image represent a fertile site of struggle involving both class dispositions and geographical power asymmetries, I strived to discuss these issues in depth in my interviews with Croatian negotiators conducted in 2007 and 2008. Negotiators were acting as leaders of teams which would participate in a number of meetings held in Brussels with the representatives of the European Commission. Some EU negotiators complained about what they perceived as the "irrationality" of conduct of certain members of Croatian teams. One negotiator, for example, referred to presentations which were out of context and which failed to meet the expectations of proper performance, which seemed to include succinct and goal-oriented communication. Some also referred to cases in which team members withheld important information, therefore betraying the idea of team work, transparent and collegial conduct. Some negotiators – and almost exclusively the female ones – asserted that Croatian representatives in their official visits to Brussels dressed in a more official and uniformed manner than their counterparts from the European Commission: men wearing what was in the interviews described as fancy ties, suits and shoes, and women nice skirt suits with stylish shoes and bags.

In comparison, in the research I am currently conducting with Croatian EU officials in Brussels, who have been permanently employed in various EU institutions following the country's accession in 2013, my questions regarding their clothes and personal image are sometimes met with indifference, circumvented with irony or dismissed as irrelevant. Questions are, nonetheless, still posed because I am interested in the ways in which their current social and financial status – which has, among the greatest majority of my interviewees, significantly improved – changes their consumption habits and overall lifestyle. It could be argued that, if there is a place in which the utopia of EU accession ever became realized, it could be within the EU institutions themselves. At least, if viewed from the perspective of Croatia, a country in which registered unemployment rate is about 17 percent[55], and the average monthly net wage is a bit less than 750 euros[56], the salaries and privileges which accompany such job posts, as well as permanence of jobs within EU institutions may, indeed, seem dream-like and utopian.

In a survey, conducted in Croatia about a decade earlier, respondents were asked to estimate, by choosing from various possible answers, who the winners and losers of the country's accession to the EU will be. Both younger and mature respondents chose "experts", "those who speak foreign languages" and "young people" to most likely be winners[57]. In many respects, Croatian EU officials seem to confirm[58] such expectations: as a rule, they had postgraduate educations, the experience of studying or working abroad, and they spoke at least one, and in many cases several, foreign languages fluently. In my interviews, they exhibited high levels of complexity and reflexivity in their answers, and they were overall very methodical and logical in laying out their arguments. Some of them conversed about their current social status somewhat hesitantly; others were straightforward and said that their current workplace changed their whole lives for the better.

Among them is a man in his thirties, previously a civil servant in a large state institution who started working in a Directorate-General (DG) in Brussels at the end of 2013. He identifies himself as coming from a middle class family: both of his parents were highly educated and held jobs which were well-respected. Even if the family's social capital never converted into the "moneyed" one, the parents still encouraged him to uphold the acquired levels of cultural capital by pursuing high-quality education and learning foreign languages. Among the positive changes which moving to Brussels brought, my interviewee mentions the ability to save money, purchase desired clothes, travel to sunnier places when he needs a vacation, as well as an over-all sense of existential security.

Climbing the slope and witnessing an utopia come true, however, may bear some (un)expected consequences as well: a position which is placed higher up the slope enhances the distance from those who are left behind, further down the slope. When talking to colleagues from his previous workplace in Croatia, my interviewee decided to stop sharing how content and enthusiastic he was about his current job post. The gap, in this case, seems to be opening between those who are accustomed to dealing with various work-related lacks and frustrations through "a lot of complaining" and those whose concerns now play out in a much wider field of possibilities and expectations.

CONCLUSION

In his book *Ideology and Utopia* Karl Mannheim draws attention to the prob-lematic task of distinguishing between a *relative utopia*, one which has the potential of being realized in the future, and an ideology. While the dominant strata in a society will defend the existing order and accuse the propositions of alternative orders of being utopian, the opposing groups will accuse the ruling order of being ideological, of concealing or distorting reality. Also, ideas and ideals which were regarded utopian at one point in historic time may become regarded as partly or completely ideological at another, so that distinguishing between ideology and utopia may be best accomplished in retrospect.

In the dominant political discourses in Croatia, EU accession was primarily framed as a matter of deciding between progress and backwardness, between rationality and irrationality, between Europe and non-Europe. The discus-sion was firmly placed within the realm of the discursive formation of the civilizational slope, but both the dominant and critical perspectives primar-ily revolved around its horizontal axis, discussing, for example, whether the country is "entering Europe" or whether it should be "escaping the Balkans". If there ever was an ideological trait of the Europeanization project which is in need of further investigation, it is the dominant assumption that a country *as a whole* may move upward on the slope. And, closely tied to this claim, another one: insisting that the acceptance of values promoted by liberal-humanitarian utopia primarily depends upon the willingness and persistence of the country's citizens to reform and adjust. This view ignores the fact that, within a certain society, there are *class* dispositions that significantly enhance the possibility of moving up the slope, and others that only enhance the formation of "passive" subjects of Europeanization.

In this chapter, I attempted to delineate the workings of the vertical, class-related axis which recounts a more complex narrative of Europeanization in which there are people who prosper, and people – whom one, for example, encounters in the Croatian rural peripheries – who remain excluded regardless of the accession date. Also, there are those who are qualified to understand and authorized to define what being Europeanized means, and others who are merely subject to those explanations. And it is in these vertical exclusions/ expulsions that we might most clearly distinguish between "Europe" as an "ideological construction"[59] and a lived experience.

NOTES

1. See Zoran Kurelić, "No Carrot and No Stick: Croatia's Simulated Democracy and the EU," in *Kroatien in der EU: Stand und Perspektiven*, ed. Beate Neuss, 47–64 (Hamburg: Verlag Dr. Kovač, 2015).

2. Tihomir Ponoš, "Croatia: An Apprehensive Fan of Europe," in *Twenty Years After: Post-Communist Countries and European Integration* (Brussels: Heinrich-Böll-Stiftung, 2009), 77.

3. Cf. Darko Šeperić, "To Europe and Back – The Croatian EU Accession Process and Its Outcomes," *SEER Journal for Labour and Social Affairs in Eastern Europe* 4 (2011): 463–80.

4. Damir Grubiša, "Hrvatski referendum za Europsku uniju: anatomija zakašnjelog(ne)uspjeha," *Politička misao* 49, no. 2 (2012): 63. Cf. also Renata Ivanović, *Analiza Komunikacijske strategije Vlade za informiranje hrvatske javnosti o Europskoj uniji i pripremama za* članstvo (Zagreb: GONG, 2011); and Dejan Jović, "Hrvatski referendum o članstvu u Europskoj uniji i njegove posljedice za smanjeni Zapadni Balkan," *Anali Hrvatskog politološkog društva* IX (2012b): 163–182. The prolonged, debilitating economic crisis also contributed to the lessening of public interest in EU-related affairs in Croatia. Grubiša, for example, states the global economic crisis, the so-called Eurozone crisis and the severe state of Croatian national economy among such factors. See Grubiša, "Hrvatski referendum".

5. Šeperić, "To Europe and Back," 467.

6. Jović, "Hrvatski referendum." Jović usefully defines euro-indifferentism as a "state and (non)acting which is based on indifferentism toward the European Union and its institutions, representatives and policies, as well as toward its survival or disintegration", Dejan Jović, "Euroravnodušna Hrvatska," *Političke analize* 9 (2012a): 64.

7. For more information about the referendum and differing interpretations of its low voter turnout of 43.51 percent, including the controversy regarding the required minimum number of voters, see Grubiša, "Hrvatski referendum" and Jović, "Hrvatski referendum" and Jović, "Euroravnodušna Hrvatska." For a more detailed analysis of euroscepticism in Croatia, see Nebojša Blanuša, "Euroskepticizam u Hrvatskoj," in *Hrvatska i Europa*, ed. Ivan Šiber (Zagreb: Fakultet političkih znanosti Sveučilišta u Zagrebu, 2011), 11–46.

8. Dipesh Chakrabarty, *Provincializing Europe: Postcolonial Thought and Historical Difference* (Princeton and Oxford: Princeton University Press, 2000), 4.

9. Cf. Ante Tomić, *Jutarnji list*, July 4, 2012, http://www.jutarnji.hr/ante-tomic--evo-zasto-cacic-mora-ostati-u-vladi/1039039/. Accessed April 20, 2015.

10. Alexander Kiossev, "Notes on the Self-Colonizing Cultures," n.d., http://www.kultura.bg/media/my_html/biblioteka/bgvntgrd/e_ak.htm. Accessed January 13, 2015. Compare with chapters 3 and 4 in this volume, on the perceived lack of "history" in the Balkans and the "catch-up" modernization of its states.

11. Ibid.

12. Ibid.

13. Ibid.

14. Cf. Zala Volčić, "The Notion of the 'West' in the Serbian National Imaginary," *European Journal of Cultural Studies* 8, no. 2 (2005): 155–75.

15. The title is a paraphrase of Slavenka Drakulić's collection of essays, *How We Survived Communism and Even Laughed* (New York: Harper Perennial, 1993).

16. Merje Kuus, "Europe's Eastern Expansion and the Reinscription of Otherness in East-Central Europe," *Progress in Human Geography* 28, no. 4 (2004): 472–89.

17. cf. Milica Bakić-Hayden and Robert Hayden, "Orientalist Variations on the Theme 'Balkans'," *Symbolic Geography in Recent Yugoslav Cultural Politics* 51, no. 1 (1992): 1–15; Milica Bakić-Hayden, "Nesting Orientalisms: The Case of Former Yugoslavia," *Slavic Review* 54, no. 4 (1995): 917–31; Maria Todorova, *Imagining the Balkans* (New York and Oxford: Oxford University Press, 1997); Larry Wolff, *Inventing Eastern Europe: The Map of Civilization on the Mind of the Enlightenment* (Stanford, CA: Stanford University Press, 1994). There is also a significant body of literature questioning, opposing and also refining some of the main tenets upon which these studies are based. See, among others: Ezequiel Adamovsky, "Euro-Orientalism and the Making of the Concept of Eastern Europe in France, 1810–1880," *The Journal of Modern History* 77, no. 3 (2005): 591–628; Ezequiel Adamovsky, *Euro-Orientalism: Liberal Ideology and the Image of Russia in France (c. 1740–1880)* (Bern: Peter Lang AG, 2006); Bojan Baskar, "Babuškini orientalizmi od blizu: analitični koncept ali komet z zahoda?" in *Včeraj in danes: Jubilejni zbornik socioloških razprav ob 50-letnici Oddelka za sociologijo*, ed. Ksenija Vidmar Horvat and Avgust Lešnik (Ljubljana: Filozofske fakultete Univerze v Ljubljani, 2011), 209–229; Andrea Matošević and Tea Škokić, *Polutani dugog trajanja: balkanistički diskursi* (Zagreb: Inštitut za etnologiju i folkloristiku, 2014); Diana Mishkova, "Symbolic Geographies and Visions of Identity: A Balkan Perspective," *European Journal of Social Theory* 11, no. 2 (2008): 237–56.

18. Attila Melegh, *On the East-West Slope: Globalization, Nationalism, Racism and Discourses on Central and Eastern Europe* (Budapest: Central European University Press: 2006), 29.

19. Melegh, *East-West Slope*, 41, 2.

20. Ibid., 40.

21. Ibid., 43.

22. Ibid.

23. During my research on Croatian negotiators (2007–2008) I interviewed six out of 13 negotiators who were, at the time, leading the country's negotiations on various "chapters", such as "transport policy", "judiciary and fundamental rights", "consumer and health protection" or "agriculture and rural development". All the interviewees

were highly educated, young and middle-aged experts, and the majority of them were employed in various state institutions such as ministries or agencies. Because negotiators were a small group of people, in order to protect their anonymity, I excluded the information which would make them easily identifiable, such is, for example, the subject of their expertise.

24. Orlanda Obad, "Imperij kao uzvraćanje udarca: predodžbe o kulturi i identitetu u hrvatskih pregovarača s Europskom unijom," *Narodna umjetnost: hrvatski* časopis *za etnologiju i folkloristiku* 46, no. 2 (2009): 111–27.

25. Melegh, *East-West Slope*, 20.

26. Karl Mannheim, *Ideology and Utopia: An Introduction to the Sociology of Knowledge* (New York: Harvest Books, n. d.), 192.

27. Ibid.

28. Ibid.

29. Immanuel Wallerstein, "Marxisms as Utopias: Evolving Ideologies," *American Journal of Sociology* 91, no. 6 (1986): 1300.

30. In this chapter, I will use the syntagma "liberal-humanitarian utopia" (cf. Melegh, *East-West Slope*), although Mannheim uses other variants, such as utopia of liberal humanitarianism, liberal-humanitarian idea, or liberal-humanitarian mentality.

31. Mannheim, *Ideology and Utopia*, 219.

32. Ibid., 224.

33. Ibid.

34. Melegh, *East-West Slope*, 20.

35. See the general Introduction to this volume.

36. In 2010 I conducted ten semi-structured interviews with agricultural entrepreneurs who were awarded EU pre-accession funds, such as SAPARD or IPARD. They were located in four different Croatian "counties" (županije). Most of them were young and middle-aged men, who led family farms. Some of them were financially successful and their business trajectories made them internationally mobile, which countered the predominant stereotype of an *inefficient and backward peasant*. Even when they were not quite successful financially, they described themselves in the interviews as individuals who possess an enterprising spirit and propensity for risk-taking.

37. Pierre Bourdieu, *Distinction: A Social Critique of the Judgement of Taste* (Cambridge, MA: Harvard University Press, 1984), 54.

38. Cf. Orlanda Obad, "Zašto nam je kapitalistička nevolja milija od svih blaga ovoga svijeta: o stvaranju dobitnika i gubitnika na hrvatskom selu," in *Komparativni postsocijalizam – slavenska iskustva*, Tvrtko Vuković and Maša Kolanović, eds. (Zagreb: Zagrebačka slavistička škola – Hrvatski seminar za strane slaviste, Filozofski fakultet Sveučilišta u Zagrebu, 2013), 165–78.

39. Cf. Ibid.

40. Caitríona Ní Laoire, "Winners and Losers? Rural Restructuring, Economic Status and Masculine Identities among Young Farmers in South-West Ireland," in *Geographies of Rural Cultures and Societies*, Lewis Holloway and Moya Kneafsey, eds. (Aldershot: Ashgate, 2004), 283–301.

41. Adamovsky, "Euro-Orientalism," 609. See also Adamovsky, "Euro-Orientalism."

42. Adamovsky, "Euro-Orientalism."

43. Ibid., 617. I am aware that the usage of terms such as bourgeoisie is contested, and especially outside of specific social and historical context. The purpose of this chapter, however, is to delineate the vertical axis of civilizational slope, and such a focus, unfortunately, does not permit me to further examine the definition and usage of a range of class-related terms in various theoretical perspectives.

44. Ibid., 623. Adamovsky notes that although in her well-known work Maria Todorova does delineate certain class-related dispositions in the examination of Westerners' perception of the Balkans, in her overall interpretation of Balkanism, "class functions" do not play a major role. See "Euro-Orientalism," 622.

45. Matošević and Škokić, *Polutani*.

46. Adamovsky, "Euro-Orientalism," 617.

47. Ibid., 618.

48. Ibid., 623.

49. Ibid., 619.

50. Kuus, "Europe's Eastern Expansion".

51. Cf. Ibid.

52. Ibid.

53. Ibid., 160.

54. Ibid.

55. As of May, 2015. See: http://www.dzs.hr/default_e.htm. Accessed June 1, 2015.

56. As of April, 2015. See: http://www.dzs.hr/. Accessed June 1, 2015.

57. Vlasta Ilišin and Ivona Mendeš, "Mladi i Europska unija: percepcija posljedica integracije," in *Mladi Hrvatske i europska integracija*, ed. Vlasta Ilišin (Zagreb: Inštitut za društvena istraživanja, 2005), 227.

58. My research is still under way and these are preliminary insights.

59. Sandra Ponzanesi and Bolette B. Blaagaard, "Introduction: In the Name of Europe," in *Deconstructing Europe: Postcolonial Perspectives*, eds., Sandra Ponzanesi and Bolette B. Blaagaard, (New York: Routledge, 2012), 3.

BIBLIOGRAPHY

Adamovsky, Ezequiel. "Euro-Orientalism and the Making of the Concept of Eastern Europe in France, 1810–1880." *The Journal of Modern History* 77, no. 3 (2005): 591–628.

Adamovsky, Ezequiel. *Euro-Orientalism: Liberal Ideology and the Image of Russia in France (c. 1740–1880)*. Bern: Peter Lang AG, 2006.

Bakić-Hayden, Milica. "Nesting Orientalisms: The Case of Former Yugoslavia." *Slavic Review* 54, no. 4 (1995): 917–31.

Bakić-Hayden, Milica and Hayden, Robert. "Orientalist Variations on the Theme 'Balkans'." *Symbolic Geography in Recent Yugoslav Cultural Politics* 51, no. 1 (1992): 1–15.

Bojan Baskar, "Babuškini orientalizmi od blizu: analitični koncept ali komet z zahoda?" in *Včeraj in danes: Jubilejni zbornik socioloških razprav ob 50-letnici Oddelka za sociologijo*, eds. Ksenija Vidmar Horvat and Avgust Lešnik Ljubljana: Filozofske fakultete Univerze v Ljubljani, 2011, 209–29.

Blanuša, Nebojša. "Euroskepticizam u Hrvatskoj." In *Hrvatska i Europa*, ed. Ivan Šiber, 11–46. Zagreb: Fakultet političkih znanosti Sveučilišta u Zagrebu, 2011.

Bourdieu, Pierre. *Distinction: a Social Critique of the Judgement of Taste.* Cambridge, MA: Harvard University Press, 1984.

Chakrabarty, Dipesh. *Provincializing Europe: Postcolonial Thought and Historical Difference.* Princeton and Oxford: Princeton University Press, 2000.

Drakulić, Slavenka. *How We Survived Communism And Even Laughed.* New York: Harper Perennial, 1993.

Grubiša, Damir. "Hrvatski referendum za Europsku uniju: anatomija zakašnjelog(ne) uspjeha." *Politička misao* 49, no. 2 (2012): 45–72.

Ilišin, Vlasta and Mendeš, Ivona. "Mladi i Europska unija: percepcija posljedica integracije." In *Mladi Hrvatske i europska integracija*, ed. Vlasta Ilišin, 197–252. Zagreb: Inštitut za društvena istraživanja, 2005.

Ivanović, Renata. *Analiza Komunikacijske strategije Vlade za informiranje hrvatske javnosti o Europskoj uniji i pripremama za članstvo.* Zagreb: GONG, 2011.

Jović, Dejan. "Euroravnodušna Hrvatska." *Političke analize* 9 (2012a): 63–5.

Jović, Dejan. "Hrvatski referendum o članstvu u Europskoj uniji i njegove posljedice za smanjeni Zapadni Balkan." *Anali Hrvatskog politološkog društva* IX (2012b): 163–82.

Kuus, Merje. "Europe's Eastern Expansion and the Reinscription of Otherness in East-Central Europe." *Progress in Human Geography* 28, no. 4 (2004): 472–89.

Kuus, Merje. Geopolitics and Expertise: Knowledge and Authority in European Diplomacy. Oxford: Wiley Blackwell, 2014.

Kurelić, Zoran. "No Carrot and No Stick: Croatia's Simulated Democracy and the EU." In *Kroatien in der EU: Stand und Perspektiven*, edited by Beate Neuss, 47–64. Hamburg: Verlag Dr. Kovač, 2015.

Kiossev, Alexander. "Notes on the Self-colonizing Cultures." n.d., http://www.kultura. bg/media/my_html/biblioteka/bgvntgrd/e_ak.htm. Accessed January 13, 2015.

Mannheim, Karl. *Ideology and Utopia: an Introduction to the Sociology of Knowledge.* New York: Harvest Books, n. d.

Matošević, Andrea and Škokić, Tea. *Polutani dugog trajanja: balkanistički diskursi.* Zagreb: Inštitut za etnologiju i folkloristiku, 2014.

Melegh, Attila. *On the East-West Slope: Globalization, Nationalism, Racism and Discourses on Central and Eastern Europe.* Budapest: Central European University Press: 2006.

Mishkova, Diana. "Symbolic Geographies and Visions of Identity: A Balkan Perspective." *European Journal of Social Theory* 11, no. 2 (2008): 237–56.

Ní Laoire, Caitríona. "Winners and Losers? Rural Restructuring, Economic Status and Masculine Identities Among Young Farmers in South-West Ireland." in *Geographies of Rural Cultures and Societies*, eds. Lewis Holloway and Moya Kneafsey, Aldershot: Ashgate, 2004, 283–301.

Obad, Orlanda. "Imperij kao uzvraćanje udarca: predodžbe o kulturi i identitetu uhrvatskih pregovarača s Europskom unijom." *Narodna umjetnost: hrvatski časopis za etnologiju i folkloristiku* 46, no. 2 (2009): 111–27.

Obad, Orlanda. "Zašto nam je kapitalistička nevolja milija od svih blaga ovoga svijeta: o stvaranju dobitnika i gubitnika na hrvatskom selu." In *Komparativni postsocijalizam – slavenska iskustva*, edited by Tvrtko Vuković and Maša Kolanović, 165–78. Zagreb: Zagrebačka slavistička škola – Hrvatski seminar za strane slaviste, Filozofski fakultet Sveučilišta u Zagrebu, 2013.

Ponoš, Tihomir. "Croatia: an Apprehensive Fan of Europe." In *Twenty Years After: Post-Communist Countries and European Integration*, 67–77. Brussels: Heinrich-Böll-Stiftung, 2009.

Ponzanesi, Sandra and Blaagaard, Bolette B. "Introduction: In the Name of Europe." In *Deconstructing Europe: Postcolonial Perspectives*, edited by Sandra Ponzanesi and Bolette B. Blaagaard, 1-10. New York: Routledge, 2012.

Šeperić, Darko. "To Europe and Back – The Croatian EU accession process and Its Outcomes." *SEER Journal for Labour and Social Affairs in Eastern Europe* 4 (2011): 463–80.

Todorova, Maria. *Imagining the Balkans*. New York and Oxford: Oxford University Press, 1997.

Volčić, Zala. "The Notion of the 'West' in the Serbian National Imaginary." *European Journal of Cultural Studies* 8, no. 2 (2005): 155–75.

Wallerstein, Immanuel. "Marxisms as Utopias: Evolving Ideologies." *American Journal of Sociology* 91, no. 6 (1986): 1295–1308.

Wolff, Larry. *Inventing Eastern Europe: The Map of Civilization on the Mind of the Enlightenment*. Stanford, CA: Stanford University Press, 1994.

Chapter 10

The Foreigners

Claudia Ciobanu

This chapter is about the affective aftermath of "mobile Europe", from the perspective of young and educated Eastern European migrants. For those "lucky ones", who have the ability to enjoy the privileges of the "borderless" EU, one of the core features of the "enlarged" Europe is mobility. Numerous possibilities to study, get training and work abroad opened up for us since the EU enlargements in 2004 and 2007. We venture moving away from our parents and siblings in a heartbeat in order to pursue interesting opportunities, we settle in other countries, we fall in love with people who do not speak our language. But what is the emotional toll this kind of life is taking on us? In this text, which is more an essay than a conventional academic study, I raise some of the issues of belonging by describing experiences and feelings that migrants deal with during their life abroad and once their study and work days in the West are over, feelings that lurk behind their successful mobility stories.

The accounts presented here are a combination of personal experience and insights retrieved from a series of interviews I conducted, as a freelance writer, over the fall of 2014 with select young people (usually in their early 30s). My interviewees are kept anonymous, being referred to just with their country of origin and their country of residence.

Finally, two short notes. First of all, this essay deals only with a narrow category of migrants. These are the "lucky" ones. The ones who can freely pursue academic, professional or romantic opportunities inside Europe. I chose to describe this kind of experience in this text because it is mine. I do not, on this occasion, speak about migrants coming from outside of established borders of Europe into the EU escaping destruction or poverty, though helping them remains one of Europe's main concerns.

With so many refugees trying to escape war, being forced to sleep in cold fields behind walls that European countries have built to stop them from coming, with kids getting sick or dying at Europe's gates, it feels almost shameless to write a text about the emotional problems of wilful migrants. I go ahead only in the hope that by shedding some light on the experiences of the "lucky" migrants, this text could help Europeans become more sensitive to newcomers, whoever they are. This text also poses a challenge to the idea of "happy mobility" from the usual promotion materials produced by the European Commission, where mobility is presented as easy and inconsequential, and where the removal of mental walls always follows the withdrawal of the actual ones. The tragedy of the refugees has exposed European mobility as a sort of rich kids' play.

Secondly, most of my interviewees are Eastern or Southern Europeans. In this essay, I write about issues specific to their moving to the more prosperous West (such as the need to help out the country left behind, the escape from social conservatism, the encounter with prejudice about "Easterners"). This text is about how some of us, Easterners, find ourselves suspended and even lost in a Europe whose internal borders have to some extent be loosened. By tracing the specific issues that come up for "Easterners" traversing the "enlarged" Europe, I also hope to have said something about migration that are shared across the continent.

It struck me after a few interviews with "foreigners": I was going through all these conversations not only for the sake of writing about it but also because this worked as a therapeutic process for me. I had reached a point where my unresolved questions about living abroad and (not) belonging felt like an open wound that I needed to at least clean up and bandage (complete healing would never be possible). I started prompting people to tell me their stories, share their burning questions and their ways of coping. In the process, I also shared my ways, my doubts.

Now, as I write this, about six months since I started the research, I am in a different place than I was when I began this work. I'm about to give birth to my daughter. Motherhood puts me in a different place literally too: having a child with my partner (the partner for the sake of whom I moved from my homeland, Romania, to Poland and became a foreigner again) will connect me with my adoptive country more, it will make my situation here more settled.

Before I begin, a comment about the chosen language of this text: English. Over the past six months, I came back to writing in Romanian after many years of speaking English exclusively. This was mainly because of the insistence of my Romanian friend who said we must recover our ability to write in our native language and with whom we eventually established a website for Romanians living in Poland. Because I am connected to my Romanian language again, I would have written this text in Romanian. I would have rooted it in my ethnic identity, in my "Romanianness", I would have used it as another chance to return to my cultural roots. But I will write it in English because I want to share it with those who also took the time to tell me their stories. One of the features of being a foreigner after all is that much of our basic communication and first-hand experience may not happen in our native language. In today's Europe, it will most likely be in English. We use English to build bonds with others. Because it gives us access to new friendships in foreign places across the continent, because it allows us to express who we are, English is in a way necessary for the survival of our souls.

THE PREMISE

One million babies born from parents who met during their Erasmus studies, the news broke the other day. It fused with other media announcements, such as adverts for "opportunities to work" all over the European Union (EU) if you are from one of the "respectable" countries in the block. Or in the US. Or in Dubai. Job offers, fully funded PhDs, exchange and training programmes, volunteering, au pairing, work and travel. So many chances to go abroad for us. Take one of them, and it will lead you to the next. To an MA and then a PhD. To a foreign boyfriend. To a nice job with an EU institution or some US company. To the impossibility of returning home, at least for now, because it started to feel too narrow, too small, too claustrophobic.

This has been our story. In Eastern Europe, it is the story of those born in the 1970s and 1980s who took advantage of the newly acquired freedom to travel abroad after the fall of communism. There was considerable migration from Romania in the early 1990s but it was only a decade later that the youth exodus really took off, not in the least because of the Erasmus EU student mobility scheme expanding to the East.

Media in our countries, as well as our families and our neighbours, often look at our lives schematically, as instances of success: the niece who got herself a great job in Brussels; the neighbour who married an American and now takes her mother every summer to the US for two months; the bright young man with an impressive academic career and so on. As long as we are abroad, those back home think we must be managing fine, even have it easy.

Being abroad does afford us a lot, otherwise it would not be that so many of us undertake this considerable change in our lives. Apart from the new opportunities, moves bring along a sense of freedom and excitement. They bring a chance to reconstruct ourselves as we wish, as being free from our histories and from social norms back home. Moves "expand our horizons", making us more friendly and open.

However, these positive features of mobility are much advertised and are thus well known. I am more drawn to the more hidden dramas of being a foreigner, "the dark souls" of the Erasmus generation. To the things we do not speak about that much. I mean the nostalgia, of course. But also the terribly confused feelings we have for our countries, our families back home, our new homes. I also mean our struggles to learn new languages and cultures, to make new friends after 30, to make meanings of our changing lives.

ENOUGH IS ENOUGH

For me, personally, a burnout moment I experienced after almost two years of doing a PhD in London, UK, was the ultimate sign that I had overdone it with being abroad and moving around. Since I turned 18, I have done plenty: I went for an undergraduate degree in Bulgaria, I did an Erasmus during my second year in The Netherlands; then went for a "study abroad" programme in Virginia, USA, during the last year of my undergraduate. I went to Budapest for an MA; came back to Bucharest for a year; then went to Athens for a summer and then for some months to Berlin, followed by some months in Sofia. And then embarked on the PhD in London. I went to most of those places because of the nice opportunities to study and, less often, for reasons like love or wanting to be in a different place.

London, with its impossible prices, did me in. Like everywhere else, I had friends, good ones, but I was not sharing my everyday life with someone. Nor the bills. Eventually, I crashed and burnt.

And so I wanted to stop. I wanted to return to Romania and remain there, finish with the travels, draw a line under it all, sum it up. And get on with "a normal life" in my country, a job, maybe a partner some day, stable friendships and patterns. But for a while I did not find work that would both be satisfying and allow me to pay my rent. And doing something meaningful is for me as important as being in the right place, with the right people. I would have found something in Romania had I been more patient. But I was not. So off I went again, to Prague, following a job that promised to be interesting. And then I met a Pole and followed him to Warsaw, where I reside now. These last two moves were particularly difficult because I had been meaning to stop for so long already. I knew I had to stop. But I moved again because I felt that the opportunity for doing engaging work and, later, for being in a relationship like I wanted, were not in Romania, but elsewhere. They were elsewhere because I had opened up my life and knew what was possible for me outside of Romania. So I followed those opportunities.

I have been in Poland for three years. About two years and a half at the time of starting these interviews with other foreigners. Poland has been a totally different story for me compared to what I had done previously. If before Poland I had been abroad always for a limited period of time, and for a specific purpose (getting a degree, for instance), I am now in Poland for an indeterminate period (who knew how the relationship would evolve?). If before I was a student or I had colleagues who were foreigners too, here in Poland I am mostly among the Poles. Thus, here, the pressure to integrate has been bigger. I could not just remain an "international" for a while and then go back home. I had to become a Pole. Learn the language, learn the place. And do it as fast as possible.

TIED TONGUES

"Childish" and "cute", this is how I feel we look to locals when we try to speak the language of the place (I suppose this is a best-case scenario, but it has definitely been a scenario of mine since I moved to Poland). For sure they appreciate our efforts, they are patient with us, speaking English if need be and trying to speak to us in the local language if we so wish. But there is often a change of facial expression when the foreigner starts to speak the local language, with the inevitable grammar mistakes and word confusions: eyes are tightening, face concentrated, all the body seemingly focused on trying to understand what will be said, often with an accompanying expression of sympathy and compassion.

For my interviewees, becoming fluent in the local language (for instance, fluent like my Moldovan interviewee living in Belgium who was mistaken for someone coming from The Netherlands) was a significant personal achievement. It meant crossing a significant threshold from being looked down at as somewhat "primitive" and "immature" or, alternatively, as a poor economic migrant suspected of being less educated, to being seen as a reasonable adult whose arguments – once they were presented adequately – can be taken into account as legitimate. It – almost – meant becoming an equal. And this is the actual starting point of integration.

Up until that point of reaching fluency, many foreigners I spoke to shared my feeling of being inevitably and systematically quiet whenever they tried "living" in the new language: going out with locals for beers in the new language and being curiously contemplative, much more than we ever were in our native tongues. Nodding, smiling politely, at most saying a few short sentences. Losing track of the conversation at points and not insisting to be brought up to speed. One of my most talkative friends, a Moldovan living in Poland, whom I now like to observe engaging freely with any new local he meets, switching among topics with the most natural ease, confessed to me he felt quite differently during his first years in Poland: earlier, he would become awfully quiet and "un-opinionated". And, consequently, he was mostly ignored.

It seems as though we bring all of our complexes to the table where we are just supposed to chat over a drink. Instead of focusing on what we do know in the new language and communicate as much as we can, we focus on the vast amounts of things we cannot say. We give too much importance to the tiny flickers of impatience when locals try to anticipate what we want to say or when they forget our limits and start speaking too fast or too colloquially in their languages. These first beers in the local languages bring out our insecurities. But this does not mean we are all insecure individuals. Most of us are quite strong. It just means that there is something unavoidable there, in the power relations behind conversations where one of the parties expresses themselves much more clumsily than the other – that brings out insecurities. That brings us back to our high school times, when we felt much more awkward and shy.

And this while most of us were breathing sighs of relief that the teenage years are over, that we have been for some time now standing properly on our feet without worrying too much about what the others think. Living abroad and getting to grips with functioning in the new language usually comes with some return to a primitive stage. We let the others smell blood again, after years of building ourselves up into invulnerable adults. It is something we do not anticipate when we move abroad. But it takes time to function again as integral beings, expressing ourselves as we want.

Then, slowly, as we move towards fluency, we get to recover part of our personalities. Never fully. Research anyway shows humans exhibit different personalities in each of the languages they speak.

THE FREEDOM AND THE OVERSTIMULATION

But, then, of course, certain freedom comes with not understanding and not being understood. Not understanding properly releases one from the responsibility of responding. Perhaps to a sexist comment that someone made. Or it makes it easier to escape the insistence of the grandmother to have more food (Eastern European grandmothers always insist on giving you more food!). You may pretend you have not understood properly all her prodding.

When abroad, we all know it, we are almost totally free from the social norms back home. We may be living in a society with quite similar mores, but they are not ours so they do seem to count less. The aunts who expect us to get married before 30 or get a better paid job are just somewhere in the distant background. We do not know the neighbours. We do not run into our high school colleagues who may prompt us with frustrating comparisons regarding our "success".

When abroad, we are as alone and as free as an individual in a huge crowd. No one cares about us and that is just fine (remember, I write here about intra-European migration mostly, about people for whom it is easy to get lost in crowds because they look similar, I write about the easy cases of migration like mine; it is certainly different for those migrants who are found to be more distinguishable from host communities and who can thus be perceived as a threat). In fact, the taste of this freedom can be intoxicating. It can turn one into an addict of being on the move.

But on the other side of this coin (freedom) there is the issue of "overstimulation" as defined by my Polish interviewee living in Austria. While being abroad protects us from various social pressures, it is also isolates us from the more usual sorts of stimuli, such as everyday news. Being abroad means it takes a while to get all the cultural references, to understand the small jokes, to catch a hint someone made during a conversation. And the foreigners I spoke to have different attitudes to this.

The Polish friend living in Austria who came up with the above concept says that for him it is a relief to leave Poland even after a short visit. Unlike his everyday life in Austria, when he is back home in Poland, he feels he is bombarded with things: from bits of information floating around everywhere (ads, announcements) that he can interpret and respond to clearly and immediately; then from understanding everything people say on the street and always getting precisely what they meant and how conservative or annoying this made them appear to him; to having access to all the media, which, in comparison to Austrian media, seem to him to be "aggressive" and banal; to the family expectations his awareness of how the society over there wants him to be in order to consider him "normal", the reminders of which "normality" he reads from nearly every street corner, banner or face on the bus.

So, my friend says, he can only be in Poland for a maximum of three days at a time. That provides enough stimulation for him.

But another of my interviewees, a Moldovan who also resides in Austria, sees this "overstimulation" differently. He acknowledges that going back to Moldova and spending time with people there comes with his feeling of reconnecting with familiar emotions, and thus perhaps making most of his daily routine. But he sees this also as a matter of inherited assumptions about cultural difference, that is, between perceptions about Austria, which is usually represented ("occidentalised") as a more "civilised", "inert" and "antiseptic" West, and Eastern Europe, which is usually represented ("orientalised") as a much more "sentimental" realm, where people tend to "wear their hearts on their sleeves". He identifies himself with this Eastern region of "too much", of "overdoing it", and it comes more "natural" for him to be in this kind of space, in this kind of energy.

For me, the overstimulation phenomenon is not a matter of East versus West because it manifests itself when I transit between one Eastern European country and another, from Poland to Romania. I remember this feeling especially from my first months in Warsaw, when I did not speak the language and I understood much less of my context than now. I remember feeling somehow thirsty in my everyday life, devoid of the rich background against which we live when we are at home. Sure, I had images and sounds of novelty. But what I did not have were the familiar newspaper titles hanging from kiosks that I could read while waiting for the bus, the posters for upcoming theatre plays and the names of the directors, the random bus conversations with old ladies who love to chat, private conversations between strangers overheard in the street.

Missing these things made my life poorer. I was secretly jealous of my partner who, when we were walking down the street together, kept noticing these things and translating and interpreting them for me. It was like he was feeding on his environment and growing from it and I was undernourished. And when I was going back to Romania for a few days, I was taking it all in with a vengeance. I was bulge consuming everything around me, keeping my ears open to public transport chats between people, catching up on TV, reading all the newspaper titles, checking out all the inscriptions on walls. It was my turn to excitedly share those little signs of belonging with my partner. I felt complete and happy doing that and only wished I could keep that going for longer.

Of course, the particular relevance this background noise of information and customs has for me has something to do with the fact that journalism is my profession. Dressing this semiotic landscape in a different, unknown language would take away the essential matter of my work, of my life.

Unlike my Polish friend in Austria, I relish in this overstimulation. Though for me too there comes a time when it is too much, usually right around the time when big family dinners begin. It is much more difficult to delay surrendering to polite smiles and nods and to stuffing yourself when you are at home.

FAMILY LEFT BEHIND . . .

. . . which is getting older.

In some cases, ageing parents are the single reason why a person living abroad might consider returning home. Such is the case for a Bulgarian living in the UK I have spoken to. She is developing a very nice academic career in her host country and back in Bulgaria it would not be possible for her to find work related to her interests. Her partner is German and, with his line of work, it is hard to imagine what he would do in the small provincial town where the Bulgarian's parents live. Plus, she sounds genuinely happy in the UK, which is not the case with all the foreigners I spoke to. Yet the strong bond she has with her parents back in Bulgaria makes returning a viable option even under these circumstances.

In some cases, we consider returning to our parents even though they were very much part of the reason we left in the first place. My interviewees of non-heteronormative sexual or gender orientations left conservative Eastern European societies behind also to separate from parents who never understood them. Seeking to live their identities openly was a crucial reason why many of them left for Western Europe in the first place, and this promise of liberty is what keeps them there. And yet, because the parents are ageing, emigrant adult children are still considering coming back.

Most of us foreigners share a strong sense of responsibility for our parents left behind, even when the terms of the parent-child relationship are not ideal. Of course, all children, regardless of where they live, feel responsible for their parents. But to me it seems that for us foreigners this feeling is more acute at times when we feel less useful – there is simply less we can do for them while away.

For me personally, this sense of responsibility has an added flavour of guilt. For having left my mother behind. For not coming back, despite her hopes I would. For living my life outside of her reach. For having a child whom she will only be able to see on holidays. For not allowing her to help me as much as she thinks parents should help kids. For not being there as she ages. For not knowing for sure what I will do to take care of her when she gets even older.

THE FULFILMENT

There is one more feeling of responsibility that some of us feel in relation to our home country. One could call it social or political responsibility.

Even if far away, we want to keep contributing to the society left behind. Because it is that society whose problems we understand best, because we care for the people and places left behind, because we want to improve a country we might one day return to. Some migrants say that they want to make a contribution, now that they have done well for themselves, and that there is no better place to help than home. The Moldovan interviewee living in Austria is financially supporting an organisation that takes care of kids with special needs. Having seen how that works in the West, he thinks he is now better equipped to help out in his home country where he understands best the context and the needs.

For me, the thought that, if I were in Romania, I would be able to contribute more to activism or political life (which is generally a priority for me) is the strongest trigger for wanting to go back. I am no patriot; like my Moldovan interviewee, I just feel that knowing the context and the language makes it possible to make a useful contribution.

When I see Polish people getting involved in all sorts of political activities, organising demonstrations, writing militant texts, coming up with slogans, I feel a strong longing to be able to do the same. I try to participate, but for me as a foreigner this is only accessible in part. It takes long to get all the background details and the nuances of language that are necessary for activism. It also takes time to crack into local activist circles and to get used to their particular norms of behaviour.

The strongest desire to return to Romania I felt during the 2013 nationwide protests to save the landscape of Rosia Montană from destruction during the planned mining work. When the protests broke out, I went to Romania immediately and joined some of the weekly demonstrations, I wrote texts about Rosia Montană and I even organised a small solidarity action in Warsaw. I did my best considering my circumstances.

By taking those steps, I got a taste for what it might be like to be politically engaged in Romania. It was especially interesting to observe the change of sentiment in my country during those protests. The language people used was completely different from the cynical passive-aggressive rhetoric that had earlier been the stereotype for Romanians. The most commonly used words on the streets in the 2013 protests denoted determination and action. Many hoped that was the beginning of changing our society more fundamentally. It would have been very satisfying to stick around and join some of the offspring initiatives that came out of the Rosia Montană protests. But this would have required a change in my life that I was not ready to undertake at that stage, just as I was beginning to settle in Poland.

The Bulgarian interviewee living in the UK shared with me that she also felt deeply touched by the protests that shook her own country in 2013. While not going back to Bulgaria to participate, she was constantly reading about developments at home, posting on social media about them and discussing with friends. That is, until someone told her that because she is so far from events she does not really have a right to comment. My interviewee said that remark broke her heart and she refrained posting her opinions publicly about those protests.

Among the people I spoke to, there is also a case of someone who recently returned to her own country, Bulgaria again, with the intention of using all the experience she had gained during nearly ten years of living abroad for the benefit of her society. According to this friend, her life was always about activism, about "doing good". She started out in Bulgaria but, once she got the first opportunity to be involved in a campaign abroad, she kept going, to study more abroad, to get a job with an NGO in Brussels, to work in Africa. Her plan was always to come back and use that experience in Bulgaria, but it took her almost ten years to return. Now she is finally back. The first year back in Bulgaria proved to be extremely hard. Sofia, her city, felt suffocating. Opportunities and friends abroad kept calling her to get moving again. Yet despite considering to leave, she ended up being patient and in the end found a new opportunity for activism back home in Bulgaria. When I spoke to her, she sounded fulfilled, for the first time in a while.

It is probably true that most of us have a stronger voice in our places of origin, where we understand the language, the history and the mores best. And yet, because I am far from returning to Romania, I try to imagine alternatives. For example, being active both in Poland and in Romania, travelling back and forth, acting as a connector helping activists in the two countries to share experiences.

In my search for a compromise, I realised that while I might not be a Romanian any more and I will never be a Pole, I am and will continue to be an Eastern European. This is the region (as opposed to a single country) that I know, where I have lived and whose people and histories I understand. This is the region where I will continue to reside and about which I will most likely write. It may only be my construction, this identity of mine, but so is any other.

HOME

Inevitably, in all those conversations, discussions of home cropped up. Unsurprisingly, this simple word means so many different things to each of the various persons I interviewed. Foreigners often refer to their home country or their home city as home. "When I go home for the holidays", they say, referring to their country of origin. At least in the beginning, it is a struggle to call the new place or the new country a home. I remember how, in my first years abroad, I was simply avoiding to use the word *home* altogether because I did not know what I was supposed to call by that name. But then those of us who spend enough time abroad get used to their new places. We might even be able to say that "I'm coming home" when returning to our adoptive countries from a trip.

But home can take other shapes. My Moldovan interviewee who lives in Belgium says she actually lives in a room, not in a country. She immerses herself in her philosophy studies, her reading and thinking. For this purposes, she only requires a desk and a chair, books and a computer. She just needs a room, whichever country it is in. There is an expression I find particularly useful to explain this phenomenon, a term I caught during my research, called "a geography of the heart". It refers to an alternative geography whose parameters are our emotions. I liked that, as a means for weaving my travels to my inner world. I found myself trying to imagine how the geography of my heart looks like. I was picturing my connections with people all over the world, with those that mean a lot to me. I was imagining it all like a flights map showing all continents with red lines uniting me to the locations where my loved ones were. This was the geography of my heart. This was the place I inhabited. This was my home.

Or, as the friend who managed to return to Bulgaria after ten years abroad puts it, it can be that all we need is a base from which to connect ourselves to a lot of other locations where interesting things are happening. In her case, this base would be Bulgaria, which would give her stability and comfort, but this would not mean that she is confined to this country. She would still travel, perhaps even for months at a time, but she would always know what she is coming back to. And she would always come back to that same place, whether it is a country, or a city, an apartment or a room.

Over the course of these interviews, I realised that my own struggle to find out where I was belonging is what has led me into this research. Because, after years of wandering around, I needed to figure out what my base was. And I had assumed that all of us foreigners, even the most adventurous of us, share that need.

But this is not necessarily equally true for everyone I encountered. My Moldovan friend from Poland considers himself a nomad and says that he would like to move on again. He says that spending six to seven years in one place is just about the right time to get to know the local culture. After such periods, his feet get restless and he wants to get going again. But he is currently forced into stability, by having a family of his own here in Poland, a wife and a child, who need to stay put.

Perhaps the most radical statement about the elusiveness of the idea of home was made by one Polish interviewee currently doing a PhD in the UK. She said that, after years of struggling with the concept of home, she found that this notion was irrelevant for her, at least in its traditional, sedentary sense (a house, a family). Born in Germany to migrant Polish parents, her reference identity (the one that is usually cultivated in the first years of life, in the kitchen, with the parents) changed as she moved and lived in various places, without ever finding an ultimate reference point. She would thus hardly think of her identity in terms of a country or nation. She finds her university to be the place where she currently feels best. Not a city, not a country, nor her family house, but the university environment, with its formal support network

(from the canteen to the campus psychologist) and the different people coming and going. Or, better than the university, she says she could imagine her
home with people of similar interests, such as queer cultures. Home for such
"strangers" is rather as a sum of people and relationships, another form of the
geography of the heart.

I like these unconventional concepts of home because they appreciate
the relevance that imagined homes have for us, wherever we find ourselves
physically in any given moment. I discussed this with my Greek friend living
in London who said that, during her first long stunt in the UK, she was constantly comparing London to Athens, finding London to be the loser. People
rush all the time, the weather is bad and the local food is not very tasty. That
Athens was very much alive as an idealised option in her mind certainly prevented her from creating a space for herself in the UK. And then she went
back to Athens for some years and realised her idealised vision of it was nothing more than that, a utopia. People were not that great, nor was the rhythm
of life. Now, on her second long stay in London, she knows better than to
compare her adopted home to a fantasy.

The same is probably true of my ideal picture of a return to a Romania
where I would be able to be very politically engaged. There is no guarantee
that, once there, I would be able to find a place for myself. But maybe I need
the idealised Romania in my head until I am prepared to settle more fully into
my life here in Warsaw. I need that idea of Romania like a child needs a parent
to still keep a hand at the back of a bike while learning how to ride.

There is no such thing as one home, not as in the nostalgias we develop
while away. And there is no full immersion into the adoptive place. There is
just our oscillating between those two places, or among many more places,
struggling to find some meaning, to have a positive impact, to create bonds
with people. Struggling to find our own ways of belonging in this changing
Europe of ours.

Part VI

CONCLUSION

Chapter 11

Can Western Europe Be at Home in the Balkans?

Slavenka Drakulić, David Morley, Zlatan Krajina
and Nebojša Blanuša

INTRODUCTION

As the title of this final chapter suggests, we wish to reverse the position that runs through much of the existing literature, of whether and how the Balkans have been seeking a home in Europe. Guided by Julia Kristeva's important idea[1] that it is only at the point at which we can imagine ourselves as strangers that we can start dealing with difference productively (as an enrichment of rather than threat to identity), we suggest that, as far as imagining a future Europe as "united in difference" goes, we need to think not only about the Balkans as part of a "growing" Europe but also of Europe as being at home in the Balkans. This approach has inspired us to engage in a conversation with two key cultural commentators of European identities, whose work has greatly contributed to a non-essentialist understanding of Europe, Slavenka Drakulić and David Morley. Drakulić is the acclaimed writer of books on life under communism in Europe and on the 1990s war in post-Yugoslav states[2]. Her numerous non-fiction and fiction books on the theme have set the tone for the understanding of the culture of living in socialism and during what enfolds as a long transition, as well as belonging and injustice. Morley's milestone scholarship on media, home and mobility[3] has put to rest orthodox, commonplace assumptions about any alleged postmodern death of geography, diminution of the relevance of borders and technological liquidation of identity. His work demonstrates that ongoing transformations of societies have to do with communications across distance as much as with inequality of access to those connections and relevant physical geographies and histories.

In the following conversation, which marks twenty years since the publication of their key respective books on the matter, *Café Europa* and *Spaces of Identity*, Drakulić and Morley reflect on their earlier arguments about Europe as a policed, but also dream-like space of possibility for those in the Balkans, and Europe as a space of multiple identities, the boundaries of which have been made ever more permeable through communication technologies and waves of EU enlargement. Speaking from particular positions ourselves (Krajina – ZK – with an interest in media and culture and Blanuša – NB – from a more political and psychoanalytical perspective, both from the University of Zagreb, Croatia), we shall be pondering Drakulić – SD – and Morley – DM – about how various issues they raised in their earlier work figure in current contexts. We particularly enquire how issues of physical and imaginary Balkan geographies intersect with matters of regional and global political economy, history and politics, and whether the ancient east/west boundary shifts terrains during the ongoing crises at Europe's southern and eastern edges. The risk of producing any incomprehensiveness, however, is entirely ours, and we take it for the benefit of learning from the specific trajectories from which the two speakers have arrived at their interaction with us, and with each other.

JOURNEYS INTO THE BALKANS, REAL AND IMAGINED

ZK: Let me start by asking where from – geographically and culturally – have you both come to think about the Balkans?

SD: I never thought about it as part of my identity. I think you're forced to declare your identity only as opposed to someone, only when somebody asks you who you are, when you are forced to do that. Normally you wouldn't. You need somebody, it doesn't have to be an enemy, but usually it is, somebody to antagonize you with questions about your identity. I, of course, was put in that situation during the war in the 1990s, in which neutral positions weren't allowed; most people had to declare themselves as either Serbs or Croats, either Catholic or Orthodox, either this or that. My reaction was to write about it. I was very lucky because I already lived with one leg abroad, and with one leg abroad you see your home country from a different perspective. Like a fish in a gold fish bowl, which doesn't know it's swimming in dirty water, until it steps out. We all used to be just "Jugosi" and "Jugovići", which was a slightly pejorative name for Yugoslavs, you heard that when you went shopping to Trieste, but that wasn't a very big problem. During the war, if you said "I'm a Serb" in Croatia, you could get yourself in trouble. For your parents' generation, guys, being Balkan or not, didn't matter! This topic was *imposed* on us.

DM: The Balkans didn't really exist for me, growing up in England in the 1960s until, as a young man, I hitchhiked through what was then Yugoslavia, a number of times, travelling to Turkey and to Greece, and later to Egypt. On my trips through Yugoslavia, I glimpsed things that I'd never seen in my very suburban

British middle class upbringing. Coming through here in the early 1970s, I met a young guy who turned out to live in Ljubljana. He took me to stay in his family house, where he lived with a single mother and his little brother, and they obviously thought this was quite normal. But I'd never come across a culture where being a single parent wasn't a matter of shame, as it still was, at that time in the UK. That stuck in my mind; I glimpsed here a little bit of a planet I hadn't ever visited before.

Of course, if a lot of this debate is about how Europe defines itself in relation to the Balkan Other, we have to recognize I'm also from the "other" side of Europe in another sense, a place that defines itself against Europe. For Britain, Europe is a continent from which it is cut off. And also, for Europe and especially for France, there's America: the "Big Bad Evil" Other. In the particular cultural studies background that I come from, one of things we were interested in was the *positive* effects of American culture in undermining conservative European traditions. Not just moaning about it, like in France, when François Mitterrand defined a European as "someone who watches American soap opera on a Japanese television". All that puts me in a rather complicated position to think about Europe at all, *before* I get to the notion that Europe is defining itself in relation to the Orient, or to the Balkans.

SD: The Swedes also say "Europe is a continent, we go to Europe".

ZK: Croatia is now part of the EU, but we also still feel that it's "there".

DM: Britain has been on the edge of Europe the whole time, and in the context of the 2016 referendum, the relations between Britain and the EU remain a subject of debate. In the past, if you were "posh" in Britain, you had to go on the "Grand Tour" of Europe to complete your education. If you were a girl in a respectable family in the 19th century, you'd have to go to Switzerland to go to the "finishing school", but these are just cultural forms of "cake decoration" that Britain wants from Europe. It's not a desire to *become* European!

There's another side to this. For me, or for anyone that comes from an ex-imperial power, I don't think we can have this discussion about Europe in terms of just the countries that are geographically "in" Europe. You can't think about France without the shadow of the French empire and its populations. You certainly can't think about Britain except in relation to its ex-imperial populations, now resident in Britain. The debate about "otherness" and identity in Britain starts off as white British people being resentful about the presence of Afro-Caribbean and Asian people. But now, if you look at the right-wing UKIP (UK Independence Party), there are a substantial number of members who are Afro-Caribbean and Asian, and they take the position "We are British, we happened geographically to have parents who weren't born in Britain, but they came from a 'British' culture and *we* were born in Britain, we've been here now for generations – what we don't like are these Eastern European migrants!" That's a whole new ethnic fault line, and many people in Britain are uneasy about their relation to people from the countries that were part of the Soviet sphere of influence – with which they feel they have less in common than they have with the immigrant families from the old British Empire.

ZK: The Balkans emerges in this book as a demonstration of the ancient premise that how we see things, including geographical entities, depends on the specific perspectives we take. How would you, from your different trajectories, then, define the Balkans?

SD: Here, in Croatia's northern Adriatic peninsula Istria, where the four of us have met, people would be terribly offended to be told they're in the Balkans. When I moved to Vienna in 1993, I learnt that the Balkans starts at Südbahnhof, the southern train station. Slovenes think that it starts at Ljubljana's central station. And so it goes further and further. Zagreb, of course, thinks that it starts somewhere more east, at the border with Bosnia. The Balkans are less a geographical, and more a mental entity, and we have to keep that in mind. No one wants to be in the Balkans because it is almost always referred to in a negative sense. It's imbued with prejudice, and in that respect Maria Todorova[4] is right. The Balkans were *created.* She also criticizes my work, saying that I too refer to the Balkans in the negative sense. Which I did, but I don't know how else you could use it at the time I was writing the *Balkan Express,* referring to unimaginable atrocities in the 1990s.

DM: Then, my question would be, is there *anyone* who would admit to being in the Balkans?

SD: Yes, Bulgarians and Romanians, because they have this mountain "Balkan" there.

DM: But that's the nearest we get to it. Todorova[5] tries to make a distinction between Balkanism and Orientalism by emphasizing the existence of those mountains, as opposed to a completely invented reality of the Orient, but this hasn't had much impact on the debate. She actually makes much more of the significance of the Orthodox Church as an identity – as "not Islam", but a different form of Christianity – to differentiate between Balkanism and Orientalism.

SD: In this part of former Yugoslavia we've made very much of this distinction, too. This differentiation between "us" and "them" through nation as a religion, and religion as a nation, was very much used in the 1990s.

DM: If you look at the possibilities raised at the point when it seemed the Greeks might "exit" from the Eurozone, you notice one point in the negotiating strategy when Alexis Tsipras considers a deal with Vladimir Putin, whereby the shared religious "Orthodoxy" of Greece and Russia re-emerges – so this strange, seemingly abstruse, religious-historical thing seems to be coming back out of the distant past . . . re-born as a cultural ghost from the realm of the un-dead.

SD: It's always been there. In Serbia, for example, they used to say "Russians and us – 300 millions". So the Orthodox is binding, as is Catholicism, in the same way. We saw this especially in Eastern Europe after 1989 and the collapse of communism. I think that we were all rather naïve thinking that everything in what we call Velvet revolution would go without much trauma. Reaction is still coming, but the first reaction was a reappearance of nation and religion. Not because it was suppressed, as it was in some countries – in Yugoslavia, for example, less so – but also because in the time of insecurity and crisis, these two things seem to be the only identities you have. Everything around you, your known world is falling apart, you're insecure, and you're back to find your identity in a very traditional, very conservative, and a very "cast-in-stone" way, which is horrifying.

WRESTLING WITH HAUNTING HISTORIES

NB: It is popular to say that we in the Balkans produce more history that we can bear, and that in this part of Europe, "past refuses to become history"[6]. In the most recent period that started in the early 1990s, this "acceleration" included jumps from late socialism to wild capitalism, and the post-Yugoslav wars. Does such a view that our recent history is a form of "accelerated", traumatic history have anything to do with the kind of "post-modern" "time-space compression", which is a Western European way of conceiving the world? Are we, the "Resterners", in this context, fodders of the West's own nightmares of itself being, as it were, at the "end of history"?

DM: That postmodernist view of the world takes you back to Francis Fukuyama[7] and the insane belief that in 1989 we had arrived at the "end of history". But that "heroic" liberal market capitalism perspective is nonsense – especially when we look, empirically, at all the history that has subsequently come back to haunt us. The postmodern defines itself, at one point, as the end of Grand Narratives. But quite early on in this debate, the Black American intellectual Cornel West[8] just says "What the hell is the rise of fundamentalist Islam if that is not the emergence of a major grand narrative?" America is getting more religious too. Another person who got onto this point early on was the Black British intellectual Paul Gilroy[9]. He described postmodernism as the psychic crisis of the white, educated, middle classes of Europe, working in the decaying public sector in what is already a declining region of the world, terrified by the rise of Japan and the Four Tigers. So the "postmodern" was perhaps a way of seeing the world that was largely generated from an incredibly narrow White Euro-American perspective that claims to speak for the whole world. It didn't help us then, and I really don't think it helps us now, to imagine that history is "ending", because there is so much traumatic history coming back, if now in new forms, especially as the political conflicts between Europe and its Others, whether in the Balkans or the Middle East, keep repeating patterns familiar almost since medieval times.

SD: The notion that "too much history" happened, as too many wars, too many confrontations etc. is just prejudice. What I see as a problem is that our past was never articulated by history as science. In the communist times, what we used to call socialism, the history of the world made only one tenth or one fifteenth of the curriculum. The rest was about the Second World War and defence against Germans. The most important role had the communist party. The fact that anti-fascism was linked only to the communist party has many serious consequences even today . . . in short, what we learned at school was more ideology than history.

The lack of knowing facts and understanding our history was one of the reasons we had the war in the 1990s and why we have a split between pro-fascists or revisionists and anti-fascists today. We never dealt with truth from the Second World War, much less this war 20 years ago, which looks to me like yesterday. Where I went to school, we never learned about Bleiburg, where Yugoslav Partisans murdered thousands of collaborators with the Croatian Nazi puppet state (Independent State of Croatia – NDH) but also civilians fleeing with soldiers, while the figures of Jasenovac concentration camp casualties were exaggerated for purposes of reparations. So I can't agree that we had too much history. We didn't know proper history in terms of factography at all.

DM: Of course, you were taught ideology. But not only here – the first thing Mrs Thatcher did was very ideological: she started reconstructing the history curriculum in British schools, to make sure you didn't get any more critiques of imperialism and empire – to make sure the story told was that of Britain's marvellous contributions to "civilizing" the world. It's been ideological all the way through. One character in Salman Rushdie's *Satanic Verses* says, "The trouble with the English is that their history happened overseas, so they don't know what it means"[10], and he is talking precisely about what the British Empire has done all over the world and how much of that complex story is forgotten, or even denied, within the "official" story of the nation.

SD: That is the essence of the problem of reconciliation in ex-Yugoslavia. We'll never get out our problems if we don't deal with facts from the past, and obviously we are not capable of that. If you do not know what really happened, then somebody can come and tell you, "they killed all of our people". How would you know if that's true? There were no independent specialists i.e. historians. In the late 1980s, political elites easily shifted emphasis from real problems to this kind of "who did what to us 100 years ago".

DM: A friend of mine, doing a project on "divided cities", tells me that in Belfast there are now 90 "peace walls", which are built to provide "security" around the edges of Catholic and Protestant territories – which is more than there were at the height of the conflict there. The reason I mention that is because one of the ways that "the Balkans" gets to be a problematic term is because it is used to imply that there is something specific ("violent", "unruly", "uncivilized") about people of this geographical region which constitutes a kind of essential deficiency, and I'm trying to argue it's not a matter of geography. It's something which is not at all geographically specific, but works in different ways in different places, depending on whether it's a division by religion, political ideology, or some other form of division. Where

I live, in East London, the poorer the area, the less the people have got, apart from their own territory, the more ferociously "territorial" they are: thinking "oh, he looks different, that stranger, I don't like him!" There's a universal tendency towards territorialism, defensiveness and of aggression towards the "nasty others", which then takes specific forms in particular geographical regions and historical moments.

NB: The main problem I see in the Balkans, particularly in ex-Yugoslavia, is a struggle between historical truth and political desire for power, for a particular definition of what has happened. How to deal with reconciliation in places like Croatia, where reconciliation is equated with national treason?

DM: The beauty of the reconciliation process in South Africa was the decision that it was more important that the truth be told than the revenge be taken. What happened to black people under apartheid in South Africa was as horrible as anything in the world. But somehow that process of "truth" and reconciliation was made to work there.

ZK: Scholars like Dejan Jović[11] and Zoran Kurelić[12] argue that unlike the former Soviet countries in Central and Eastern Europe, Yugoslav successor states were never entirely transformed from communist to liberal democratic societies, precisely because, following the hybrid identity of the Non-Aligned Yugoslavia (a mixture of socialism and market economy), the 1990s change was not desired nor undertaken from within, but only to please others, like the EU's accession conditions. To quote Mieczyslaw Boduszynski, our politicians "fake", that is, perform a "hybrid" kind of democracy, just "to meet concrete political ends and pacify external critics"[13].

SD: The entire history of this part of Europe, in a very banal and condensed way, is as follows: there's feudalism, then comes communism. You go directly from one kind of society into another, without passing through what, for example Western Europe, passed; revolutions, like the French, the bourgeois revolutions, we did not have, and our values, mentalities and habits did not change so fast. We are still stuck with the mentality of 25 years before, as during communism we were still stuck with many elements of feudal mentality. And now people are surprised to see democratic institutions here which are non-functional. You can develop democratic institutions in 25 years, but you can't have democracy! People behave exactly the same as they did during communism, we have tribalism, corruption, and clientelism as before. "I'll do things for you, I'll employ you first because you're my best friend and my daughter and my *kum*/best man". So, what did we gain in these 25 years? We gained freedom, but freedom involves responsibility, and responsibility here does not work. Neither politicians want to take it, nor ordinary people. Generations of people had authoritarian governments, first the king, then an authoritarian quasi-king like Tito. Now we don't any longer have a communist "we", the common identity, but a nationalist "we", where everyone is expected to adhere to this new word *domoljublje* (love for homeland). Where do you learn about an anti-authoritarian culture? Most certainly not from our past . . .

DM: It's quite interesting how we might bring in here Mrs Thatcher's transformation of British culture towards a greater individualism, when she declares
"there's no such thing as society, only individual men and women". The whole
Thatcherite hegemony which has now lasted, God help us, more than 30 years,
over that period has transformed the notion of what a "person" is in Britain.
Nowadays in the UK it's only "common sense" that a person has to be very
individualist, has to keep fit, be self-entrepreneurial, a self-developer, self-ish.
In the consequent death of all the public forms of collectivism of the post-war
Welfare State, I see the dying of all of the things I treasured about British
society. But things like "individualism" can mean different things in different
places. Slavenka, you wrote about how people in Eastern Europe haven't ever
been allowed much sense of individuality at all, under communism. While
I hate how individualist Britain has become, I can still see that sometimes, even
individualism can be positive, in the face of the conservative forms of authoritarian collectivism.

ZK: Let me hang onto the issue of temporality for a bit more. Slavenka has
demonstrated that communism modelled itself as an "eternal" system[14]. It furnished a sense of dead time, whether at the level of narrating its ideology as the
only one conceivable, or at the everyday level of queues in post offices where
people stood waiting – during their own office hours – until the clerk comfort-
ably brewed coffee for themselves before providing service to anyone at the
counter. Now, across Europe austerity and the neoliberal project are being nar-
rated as being "without alternative", which is exactly what pre-1989/1990 communist regimes were telling its citizens about their own "inevitability" ("iron
laws of history"). Could we draw a parallel between this sense of "suspended
future" (the brighter tomorrow was constantly being promised and delayed)
and the ways in which now the future is being infused with a profound sense of
uncertainty ("crisis" has become permanent)?

DM: One of my teachers, Stuart Hall, always said that the key date for him in his
whole intellectual life was 1956. Coming from the Caribbean and writing about
post-colonial studies, he said that he found himself being dragged into politics
"backwards" against the simultaneous invasions of the British paratroops in
Suez and the Soviet tanks in Budapest. He was thinking about *both* capitalist and communist forms of oppression. I think that the recognition (or even
glimpse of) political alternatives, recognized by things like the Non-Aligned
Movement of the 1960s was very important. I've come to think that there was
something well worth recalling in the Non-Aligned Movement. I'm fascinated
to see that, in fact, it does (notionally) still exist, with ongoing committees and
an organizational structure, even if, these days, it doesn't do much. I've always
been given this understanding of it as an "empty dream" that nobody should ever
have bothered about. But I'm now wondering whether there we might usefully
still go back and reconsider it: perhaps that wasn't necessarily just a historical
"blind alley".

ZK: It is certainly problematic that even critique itself is increasingly being called
"radical" (e.g. Greece's views of "bailout" conditions set by the Troika – IMF,

ECB and EU Commission – as "humiliating" ultimatums), when it is the essence of democracy to appreciate different viewpoints. That really downplays the substance and vitality of any discussion.

DM: Chantal Mouffe[15] has this notion that, if we're going to understand democracy, we have to understand that it is above all else an "agonistic" process, a process of disagreement, which won't produce an answer that we all agree on. Whatever social and political arrangement we might want in the future, it is going to depend on recognizing and validating disagreement.

TRIBALISM, REGIONALISM AND MOBILE GEOPOLITICS

NB: During this so-called period of transition some places in the Balkans have witnessed a large scale re-traditionalization, fuelled by the Catholic Church and its re-emergence as a kind of renewed ideological force or "state apparatus". Croatia was alerted to a peculiar form of an "occupy" protest, with a tent, erected in front of the ministry of war veterans in Zagreb, and held for more than a year, heavily ornamented with wartime nationalistic symbols, and warmly sympathized and supported by the Church. Is it trying to put itself in the "shoes" of the communist party as the ultimate political arbiter and interpreter of history, given that the unfinished democratization of the Balkans has produced such ideological "vacuum"? Does this sound to you, as it does to me, as a rather "ironic" return, especially as it is happening in this hyper-technologized world, to a pre-modern frame of mind, where the Church seeks to freeze time, or this is just a "farce"?

SD: Why in the country of a long tradition of authoritarian governments would not the institution like Catholic Church try to get as much power as they can? If I ruled the Catholic Church in Croatia, I would certainly try to do that and they're doing it very successfully. There was Tito, communist party, and then comes the Catholic Church. It's not farce; it's very real, I'm afraid. And it is a consequence of the post-1989 identity crisis but also a consequence of 1991–1995 wars. When they say there are 95% Catholics in Croatia, it only means that they want to distinguish themselves from the others who are non-Catholics. It doesn't mean that these are believers or church goers. It is only to equate Catholic with Croat, and vice versa, as opposed to the orthodox, who are Serbs.

DM: That seems to me also to be expected, given the historical roots, in the Latin phrase about Croatia being designated by the Pope as the "front wall" of Christianity: *antemurale christianitatis*. That goes very deep, when you think (as Umberto Eco suggests) about the church as a medieval equivalent of a powerful, transnational broadcasting system! One of the threads related to this is the whole story of modernization and progress, as told by people like Max Weber[16], as being about the presumption that the future will be scientific and secular. Quite separately from the communist opposition to religion on ideological grounds, there's been a presumption in the last 200 years or so, that the future will automatically or necessarily, be more secular – but that is manifestly not happening. We're surrounded by the growth of religious modernities. Look at all the very religious, very rich, very successful, very authoritarian societies all over East Asia. So, let's not imagine that this religious issue is something specific just to the Balkans. It's a general problem and I don't think that secularization necessarily offers the solution.

SD: In the Balkans, many people tend to treat identity as if it is something that might be stolen from them. I personally like to define identity as a sandwich, with layers of local, regional, national, European, but also many-faceted individual identities, which add to each other. But nationalism sees identity as cast in stone. Maybe the problem is also that there is no such thing as, and maybe it is only being created slowly, European identity. But we are more and more having national identities coming back on the agenda. Of course, one of the reasons is a bad financial situation, and the other is immigration, which has turned out being a very useful political argument and also a racial issue across Europe.

Huge waves of immigration came before the current one from the Maghreb into Italy, Serbia or Bulgaria. One came from Albania with the collapse of its financial "pyramid" structure in the late 1990s, and there was earlier one following the Bosnian war. About 50,000 Albanians came on the sea, as well as almost 40,000 people from Bosnia. There was this image, by an Italian photographer, of the Albanians coming to Bari, on a huge merchandise ship that had thousands people hanging on every possible inch. About 20 years later this boat disappears from view. What happened was not "integration", as it is usually called, but assimilation. Second generations are already finishing Italian schools. A friend of mine, who is Bosnian, came from Srebrenica when she was ten, and she is now a well-known Italian writer.

ZK: The issue is also how different generations share the present moment. Speaking from my own generation born in the early 1980s (the last one to be admitted in Tito's pioneers), we are pulled into battles which are not necessarily our own: in 1995 I had difficulty enrolling in high/secondary school because, even though I was born in Croatia, my blood wasn't "pure" enough, given that my parents were born elsewhere in Yugoslavia, and now in 2015, some right-wing politicians pester the public by asking "where were you in 1991 (when the war broke out)?" Members of parliament are always ready to couch discussions as diverse as food safety, gay rights and privatization of shipyards, in terms of Second World War cleavages. All the same time, the young and educated either remain unemployed, or happily report about getting a job in Germany or Ireland, because they see "no future" for themselves in the Balkans.

DM: Dates are funny things. I noticed, Slavenka, reading one of your essays, that you were born in the same year as me, 1949. My generation in Britain is recently referred to as the "lucky guys", the "baby boomers". We got free education, there were jobs; we could buy houses when property was cheap.

SD: Life was good for us in this part of Europe, too. We lived in peaceful times, we could travel abroad, buy books, learn English, watch American movies.

We, my generation, were really the last believers in socialism in Yugoslavia. We were not liberal, but depoliticized, besides we had the gerontocracy principle. Old politicians, many of them from Partisan times, treated us as babies.

DM: I keep finding myself wondering whether there is anything to be rescued from that past, which is not just nostalgia. Two years ago I was with a group of Croatians in Dubrovnik for a conference. On the way back, we ran into an air traffic strike, which kept us stuck in the airport for six hours, but actually we had a really good time, having an improvised picnic, which they constructed out of bits and pieces that could be bought in the airport shop, and we were eating at a makeshift picnic table made from an old crate. And the joke that kept being made that it was because they still had Tito's "Pioneers" spirit. It was a fantastic occasion, with people dealing playfully, but collectively, with a difficult situation. Čvoro's chapter in this book talks about conceptual art projects also including these rather playful forms of dealing with the past – and maybe, although it sounds trivial, it is, in fact, an important level at which to address the issue.

SD: But I'm sorry to say that your generation, Zlatan, is depoliticized too. They are de-motivated when they see this terrible corruption. They know that youth today go into politics in order to get money. And then they expect somebody else to bring some kind of solution to their problems. It was amazing to see Thomas Piketty giving a lecture in the National Theatre in Zagreb in 2015. At the end a person from the audience said, "You know something about the economy? Please tell us what to do!" (Laughter) That's how it works! There's still this idea, even hope that the solution will come from outside.

DM: That's exactly the parallel with the Egyptian problem; there again, there was a crazy notion that a democratic process could be imposed, very quickly, from above, on a population quite unfamiliar with and unprepared for any form of democracy, as we might understand it.

SD: The four of us arrived here today driving up this little road, which was recently widened. My neighbour from the village, knowing that the minister of foreign affairs has her house here too, asked me if it is true that the road was widened because of the minister! Because it's absolutely normal that a politician who comes from any small place builds a road for himself, or brings electricity, as it was before. People have learnt to expect things get done from above, that is, corrupt. Political elites are identified with – democracy. And when political elites are bad, we automatically distrust democracy as such! This is why things develop very slowly here.

ZK: What does then happen to the elemental idea that has guided the development of Europe as a "Union", which was a kind of negation of whatever lied east of its protected borders? Is the EU enlargement and the influx of young and educated labour migrants from Central and Eastern into Western Europe, and of the refugees from Africa and the Maghreb in any way challenging the old Euro-centric cartography?

DM: In 1995, Kevin Robins and I were writing about the definition of Europe, and about the northern border of the Balkans or the south-eastern border of Europe – whether you define it as falling in Croatia or just outside of Klagenfurt. But I don't think it's in the same place any more. The pictures we're seeing daily, of would-be migrants from North Africa drowning in the Mediterranean off Italy, re-frames the question of where the southern and the eastern borders of Europe will be. The question of patrolling those borders and the EU's plans for the processing of would-be migrants in North Africa rather than in Italy, shifts the terrain. For me, the really spectacular issue was Greece, especially at the point when their finance minister showed his middle finger (at the Subversive festival in Zagreb) as a gesture to the Germans. Then the Greeks came up with that negotiating tactic of saying to the Germans "it's time you paid war reparations, if you want to see the money you say that we owe you". That was crude, but it speaks directly to the crux of the matter, because it was German archaeologists who invented the notion of Greece (in the 19th century) as the foundation of the classical European civilization. That relation is now in crisis, given that the Balkan geographical territory is "in between" Europe and the Great Beyond. If Greece finally leaves Europe – which it still may, one day – the Balkans won't be a "missing bit" of the puzzle of essential "Europeanness". The Balkans will then seem even "further away", because there'll be nothing that Europe identifies with beyond, on the other side of the Balkans.

I'm less satisfied with the notion of "East/West divide" than I was in 1995. Everywhere is an East and West to somewhere else: these are relative concepts. Recently, I went to an exhibition in Istanbul about the way that the "white Turks" have orientalized the Eastern districts of Anatolia! Istanbul is now a massive receiver of migrants from elsewhere, and Asian migrants are also coming into Serbia. Dipesh Chakrabarty talks about "East" and "West" as conceptual categories, where time and space are meshed together[17]. It's hard to say "West" without thinking about what is newer, better, and "progressive"; similarly, it's hard to think of "East" without thinking about tradition, corruption, and decay. They're temporal categories as much as they are geographical; but the emerging economy of the world is China, and so the future is actually moving *East*! Classically, in Europe we think of history as a "process" running from East to West; the sun of capitalism rises in Venice, then Paris takes over, then Amsterdam, London, then New York. . . . Forget it, now it's in places like Shenzhen that the future is being scripted.

SD: Having lived much of my life in socialism, I see this east/west division again re-emerging as a political element in Russia antagonizing Ukraine.

DM: But that's now a different East/West split than it was before. When I switch on the television to watch European Championship football in Britain, I have to watch the Russian "Gazprom" adverts because they're now the sponsor of the Champions League. The way in which they are now in a position to use energy resources as a negotiating tactic against the West, just as they already do in the

Ukraine, is political dynamite, but it's not only a question of the "hard" politics of resources – it's also about soft forms of cultural power.

SD: Ukraine is considered a "black hole" in Europe, a huge country that neither Europe nor Putin wants. Europe couldn't solve the problem in Bosnia, how will it do it in a much bigger country much further away? I see it also as a problem of the otherness, are they "they"? It's kind of an old Roman Empire problem and the invasion of the barbarians on its borders. Not having its own foreign policy, Europe still depends on America. Plus, we should also remember the kind of capitalism with no border on the profit, of this enormous, to use Naomi Klein's expression, "greed", can it go on like this? Only a strong state can put a stop to it, and the state exists less and less. In that context, the case of Greece is very paradigmatical.

NB: Euro-crisis actually reanimated an old narrative of "being exploited by others" for example, in the fears of young Spaniards of being enslaved by Germany, in the Italian indignation with French and German leaders' arrogance, etc. Furthermore, this sentiment is obvious in the Germans declaring that the concept of multiculturalism is dead, in Greeks' revolt against the "occupation", with depictions of Angela Merkel in Nazi uniform, and comparing the 2011 tumults in Athens with Czechoslovakia in 1968, where rating agencies were compared with the Russian tanks enforcing limited sovereignty. In such North vs. South polarization, it seems that Greece is symbolically returning onto the map of the Balkans. Is the status of the Balkans now assigned to "PIIGS" (Portugal-Italy-Greece-Spain)? Where is the border of such Yugoslavization of the EU?

DM: There's a good reason to think about historical analogies between contemporary Europe and medieval Christendom. Over the last 25 years the debate initiated by the Northern League ("Lega Nord") in Italy has been basically about the idea (preposterous though it sounds) to build a line just south of Rome and cut the south of Italy off, and solve the problem that way. What comes to my mind is the Hanseatic League from the 15th century, built around the northern German and Baltic ports. If you look at the politics of which countries took the hardest line against the Greeks, in the crisis of summer 2015, it was exactly the countries of North West Europe, where the Hanseatic League was founded. There's a Europe that looms in the future, of which Northern Germany and Scandinavia would be the key part. It would be the rich North-Western part of Europe. It's not just that Greece might still leave or get kicked out, which is crucial, given that, as I said earlier, Greece has historically provided the very definition of what Europe is and where it comes from. (Even if, as Martin Bernal's "Black Athena" shows, the North African roots of Greek culture were written out at the beginning[18].) But this all involves a potential reconstruction of Europe, which could be rather more radical than anybody understands at the moment. It's not just about Greece; other European countries or regions like the south of Italy, may either be pushed out of Europe or relegated to some very "secondary" status. However, to go back (finally!) to your question, yes, there is a narrative about being exploited, but there is also (an even worse) narrative about being abandoned and not even being thought worth exploiting. That's an even worse prospect for the future, of just being discarded (which comes close to what writers like Agamben are concerned about).

SD: Ukraine is just that, abandoned, and treated as not being worth exploiting. That's a definition of the EU's attitude to Ukraine. Before Ukraine, it was Bosnia and Croatia. Are we all so different? We look not at the things that connect us, but which disconnect us, and in that light, the whole future of the project of the EU is really frightening.

NB: Giorgio Agamben[19] tried to revive the idea of Southern EU, originally proposed to Charles de Gaulle by another philosopher, Alexandre Kojève[20], just after the Second World War. Agamben's newspaper article entitled "The 'Latin Empire' should Strike Back" glorifies Kojève's idea that Germany would soon become Europe's main economic powerhouse and that France would be downgraded to a "secondary power" within Western Europe[21]. He said, "If we do not want Europe to inevitably disintegrate as many signs seem to indicate it is political reality should be turned into a 'Latin Empire', with France as a leader, along with Spain, Italy and other Mediterranean nations"[22].

DM: I certainly think Europe is going to be a shrinking, and more tightly defended territory. There may still be a *notional* Europe, which at a formal level is quite inclusive, but it won't be anything like what Europe is today: it will have a very small number of rich, powerful countries at its centre, more so, even than it does now.

SD: At present, there is an interesting development which may help to curb the current rise of nationalism. It's regionalism. I see how it works here. Istrians feel that they're part of the region more than of the nation. In the census of 1990 a great number declared themselves Istrians, which made authorities go berserk, because you can't be Istrian. But food here is a poor version of Italian and Slovene cuisine, and of course they go to Italy every other day to buy groceries and to Slovenia to buy petrol. For Istrians, Croatia is "there", on the other side of the mountain Učka. Regionalism could be good in terms of connecting people over the real or no longer real borders, because what we got was EU as constructed from above, and nothing was done, so to say, from below. I walk the streets here and I speak three languages immediately. An Italian lives in that house and a Slovene lives in the house next to it, and it doesn't feel like somebody is taking or stealing something away from you, but adding. Being Istrian does not mean "not being Croatian". It means Istrian and Croatian and Balkan and East European. In southern Sweden they feel more Danish and have a bridge going from Malmö to Kopenhagen, which is not only for trade. Thus the idea of regionalism, where you speak more than one language and food is of mixed cuisine, might take us somewhere, imagining multiple identities as a political project, perhaps.

NB: David, in your 2014 lecture at the Subversive festival in Zagreb, you discussed EU's actions concerning various transcontinental communication and transport networks and their power to regulate, constitute and exclude different categories of people and to constitute the territory. You described the so-called "Corridor 8" project as a reopening of the Silk Road and an imaginary return to the 19th-century Bismarck's dream to build a railway from Berlin to Baghdad and further, to the Indian Ocean. Along with other processes, especially with Eastern countries accession to the EU, can we describe this scheme as the final realization of the German empire?

DM: The whole notion of geopolitics, as invented by German intellectuals in the late 19th century, concerns me more and more. In both *Spaces of Identity*[23] and the book that followed, *Home Territories*[24], I discussed a world in which we have to think about virtual as well as actual geographies, whether in the form of satellite broadcasting or internet connections or whatever. What I'm trying to think about now in my book *The Geopolitics of Communication*[25] is how to re-model those old notions of geopolitics and imperial rivalries, because, to my mind, they still go a long way to explaining things. When we are talking about the Ukraine, it is important to remember that in an earlier period, Ukraine was part of the Polish empire. There's often another historical structure there that lurks in the background of contemporary events. What interests me is thinking again about the classical questions of geopolitics but now in the "re-vivified" form that they achieve in this world of virtual communications. If you look at an old *Oxford English Dictionary*[26], it defines "communication" as a noun concerned with transport as much as with the sending of messages. But nowadays we think of communication entirely as a matter of rhetoric, as only a matter of information. However, if you look at the way transport links like the high-speed railways, have reshaped Europe, they were built on the principle of allowing businessmen from particular northern European cities to go somewhere, do a day's business and get "back home" in time for dinner. But the problem is that the more those parts of Europe are connected, the more disconnected the rest of Europe is. That's why I invoke that Bismarck story. I want to insist that those old questions about the geopolitics of transport are as important as all this stuff about television and the internet that have been so much the focus of recent debate.

THROUGH THE SCREEN: EUROPEANS AND THEIR OTHERS

ZK: There is a powerful and disturbing notion in *Spaces of Identity*, David, that the presence of difference is increasingly mediated via television and computer screens, to the point at which we all, sooner or later, and whether we like it or not, become "armchair anthropologists" or "nightly witnesses of the strange customs of Others"[27]. You go on to argue that "screening the Other" is actually about screening out "our" fears of the outside world from which the screen will shield us just as the national border control will protect us[28]. In this particular context, the screening of Bosnia and Croatia during the post-Yugoslav wars, but also Kosovo and Serbia later, for better or worse, made the Balkans present in the homes across Western Europe. But now it seems as though, since trouble has moved further towards the east of Europe, the Balkans have gone from the everyday news screen altogether (in spite the European Commission's repeated attempts to create a sense of belonging in the EU via shared television pro- grammes and similar schemes). How do you see the actual use of the media in representing difference in Europe?

DM: What you see in the media in most northern European countries is almost exclusively pictures of migrants' distress, of these poor, desperate people, drowning on boats just off the coasts of Mediterranean countries. You see the failure of migrant hopes; you are shown death and disaster. But I'm quite interested in trying to think about different forms of representation of these issues. The Swiss video maker Ursula Biemann has a series of works, which are potentially very productive, because she approaches the question of migrants coming to Europe from their own perspective. She goes to the camps on the far side of the Sahara desert where they meet, and you see them in this moment of optimism, when things are still possible, as they set off across the Sahara with their Tuareg guides. You have to remember that actually, an awful lot of them are successful. Europe represents to itself the continual failure of migrants to get into Europe, but most of the time, migrants *are* getting into Europe. They are coming in container ships, in all kinds of ways . . . percentage-wise, illegal migration is a much better bet than is shown in the European media!

SD: Showing the images of migrants in distress is perhaps meant to act as a message to them back home: "Don't do it, you'll die".

NB: To describe the role of flickering TV screen as a sort of limited preparatory device for facing the war, as well as how the war profoundly changed people in the Balkans, David, you cited some lines from Slavenka's books, one of which is rather important here: "For a long time we have been able to fend off the ghost of war; now it comes back to haunt us, spreading all over the screen of our lives, leaving no space for privacy, for future, for anything but itself"[29]. It describes how the spectre became the real, how it became a pure horror. In other words, the reality of war was not any more separate but became our reality. And this spectre has kept returning, in the forms of haunting discourses about friends and foes, victims and perpetrators, imbued by interpretations from the previous wars and ancestors' unhealed wounds. Another layer of spectrality was filled with western images of uncivilized tribal conflicts and viral metaphors calling for the quarantine and distancing from this area. I'm interested here in these "screens of our lives" as virtualities with the real effect. They could be produced by screen- ing technology but they were here before such technology. Are they necessary to keep us together as collectivities and against our proclaimed enemies and/or inferiors? Is it possible to live without spectres? If not, what kind of spectres do we need?

DM: In the front of *Spaces of Identity*, Kevin Robins and I quote the Cavafy poem that says "What's happened to the Barbarians? These people were some kind of a solution – if we haven't got them, what are we going to do?"[30] Ghassan Hage has a parallel, psychoanalytic, notion that the value of the barbarians (the migrants, the others) is that their presence is used as an alibi to explain why "we" are not happy[31]. What happened at a certain moment in the post-Yugoslav wars, as televised in Europe, did have a kind of visceral effect. But of course, if it's only on television, it could be anywhere, it's not "real". As a viewer, you are protected from it, just like with any other screen, if you've had too much of it, you just change to another channel. So it's a peculiar thing, you feel informed, you feel perhaps you've taken a moral position, donated to a charity for refugees or something. But most of the time it's just a morally edifying spectacle of the woes of Others.

SD: I tried to describe this in *Balkan Express*. Television wanted to distance us from the war in the Balkans in the early 1990s. It was saying that the war was happening "there": in Vukovar, in Dubrovnik. Even two streets away was not "here". So it was constantly trying to push the war away. You come to think that it doesn't concern you. What I tried to capture are those small moments of preparation, which were perhaps not conscious, but you see around you people buying sugar and flour, stocking them, thinking, "we don't know if something's gonna happen, but it's better to be "prepared"". On one level, it was very abstract. War, for people in Zagreb, was happening "far away" (about 40 kilometres!) in neighbouring towns of Karlovac and Sisak. Until Zagreb was bombed, war did not materialize. Even refugees were put in some centres and hotels, so it was on the whole more abstract and distanced than not. War was happening "somewhere else".

DM: Concerning the ways in which all this was screened in northern Europe (which always implied attitudes like "Thank God I'm not there"; "how weird those people are"; "I'm not like them"; "isn't this dreadful"), I recall that a friend of mine in Sydney supervised a PhD thesis by someone from Macedonia, a study of how, during the war in Yugoslavia, in the suburbs of Sydney, there were many Serbs and Croats living there. Members of each community "back home" were sending them unedited, raw video footage of atrocities of what had happened to their families, which was stuff that was way beyond what you'd see on ordinary television. The arrival of that footage then sparked riots in the suburbs of Sydney. It was a very strange virtual form of long-distance "viralization" of trauma and some people responded to it by re-starting the war in their own, far-away Australian suburbs. In Sydney they were doing it only with fists, not with guns, but they were fighting! So the wars then were re-located to a quite distant territory and re-staged there.

However, as we seem to be coming to an end of our discussion, let me also say, on a rather abstract level, that I was reminded by this discussion of a big EU meeting in which they were once discussing some policy, where Umberto Eco was present. He interrupted them to point out that there were difficulties in the policies they were proposing. And so they asked "OK, so what do *you* think we should do about it, if you're so clever?" And he said "No, no, no, I'm an intellectual, my job is only to define problems more clearly – *your* job is to solve them!" So I'm thinking about us here: I think we're maybe giving ourselves a bit of a hard time, like we're also trying to identify the solutions to all these problems – but that may be above our pay-grade.

SD: I agree with Eco, we can only describe problems and ask unpleasant questions, maybe also million dollar questions. But we're obviously not paid to answer them.

ZK: OK – so I'd better start fundraising!

NOTES

1. Julia Kristeva, *Strangers to Ourselves* (Harvester Wheatsheaf: New York and London, 1991), 13.

2. Slavenka Drakulić, *Café Europa: Life After Communism* (New York: Penguin Books, 1999/1996); *The Balkan Express: Fragments from the Other Side of War* (Zagreb: VBZ, 2012/1993); *How We Survived Communism And Even Laughed* (Zagreb: VBZ, 2013/1992); *They Would Never Hurt a Fly: War Criminals on Trial in the Hague* (New York: Penguin Books, 2005); *A Guided Tour Through the Museum of Communism: Fables from a Mouse, a Parrot, a Bear, a Cat, a Mole, a Pig, a Dog, and a Raven* (New York: Penguin Books, 2011).

3. David Morley, *Television, Audiences & Cultural Studies* (London and New York: Routledge, 1992); *Home territories: Media, Mobility, and Identity* (London and New York: Routledge, 2000); *Media, Modernity and Technology: The Geography of the New* (London and New York: Routledge, 2006); *The Geopolitics of Communication* (Oxford, UK: Blackwell, forthcoming); with Kevin Robins, *Spaces of Identity: Global Media, Electronic Landscapes, and Cultural Boundaries* (London and New York: Routledge, 1995).

4. Maria Todorova, *Imagining the Balkans* (New York and Oxford: Oxford University Press, 1997).

5. Ibid.

6. Vjeran Pavlaković, "Croatia's (New) Commemorative Culture and Politics of the Past," in *Avanture kulture: Kulturalni studiji u lokalnom kontekstu*, eds. Sanja Puljar D'Alessio and Nenad Fanuko (Zagreb: Jesenski and Turk and Croatian Sociological Society, 2013), 139.

7. Francis Fukuyama, *The End of History and the Last Man* (New York: Free Press, 1992).

8. Cornel West, "Decentring Europe," *Critical Quarterly* 33, no. 1 (1991): 1–19.

9. Paul Gilroy, "Remarks on postmodernism," in discussion at National Film Theatre, London, cited in Ien Ang and David Morley "Mayonnaise culture and other European follies," *Cultural Studies* 3, no. 2 (1989): 133–44.

10. Salman Rushdie, *The Satanic Verses* (London: Viking, 1988), 343.

11. Dejan Jović, "1989: godina koja nam se nije dogodila," *Politička misao portal* 2014, http://politickamisao.com/1989-godina-koja-nam-se-nije-dogodila/. Accessed October 10, 2015.

12. Zoran Kurelić, "No Carrot and No Stick: Croatia's Simulated Democracy and the EU," in *Kroatien in der EU: Stand und Perspektiven*, ed. Beate Neuss (Hamburg: Verlag Dr. Kovač, 2015).

13. Mieczyslaw P. Boduszynski, *Regime Change in the Yugoslav Successor States* (Baltimore, MD: Johns Hopkins University Press, 2010), 46.

14. Drakulić, *How We Survived*, 22.

15. Chantal Mouffe, *On the Political* (London: Routledge, 2005).

16. Max Weber, *The Protestant Ethic and the Spirit of Capitalism* (New York: Scribner, 1958).

17. Dipesh Chakrabarty, *Provincializing Europe: Postcolonial Thought and Historical Difference* (Princeton and Oxford: Princeton University Press, 2007).

18. Martin Bernal, *Black Athena: The Afroasiatic Roots of Classical Civilization* (New Brunswick, NJ: Rutgers University Press, 1987).

19. Giorgio Agamben, "The 'Latin Empire' should strike back," *Presseurop,* March 26, 2013, http://www.presseurop.eu/en/content/article/3593961-latin-empire-should-strike-back. Accessed November 15, 2015.

20. Alexandre Kojève, "Outline of a Doctrine of French Policy," *Marxists Internet Archive* 1990/1945 https://www.marxists.org/reference/subject/philosophy/works/fr/kojeve2.htm. Accessed December 2, 2015.

21. Ibid.

22. Ibid.

23. Morley and Robins, *Spaces*.

24. Morley, *Home Territories*.

25. David Morley, *The Geopolitics of Communication* (Oxford, UK: Blackwell, forthcoming).

26. *Concise Oxford Dictionary of Current English* (Oxford: Oxford University Press, 1964).

27. Morley and Robins, *Spaces*, 7–8.

28. Ibid.

29. Slavenka Drakulić, *The Balkan Express: Fragments from the Other Side of War* (Zagreb: VBZ, 2012/1993), 18.

30. Constantine P. Cavafy, *Poems* (London: Hogarth Press, 1971).

31. Ghassan Hage, "Nation-building-dwelling-being," *Communal/Plural*, vol. 1. (1993): 73–104.

BIBLIOGRAPHY

Agamben, Giorgio. "The 'Latin Empire' Should Strike Back." *Presseurop,* March 26, 2013. http://www.presseurop.eu/en/content/article/3593961-latin-empire-should-strike-back. Accessed November 15, 2015.

Bernal, Martin. *Black Athena: The Afroasiatic Roots of Classical Civilization.* New Brunswick, NJ: Rutgers University Press, 1987.

Boduszynski, Mieczyslaw P. *Regime Change in the Yugoslav Successor States.* Baltimore, MD: Johns Hopkins University Press, 2010.

Cavafy, Constantine P. *Poems.* London: Hogarth Press, 1971.

Chakrabarty, Dipesh. *Provincializing Europe: Postcolonial Thought and Historical Difference.* Princeton and Oxford: Princeton University Press, 2000.

Concise Oxford Dictionary of Current English. Oxford: Oxford University Press, 1964.

Drakulić, Slavenka. *Café Europa: Life After Communism.* New York: Penguin Books, 1999/1996.

Drakulić, Slavenka. *The Balkan Express: Fragments from the Other Side of War.* Zagreb: VBZ, 2012/1993.

Drakulić, Slavenka. *How We Survived Communism And Even Laughed.* Zagreb: VBZ, 2013/1992.

Drakulić, Slavenka. *They Would Never Hurt a Fly: War Criminals on Trial in the Hague.* New York: Penguin Books, 2005.

Drakulić, Slavenka. *A Guided Tour Through the Museum of Communism: Fables from a Mouse, a Parrot, a Bear, a Cat, a Mole, a Pig, a Dog, and a Raven.* New York: Penguin Books, 2011.

Fukuyama, Francis. *The End of History and the Last Man.* New York: Free Press, 1992.

Gilroy, Paul. "Remarks on Postmodernism." In discussion at National Film Theatre, London. Cited in Ang, Ien and Morley, David. "Mayonnaise Culture and Other European Follies." *Cultural Studies* 3, no. 2 (1989): 133–44.

Hage, Ghassan. "Nation-Building-Dwelling-Being." *Communal/Plural* vol. 1 (1993): 73–104.

Jović, Dejan. "1989: godina koja nam se nije dogodila." *Politička misao portal* 2014, http://politickamisao.com/1989-godina-koja-nam-se-nije-dogodila/. Accessed October 10, 2015.

Kojève, Alexandre. "Outline of a Doctrine of French Policy." *Marxists Internet Archive* 1990/1945, https://www.marxists.org/reference/subject/philosophy/works/fr/kojeve2.htm. Accessed December 2, 2015.

Kristeva, Julia. *Strangers to Ourselves.* New York and London: Harvester Wheatsheaf, 1991.

Kurelić, Zoran. "No Carrot and No Stick: Croatia's Simulated Democracy and the EU." In *Kroatien in der EU: Stand und Perspektiven*, edited by Beate Neuss, 47–64. Hamburg: Verlag Dr. Kovač, 2015.

Morley, David. *Television, Audiences & Cultural Studies.* London and New York: Routledge, 1992.

Morley, David. *Home territories: Media, Mobility, and Identity.* London and New York: Routledge, 2000.

Morley, David. *Media, Modernity and Technology: The Geography of the New.* London and New York: Routledge, 2006.

Morley, David. *The Geopolitics of Communication.* Oxford, UK: Blackwell, forthcoming.

Morley, David and Robins, Kevin. *Spaces of Identity: Global Media, Electronic Landscapes, and Cultural Boundaries.* London and New York: Routledge, 1995.

Mouffe, Chantal. *On the Political.* London: Routledge, 2005.

Pavlaković, Vjeran. "Croatia's (New) Commemorative Culture and Politics of the Past." In *Avanture kulture: Kulturalni studiji u lokalnom kontekstu*, edited by Sanja Puljar D'Alessio and Nenad Fanuko, 139–151. Zagreb: Jesenski and Turk and Croatian Sociological Society, 2013.

Rushdie, Salman. *The Satanic Verses*. London: Viking, 1988.

Todorova, Maria. *Imagining the Balkans*. New York and Oxford: Oxford University Press, 1997.

Weber, Max. *The Protestant Ethic and the Spirit of Capitalism*. New York: Scribner, 1958.

West, Cornel. "Decentring Europe." *Critical Quarterly* 33, no. 1 (1991): 1–19.

Index

About the Contributors

Nebojša Blanuša is assistant professor of political psychology at the Faculty of Political Science, University of Zagreb, Croatia. He has been involved in a number of research projects such as the FP7 "Social Performance, Cultural Trauma and Re-establishing Solid Sovereignties". He is the author of *Conspiracy Theories and Croatian Political Reality 1980–2007* (2011) and a number of articles on the Balkans, Europe and the European Union (EU). In 2015, he was a visiting fellow at the Center for Cultural Sociology at Yale University, New Haven, Connecticut.

Claudia Ciobanu holds an MA in political science from the Central European University in Budapest. Based in Warsaw, Poland, she is a freelance reporter contributing to various international media and an editor of Romanian magazine *Mamaliga de Varsovia*. She is currently working on a book about the dark side of European mobility.

Uroš Čvoro is a senior lecturer in art theory at UNSW Art & Design, Sydney, Australia. His research interests include post-socialism, transitional societies, representations of nationalism and contemporary art and politics in the countries of former Yugoslavia. His most recent book is *Turbo-folk Music and Cultural Representations of National Identity in Former Yugoslavia* (2014).

Ivaylo Ditchev is professor of cultural anthropology at Sofia University. He works in the field of politics, urban cultures and media. His latest book is on mobility and citizenship, entitled *Desire to Leave, Right to Stop* (2013). He is the editor-in-chief of the online journal on cultural studies *SeminarBG*.

Slavenka Drakulić is an author whose novels and non-fiction books about the war in the Balkans and life under communism [*Holograms of Fear* (1992); *Marble Skin* (1994); *How We Survived Communism* (2004); *Balkan Express* (1994); *Café Europa* and *They Would Never Hurt a Fly* (1999)] have been translated into many languages. Her numerous essays have appeared in a variety of newspapers and magazines. She is the recipient of the 2004 Leipzig Book Fair Award for European Understanding. At the Gathering of International Writers in Prague in 2010, she was proclaimed as one of the most influential contemporary European writers.

Zlatan Krajina is an assistant professor in media studies at the Faculty of Political Science, University of Zagreb, Croatia. He was awarded MA and PhD in media and communications from Goldsmiths, University of London. He has written about Orientalism in the media. His research also involves the ethnography of everyday media consumption in urban spaces, which was the focus of his monograph *Negotiating the Mediated City* (2014).

Noémi Lendvai is a senior lecturer in Comparative Public Policy at the School for Policy Studies, University of Bristol, UK. Her research interests cover post-communist welfare states, EU integration, EU social policy, authoritarian neoliberalism and critical comparative research methods. Her latest book, co-authored with John Clarke, David Bainton and Paul Stubbs, is *Making Policy Move: Towards a Politics of Translation and Assemblage* (2015).

Milena Marinkova is a teaching fellow at the University of Leeds, UK. Her research in contemporary literature and culture is informed by broader debates in postcolonial theory and transnational writing about identity, representation, affect and embodiment. She is currently completing a monograph which interrogates "the Balkan" as a trope in contemporary Canadian and Australian fiction.

Suzana Milevska is a curator and theorist of art and culture with a PhD in visual cultures from Goldsmiths College, London. Her projects focus on postcolonial critique of identity politics. She was the first Endowed professor for history of Central and South Eastern European Art histories at the Academy of Fine Art in Vienna and a visiting professor at the Technical University Vienna. In 2010 she published the book *Gender Difference in the Balkans* (2010) and edited *The Renaming Machine: The Book* (2010).

Monika Metykova is a lecturer in media communications and journalism studies at the School of Media, Film and Music, University of Sussex, UK.

Her research interests include media/journalism and democracy, migration and European media spaces and policy. She has recently co-edited a special issue of *Media Studies* on "Media Systems Twenty-Five Years After the Revolutions of 1989". Her upcoming book is *Diversity and the Media.*

David Morley is a professor of communications at Goldsmiths, University of London. His work spans issues of media consumption, the role of media in the constitution of "electronic landscapes" and the development of non-Eurocentric and non-media-centric media studies. He was a research fellow at the Centre for Contemporary Cultural Studies in Birmingham. His books include *Media, Modernity and Technology* (2006), *Home Territories* (2000), *Spaces of Identity* (with Kevin Robins) and *Television* (1995), *Audiences and Cultural Studies* (1992), amongst many others.

Eunice Castro Seixas holds a PhD in sociology. She is currently affiliated with the School of Psychology at the University of Minho, Portugal, where she works as a research assistant on justice psychology. She has published papers on democratization, developmental aid and transitional justice in Bosnia and Herzegovina, and civil society and human rights narratives in the Russian Federation.

Orlanda Obad is a senior assistant at the Institute of Ethnology and Folklore Research in Zagreb, Croatia. Her research interests include symbolic geographies of the Balkans, EU enlargement in the Western Balkans, postcolonial theory and the critique of Balkanism. She participated in two related projects: COST Action "Remaking eastern borders in Europe" and Austrian Science and Research Liaison Ljubljana Office project "Negotiating Europe(anness)".

Piro Rexhepi holds a PhD in politics from the University of Strathclyde, UK. He is currently a research fellow at the Max Planck Institute for the Study of Religious and Ethnic Diversity. His research is located in Critical and Queer Theories in International Relations with special interest in Islam and South-eastern Europe.

Paul Stubbs is a UK-born sociologist who is currently a senior research fellow in the Institute of Economics, Zagreb. His main research interests are in social movements and grassroots activism, social policy and social protection. His latest book, co-written with John Clarke, Dave Bainton and Noémi Lendvai, is *Making Policy Move: Towards a Politics of Translation and Assemblage* (2015). He is also co-editor (with Rory Archer and Igor Duda) of *Social Inequalities and Discontent in Yugoslavia* (2016).